Greening the Car Industry

For Kara, Annika and Erin

Greening the Car Industry

Varieties of Capitalism and Climate Change

John Mikler

Lecturer, University of Sydney, Australia

Edward Elgar

Cheltenham, UK • Northampton, MA, USA

Published by
Edward Elgar Publishing Limited
The Lypiatts
15 Lansdown Road
Cheltenham
Glos GL50 2JA
UK

Edward Elgar Publishing, Inc.
William Pratt House
9 Dewey Court
Northampton
Massachusetts 01060
USA

A catalogue record for this book
is available from the British Library

Library of Congress Control Number: 2009930433

Mixed Sources
Product group from well-managed
forests and other controlled sources
www.fsc.org Cert no. SA-COC-1565
© 1996 Forest Stewardship Council

FSC

ISBN 978 1 84720 652 7

Printed and bound by MPG Books Group, UK

Contents

Figures

Tables

Abbreviations

4WD	four wheel drive
AAM	Alliance of Automobile Manufacturers
ACEA	Association des Constructeurs Europeens d'Automobiles
CAFE	corporate average fuel economy
CCFA	Comite' des Constructeurs Français d'Automobiles
CEO	chief executive officer
CERES	Coalition of Environmentally Responsible Economies
CME	coordinated market economy
CNG	compressed natural gas
CO_2	carbon dioxide
ECMT	European Conference of Ministers of Transport
EIA	Energy Information Administration (US)
EPA	Environment Protection Agency (US)
EU	European Union
FCV	fuel cell vehicle
GCC	Global Climate Coalition
GRI	Global Reporting Initiative
ICC	International Chamber of Commerce
IEA	International Energy Agency
JAMA	Japan Automobile Manufacturers Association
KBA	Kraftfahrt-Bundesamt
LME	liberal market economy
LPG	liquefied petroleum gas
METI	Ministry of Economy Trade and Industry (Japan)
MITI	Ministry for International Trade and Industry
MNCs	multinational corporations
NGO	non-government organization
NHTSA	National Highway Traffic Safety Administration (US)
OECD	Organisation for Economic Co-operation and Development
OICA	International Organization of Motor Vehicle Manufacturers
SUV	sports utility vehicle
UNCED	United Nations Conference on Environment and Development

UNEP	United Nations Environment Programme
UNFCCC	United Nations Framework Convention on Climate Change
US	United States
VDA	Verband der Automobilindustrie
VOC	Varieties of Capitalism
WBCSD	World Business Council for Sustainable Development
WVS	World Values Survey

Preface and acknowledgements

The origins of this book are in research undertaken for my PhD from 2003 to 2006. However, the thinking behind it comes from my time in the Australian Commonwealth Public Service. Commencing as a keen economics graduate with the Department of Industry, Technology and Commerce in 1990, that which non-economists take for granted soon became obvious as I observed the policy process and its machinations. This is that all organizations, whether government departments, non-government organizations or firms, are complex. They are made up of human beings, operating in institutionally diverse environments, and motivated by a range of factors. For firms in particular, it seemed to me that while profits may be a key motivator, how these are defined and achieved is not an easy question to answer. This gave me the impetus to undertake study in politics and international relations, and eventually complete a PhD. As an academic now, it still seems odd to me that, even in the politics literature, while states, international organizations and civil society are reasonably well *drawn*, firms are mostly (albeit with some notable exceptions) simply *sketched* as instrumental profit seekers.

Being narrowly sketched as such, the potential for firms to take environmental concerns into account is usually seen in terms of presenting them with things to which they can react. The arguments go something like this. Threats are required, such as attacking their financial bottom lines via penalties for non-compliance with regulations, or taxing their products so that changes in market forces present them with no alternative but to change what they offer consumers. Alternatively, incentives are required such as subsidies for new products, or new market opportunities stemming from instruments such as emissions trading schemes. In the absence of state intervention, it is optimistically hoped that increased consumer desires for environmental responsibility may produce change, along with the idea that there are stakeholders with whom firms wish to form relationships in order to improve their financial performance. In short, firms are treated as the objects rather than the subjects of study.

So, I wanted to examine how firms are political actors along with others that are more central in political science, such as states, social movements and international organizations. Being worried about the environment, and recognizing the growing prominence of the global environmental concern of climate change, I thought I should look at an industry sector that 'matters' (in terms of size and economic influence), preferably one composed of large corporations (preferably multinational corporations) and one that contributes to the environmental problem of climate change to such a degree that it will have to change quite dramatically to effect real change. I chose the car industry, and this book is the result. I hope it is helpful. In many ways, it is a piece of unfinished research that raises as many questions as it answers. Maybe this is the case with all research. Hopefully, the findings are intriguing enough for the paths to future study suggested to be taken up by some of its readers.

As is always the case, in doing the research for this book I received help from many people who deserve recognition. I am bound to leave someone out, and I hope they will forgive me if I do. My greatest thanks goes to Jason Sharman, who read many drafts of the chapters in this book and was instrumental in helping me to shape the research and present the results of it. I am also indebted to other members of the Department of Government and International Relations at the University of Sydney, and could easily thank all of them here. It is rare to find such a harmonious, supportive *team* of people! The following deserve special mention: Linda Weiss, Allan McConnell, Rodney Smith, Betsi Beem, Darryl Jarvis, Diarmuid Maguire, Rod Tiffen, Graeme Gill, Deborah Brennan, Lyn Carson, Ariadne Vromen, Susan Park and Shelly Savage. Also Dick Bryan from the Department of Political Economy.

For their constructive feedback on an early conference paper I would like to thank Jeff Harrod, Helge Hveem and Gerd Junne. For their constructive suggestions on my thesis, I thank Stephen Wilks, Russell Lansbury and Andrew Griffiths. Their advice, along with that of David Marsh and Neil Harrison, helped me to shape my thesis into this book.

More tangentially (in the sense of wide-ranging, mind-expanding discussion), Susan Shaheen helped me with some of my early thoughts on tackling the issues, as did Nic Lowe, the charismatic Director of CarShare Australia. John Wormald helped me to better understand how one may conceptualize the car industry as both global and national. Also thanks to Stuart White, Tom Berry and the staff of the Institute for Sustainable Futures at the University of Technology Sydney for their assistance.

I would also like to take this opportunity to say a big thank you to all the people at Ford, Toyota, BMW and Volkswagen who agreed to be involved. Your time and enthusiasm for this project, not to mention your freely-offered opinions, helped the research to 'come alive' in the latter stages of the book, and I hope I have not done you any disservice in how your comments have been reported. None is intended, and I am truly grateful. While on the car industry, I should also thank Carole

Bartholomew of the Victorian Department of Innovation, Industry and Regional Development, whose advice was helpful, and who got me a ticket to the International Automotive Conference in Melbourne in 2005. My good friend Robyn White also deserves thanks for introducing me to her and putting me up while in Melbourne.

This book started as a PhD, and other students toiling away on a remarkably eclectic range of topics, yet who provided incredible support and advice include Kriszti Molnar, Siobhan O'Sullivan, Lavina Lee and her husband John (especially for getting me a ticket to a conference where I met two very interesting and helpful executives from the Australian branch offices of Audi and Jaguar), Marcus Chadwick, Young Ju Kwon, Tony Stapledon, Nigel McCarthy, Sungyoung Kim, Adam Lockyer, Soojin Yoon, Dwane Byrne, Matthew Brazil and Debra da Silva.

Last, but not least, I must thank family and friends. You have all been so supportive and willing to listen to my diatribes about cars, capitalism and the environment with (almost) no complaints. My biggest thanks of all goes to my wife and best friend, Kara. She encourages and supports me in so many ways. I don't always make this easy. I am ever grateful to my parents, Stella and Sid, for imbuing me with a sense that anything is possible, and therefore playing a large part in getting me to the point where I could imagine taking the time and putting in the effort to undertake such a project. I wish they had lived to see the results. Thanks are also due to my Aunt Teresa Moffett, for all her support. Finally, I must thank my daughters Annika and Erin, the first of whom was born at the beginning of this project, the latter at its conclusion. They both continue to teach me the most important lessons of all, including that a good meal is cause for dancing in your seat, and that however big the problem, however confusing the issues, you can always come home and pretend you are a tiger!

John Mikler
Sydney

A Note on Events in the Car Industry as the Book was Going to Press

Any piece of research is dated once published. Even so, the analysis employed in this book suggests that recent developments in the international car industry should not have been unexpected. For example, the prediction that European and Japanese car firms will find it easier than US firms to adjust to future imperatives has been quite dramatically borne out. Similarly, although fully electric cars are not considered, the fact that US firms are currently playing 'catch up' with their Japanese counterparts in respect of such vehicles is also not surprising. Therefore, in addition to providing a historical snapshot, hopefully the reader is provided with an analytical framework for understanding ongoing developments.

1. Introduction

> The ground rules of profit make it hard to be a friend to the environment.
>
> (David Suzuki, 1993: 137)

> The formulation of strategy is generally treated as a rational process of matching corporate capabilities to market demands. But this does not always account well for the heterogeneity observed in corporate strategies towards complex environmental issues.
>
> (Levy and Rothenberg, 2002: 173)

Why should firms address environmental problems? It's a simple enough question. When it comes to problems that threaten the future of the planet, such as climate change, it is also crucial for the future of humanity. The simple answer is that they *must* take a leading role in addressing such problems. This is because it is not society that is responsible for environmental degradation. Neither are governments. Both may be important for finding solutions, but ultimately the actors responsible for environmental damage are firms, because environmental damage occurs in the production process and the act of consuming the outputs of it. This is clearly a contentious position. One thing it is not is idealistic. If business does not address the central role it plays in causing or ameliorating the environmental impacts of its activities, we are potentially doomed.

Yet, the liberal economic model is based on the premise that the business of business is business, not just in fact but as a virtue – i.e. it is *right* that this be the case. If this is true, then the likelihood of business taking a leading role is slim.[1] More accurately, it is seen as unlikely in the absence of changes in the material incentives offered by market forces or effective state regulation. Even so, corporations are increasingly keen to represent themselves as 'green'. In the case of the car industry there is evidence that concern for the environment may be more than just rhetoric. Car firms have made significant commitments to incorporate environmental concerns in business strategies (OECD, 2004; ACEA, 2002; Deutsche Bank, 2004; Austin et al., 2003). The car industry is dominated by multinational corporations (MNCs), and the world's largest manufacturing sector. It also produces a product that has major environmental impacts. Therefore, any behavioral change occurring within it is central to the debate on addressing the environmental impact of business.

This book asks the question: what *motivates* car firms to actually make environmental commitments? The reason for asking this is that if one understands the key motivators of firms, one has the basis for answering questions of whether or not the commitments they make are likely to be real or simply 'window dressing'. The issues raised by the question are complex. Multiple interrelationships are involved between states, business, markets and society. Theoretically, there are also multiple perspectives for considering the puzzle. Disciplinary boundaries will inevitably be crossed and readers with an interest in regulatory governance, international business and management, global environmental politics and the role of civil society, among others, should all be interested in the findings.

The book takes as its starting point the dichotomy between material factors and rationalist ways of viewing the world, versus normative perspectives that emphasize the role of institutions. The case is made for why the latter approach has more explanatory power. A belief that states remain central, rather than the view that global markets are now in charge, informs the analysis because firms remain embedded in their home states. They are therefore subject to normative factors that constitute capitalist relations of production that have become institutionalized over time there. Recognizing this, the analysis employs the Varieties of Capitalism (VOC) approach.[2] If environmental damage occurs in the production process and the act of consuming the outputs of it, then capitalist relations of production should be at the heart of answering questions about firms' motivations. The findings demonstrate that car firms' motivations for taking the environmental impacts of their actions into account, and how they do so, are fundamentally a matter of differences in such capitalist relations. Specifically, in this book, they are about the different capitalisms of Germany (and to some degree the European Union), the United States and Japan.

This introductory chapter first briefly highlights the global economic and environmental importance of the car industry, and places this in the context of the growing awareness of environmental issues from the 1990s onwards. It then introduces how addressing the environmental damage resulting from the car industry's activities may be considered in the light of contrasting theoretical perspectives on addressing environmental externalities resulting from the actions of economic actors. The mainstream rationalist liberal economic perspective, which focuses on material factors, is contrasted with institutional perspectives, which focus on normative factors. The idea that the influence of firms' home states remains important, for both material and institutional reasons, is then introduced along with the VOC approach. Finally, the contribution of the book and the substantive questions it seeks to answer in light of the actions of the car industry and contrasting theoretical perspectives are presented. The chapter concludes with the hypothesis to be explored. This is that both material and institutional perspectives are relevant to understanding and explaining the car industry's environmental initiatives, but national institutional variations in capitalist relations of production, as suggested by the VOC approach, are crucial for understanding what might motivate such initiatives in firms of different nationalities.

THE GLOBAL ECONOMIC AND ENVIRONMENTAL IMPORTANCE OF THE CAR INDUSTRY

The car industry has been described as 'the economic sector most emblematic of modern times and of the polluting consequences of modernity' (Orssatto and Clegg, 1999: 264; see also Womack et al., 1990). Its economic and environmental significance mark it as a crucial case for study because, more than any other manufacturing sector, it possesses the material capabilities to either reduce or increase global environmental damage. The following outlines some key aspects of the industry's global economic significance. In light of this significance, the manner in which the industry's products are a major cause of global environmental damage is then outlined. This provides some background for the subsequent discussion of alternative approaches to addressing the industry's environmental impacts.

Economic Significance

MNCs are perhaps the most important economic actors shaping the contemporary global economy. The car industry is the archetypal example of an industry sector dominated by MNCs. It manufactures and distributes its products on an integrated global scale and today is often taken as 'a paradigm case of a globalised industry' (Paterson, 2000: 264). Most of the largest car manufacturers have over 40 per cent of their production outside their 'home' state (Paterson, 2007: 98), and in addition to the finished product being produced and traded internationally, the international dimension of the product is embedded in its production. This is because various parts and components are produced in different countries, so that the final product itself is global in character (Braithwaite and Drahos, 2000: 440–441; see also Dicken, 2003: 355–369). Furthermore, collaborative agreements between firms of different nationalities, and often cross-ownership, mean that a 'global connectedness' exists in research and development, the dissemination of new production techniques and other technological advances.[3]

The car industry dominates global manufacturing. Vehicle production is the largest manufacturing sector in the world. Five of the world's top ten businesses by sales are car manufacturers, with another three in the top 45 (*The Economist*, 2002a: 62). The industry contributes 4 to 8 per cent of total GDP for Organisation for Economic Co-operation and Development (OECD) countries, and leads all other industries, including information technology, in research and development (UNEP and ACEA, 2002: 12). In fact, on the basis of the value of the industry's output, the Organisation Internationale des Constructeurs d'Automobiles (OICA, 2006) declares that if vehicle manufacturing was a country it would be the sixth largest in the world.

Yet, while being globally significant, the industry is also nationally concentrated. Table 1.1 presents turnover, investment and production figures, including for the top three countries in the world where this is undertaken: Germany, the US and Japan. It shows that the industry's total turnover in 2004 was almost €1.9 trillion, its investment totaled nearly €85 billion, and it produced over 66 million vehicles worldwide in 2005 (of which 46 million, or 69 per cent of the total, were cars). By location of economic activity, the industry's three major hubs account for 58 per cent of its turnover and investment, and over 40 per cent of its production. Therefore, it is clear that in addition to the industry's global economic significance, it is of particular significance to the world's three largest industrialized states where 40–60 per cent of its global economic activity is located. These figures are magnified if the whole of the European Union (EU) is included, in which case, four-fifths of world car output is produced in the US, EU and Japan (Dicken, 1998: 319).

Environmental Damage

Given the economic importance of the car industry, and significance in the world's three largest industrialized states, there is also ample evidence of the environmental damage caused by cars. The following is a brief summary.

Transportation accounts for around 23–25 per cent of total carbon dioxide (CO_2) emissions, with up to 85 per cent of this accounted for by road transport (UNEP, 2003; Paterson, 2000). This is exclusive of related activities linked with transportation such as fuel extraction, processing and transport, and the manufacturing process. If these are included, passenger cars alone are responsible for up to 33 per cent of the OECD's CO_2 emissions.[4] Just a 10–15 per cent reduction in passenger cars' contribution to CO_2 emissions would meet half of Germany or Japan's emission reduction commitments under the Kyoto Protocol to address climate change (UNFCCC, no date a, no date b, no date c).[5]

Table 1.1 Turnover, investment and production volumes

	Turnover (€million)	Percentage of total	Investment (€million)	Percentage of total	Production – cars and commercial vehicles (units)	Percentage of total	Production – cars (units)	Percentage of total
Germany	227 666	12	11 900	14	5 757 710	9	5 350 187	12
US	425 106	23	30 416	36	11 980 912	18	4 321 272	9
Japan	435 610	23	6 450	8	10 799 659	16	9 016 735	20
Germany, US and Japan total	1 088 382	58	48 766	58	28 538 281	43	18 688 194	41
World total	1 889 840	100	84 801	100	66 465 768	100	46 009 207	100

Source: OICA (2006).

In terms of exhaust emissions other than CO_2, cars contribute 90 per cent of all carbon monoxide emissions, and are a major cause of acid rain through the sulphur oxides they emit. Road transport also accounts for 48 per cent of nitrogen oxide (NO_x) emissions in OECD countries on average, and around 60 per cent of this is accounted for by cars (Paterson, 2000: 258–259). In addition, cars are a prime cause of the depletion of the world's resources – for example, car use accounts for 63 per cent of US oil consumption (Freund and Martin, 1993).[6] Of all land-based modes of transport, cars are the most energy intensive, with petrol-powered cars consuming, in aggregate, more energy and producing more greenhouse gas emissions than any other type of vehicle (IEA, 1993: 14). The industry also produces over 3 million tonnes of scrap and waste every year (Hawken et al., 1999: 23).[7]

Based on current growth rates, the number of vehicles worldwide is projected to increase from around 700 million at present to 1.1 billion by 2020, so the environmental impacts of the industry will increase substantially unless dramatic changes are made (Burns et al., 2002). It is not surprising that the US Environmental Protection Agency declares that driving a car is 'the single most polluting thing that most of us do' (Maxton and Wormald, 2004: 31).

Given their economically powerful position, car firms have historically put strong political pressure on governments against environmental regulation. They have supported national lobby groups such as the Coalition for Vehicle Choice in the US, and international lobby groups such as the Global Climate Coalition (GCC) and the Climate Council. These consistently lobbied governments against emission controls to reduce greenhouse gases, on the basis that the result would be severe economic impacts (Beder 2002; see also Porter and van der Linde, 1995a; Newell and Paterson, 1998; Bradsher, 2002; Levy and Rothenberg, 2002). US firms resigned their membership of lobby groups like the GCC prior to its ultimate demise in 2002 in favor of openly embracing (or at least declaring) support for environmental commitments.[8] In fact, all car firms now announce their support for, and membership of, environmentally-motivated industry organizations such as the World Business Council for Sustainable Development (WBCSD: 2004). Even so, there remains vast scope for efficiency improvements by the industry. For example, the US industry has made most of its profits since the mid-1990s from the sale of light trucks, primarily in the form of large, heavy, gas-guzzling pick-up trucks and sports utility vehicles (SUVs). These vehicles now account for over half the total US passenger 'car' market. Far from seeking to differentiate themselves from the production and sale of these vehicles, European and Japanese manufacturers are producing similar vehicles to compete for US market share (Bradsher, 2002).[9]

Overall, the industry's size and global economic significance is mirrored in the environmental damage caused by its products. Without action, its environmental impacts will inevitably worsen based on current market trends. However, as environmental concern has risen in prominence since the early 1990s, there is cause to think action may be forthcoming. This is the subject of the following section.

THE ENVIRONMENT GOES MAINSTREAM

These days, it is easy to take it for granted that the environment matters. Environmental concern spans the political spectrum from left to right, as well as from governments to firms and society. It is not so much a question of whether the environment should be a concern, but how environmental impacts should be addressed. This was not always the case. The Club of Rome's (1972) *The Limits to Growth* helped to set the agenda in the early 1970s, as did Carson's ([1962] 1999) *Silent Spring* that preceded it. To be an environmentalist back then was to be on the political fringes, but the 1990s marked the beginning of the period over which the environment went mainstream.

This book primarily considers the period of time from 1990 to 2004. There are five observations to make about why this period of time is pertinent. The first four relate to the rise in environmental awareness generally, or the way in which it went mainstream. The fifth relates to the material conditions faced by the car industry specifically, in the sense that these may be held relatively constant over this period of time as environmental awareness became a feature of the political landscape.

First, international organizations significantly raised the profile of environmental concerns over this period. For example, the United Nations Environment Programme (UNEP) views the 1992 Rio Earth Summit as a watershed in the discussion of environmental sustainability from which sustainable development initiatives have sprung (UN, no date a),[10] such as the Kyoto Protocol signed in 1997 and subsequently ratified by nearly all its signatories (UNFCCC, no date a, no date b, no date c).[11] Even economically-focused international organizations such as the World Trade Organization (WTO) recognized that, going into the 1990s, 'environment, gender and labor concerns are on the agenda in ways that would have been deemed illegitimate in the 1970s' (O'Brien et al., 2000: 231). They realized that ignoring the views of increasingly noisy and angry protestors and social movements undermined their agendas. The WTO's answer was to establish its Committee on Trade and Environment in 1995 at its inception. Throughout the 1990s, a series of international agreements with business also emerged such as the United Nations' (UN) Global Compact, announced in 1999. This brings companies together with UN agencies, labor and civil society to support nine principles in the areas of human rights, labor and the environment. Another such agreement is the Global Reporting Initiative, started in 1997 by the Coalition of Environmentally Responsible Economies (CERES), and now an official collaborating centre of the UNEP that works in cooperation with the Global Compact (GRI, 2002; see also UN, no date b).

Second, authors like Florini (2003a and b) identify the concept of corporate social responsibility (CSR) as having come to the fore as an ideological shift with its genesis in the 1990s. As a concept, CSR includes environmental sustainability among a range of other responsibilities, such as those in respect of labor standards, human rights, disclosure of information, corporate governance, public safety, privacy protection and consumer protection. There is a growing body of research that shows environmental sustainability and other socially responsible behavior on the part of MNCs, such as those in the car industry, to be voluntary initiatives. Such initiatives are further identified as being global (see also OECD, 2001a, 2001b; Holliday et al., 2002). For example, the WBCSD was established at the same time as the 1992 Rio Earth Summit and has been working ever since to be at the forefront of the business response to sustainable development. A coalition of 165 companies drawn from 30 countries and 20 industry sectors, it also links a network of 43 national and regional business councils and partner organizations in 39 countries. It includes all the major car firms in its membership, and has been regarded as a manifestation of a broader acceptance by corporations of the importance of environmental issues as a key component of CSR (WBCSD, 2000).[12] At the same time, as already mentioned, industry associations like the GCC, established to resist attempts to address climate change, went into demise because membership of them tarnished firms' reputations to such a degree as to be unacceptable to them (Beder, 2002: 238–239).

Third, even outspoken critics of international capitalism vis-à-vis the environment suggest that we are actually witnessing a fundamental change in how firms do business worldwide as they incorporate environmental sustainability concerns in their operations. For example, before the mid-1990s, Hawken et al. (1999: 24) find there is not much evidence of the car industry proactively addressing environmental concerns, with any gains the result of social activism or government regulations. Similarly, in Suzuki (1993: 137 and 139), a strident critic of capitalism, globalization and the environmental degradation it causes worldwide, declared that 'the ground rules of profit make it hard to be a friend to the environment'. Indeed, he said that 'amid . . . the suicidal demand for steady growth, happy stories are few', singling out the international car industry for the enormous social and ecological costs it imposes on societies above all other industries. But by 2002 he notes a philosophical shift within corporate hierarchies, the results of which include General Motors supporting a 50 per cent tax on petrol for environmental reasons (Suzuki and Dressel, 2002: 289–290). To illustrate the point, he cites the speech by Ford's Chairman to a Greenpeace business conference on 5 October 2000:

> We're at a crucial point in the world's history. Our oceans and forests are suffering; species are disappearing; the climate is changing . . . Enlightened corporations are beginning to . . . realize that they can no longer separate themselves from what is going on around them. That, ultimately, they can only be as successful as the communities and the world that they exist in. . . . I personally believe that sustainability is the most important issue facing the automotive industry in general in the 21st century. (Suzuki and Dressel, 2002: 290–291)

Within the space of a decade, Suzuki's attitude changed from pessimism to a decidedly more optimistic view of business environmental responsibility, with the car industry at the forefront of moves by big business towards environmental sustainability.[13]

Fourth, environmental reporting by firms in many cases preceded reporting on CSR more generally. Starting in the late 1980s to early 1990s, an increasing number large corporations, mostly MNCs, began producing such reports.[14] US car firms were among the first to do so,[15] followed by German and Japanese firms. Such reports represent a desire by firms to represent themselves as environmentally concerned (whether in image or fact), suggesting the rise in prominence of environmental considerations as of strategic importance in this timeframe.[16]

Finally, and specifically for the car industry, between 1990 and 2004 environmental concerns and their impact may be considered in the context of relatively constant material factors. This is because the oil price was reasonably stable. For most of the 1990s the spot price for crude oil was US$15–20 per barrel. From 2000 to 2003 it increased slightly to US$20–25 per barrel. However, thereafter there was a price shock that saw the price nearly double to US$50 per barrel by 2005. In 2008 it passed US$100 per barrel on its way to around US$140 per barrel, before plummeting to less than half this price by the end of the year (EIA, 2008). As such, a *ceteris paribus* analysis based largely on fuel economy and the cost of running a car in terms of fuel purchased is only meaningful up until 2004, after which market uncertainties generated by the material imperatives of volatile oil prices unavoidably come to the fore. So, to some extent this book may be conceived of as a historical snapshot, and this is entirely appropriate because the question asked is not whether firms respond to market forces (clearly they do), but whether their desire to represent themselves as green counts for anything beyond these, as opposed to just being 'window dressing'.

This last point raises the institutional approach to be taken in the book, rather than the more mainstream rationalist, liberal economic approach that is usually applied. The two approaches are contrasted in the following sections.

ADDRESSING ENVIRONMENTAL EXTERNALITIES: MATERIAL 'CALCULUS' VERSUS INSTITUTIONAL 'CULTURE'

Environmental problems are usually characterized as cases of market failure due to externalities. Simply put, externalities occur when factors that should be taken into account by markets are left external to them. The primary reason for this is that property rights in respect of the environment are often ill-defined – i.e. it is not clear who owns the environment, and so it is often the case that economic actors responsible for environmental damage are not made responsible for the environmental impacts of their actions. Due to ill-defined property rights, the environment is often a public good – i.e. it is in the public domain and can be jointly consumed by several agents simultaneously. The result of environmental externalities arising from a lack of property rights because of the environment's public good nature is market failure, in the sense that the prices of goods and services do not reflect the environmental impacts of their production and consumption. More specifically, costs to the environment arising from economic activity are not borne by those engaged in the economic activity and are therefore not reflected in prices.[17]

Far from market failure being unusual, 'environmental externalities are pervasive' (Ekins et al., 1994: 7). Because the environmental costs of economic activity are incorrectly priced by markets, and economic actors can ignore the negative environmental effects of their actions, the costs of environmental externalities are often borne by others who were not responsible for them. Specifically, they are often borne collectively by society. When the public good attribute of the environment is a global or transborder phenomenon, as is the case with climate change, the environment is said to be in the realm of the 'global commons': the costs are borne by us all.

What then might motivate firms to address their environmental impacts? Ameliorating the problem of pervasive, often global, environmental externalities may be approached in two ways. Mainstream liberal economic perspectives are challenged by institutional perspectives. Both are considered below, along with the major divide between them: rational choice versus norms as the basis for action.

The Liberal Economic Perspective

The liberal economic perspective is the mainstream view that informs analysis in the business/government/environment debate. So profound is the acceptance of this perspective in debates about environmental sustainability that it may be called 'hegemonic' (Harrison, 2000: 20). Liberal is a somewhat 'rubber' term to the extent that it has been given different definitions by different commentators, but it is used here to refer to approaches in economics, political science and international relations that apply the ideas of individual autonomy, freedom and rationality to firms, the state, interstate relations and international economic relations generally (see, for example, Wallerstein, 1995; Burchill, 1996).[18] Broadly speaking, it refers to those theories in which 'people behave in self-interested and broadly rational ways', with rationality defined on the basis of a priori utilitarian assumptions (Goldstein and Keohane, 1993: 5).[19] In the case of firms, they are constructed as rational profit maximizers, making rational choices employing 'instrumental logics of calculation (calculus logics)' to achieve their material ends (Hay, 2006a: 4; see also March and Olsen 1989 and 1998; Hay, 2006b). Fundamentally, this mainstream view therefore employs a materialist perspective through which firms act instrumentally to make profits in markets, or to increase their material power in terms of market outcomes. In a nutshell, rationality is defined in terms of choices that maximize material profit and power outcomes.

The implications are clear. Without state intervention, environmental externalities will never be internalized as firms responsible for them can rationally ignore the cost of them. State intervention is required to increase the price of environmental resources so that 'trade can take place on the basis of prices reflecting true social costs' (Ropke, 1994: 17).[20] Without such intervention, market forces will not internalize the value of environmental externalities in market transactions.

Such a perspective has proved to be a parsimonious way of explaining firms' behavior. However, there are four inherent epistemological foundations underpinning it that are problematic. First, rational choice models are ahistorical. Rationality is assumed to apply at all times, and therefore questions such as path dependency, and timing and sequencing of events are not considered important determinants of outcomes. Second, rational choice models aim for generalizability. 'Rules of the game' are examined and equilibrium solutions posited that result from these. It follows that in addition to such solutions applying at all times (i.e. ahistorically), they apply in all cases. Third, rational choice models exogenize the interests, identities and preferences of actors. The limited understanding of actors' motivations that results means that their behavior is constrained to certain utility (in terms of profit or power) maximizing assumptions. Fourth, rational choice models focus on methods with the research agenda set by the model. By incorporating ahistoricity, generalizability and exogeneity of actors' interests, identities and preferences, parsimony is certainly more likely and one can also say that any resulting model will be widely applicable in theory (or more accurately by definition). However, the end result is that most of what remains to argue about is methods (see, for example, Green and Shapiro, 1994; Pierson and Skocpol, 2000; Boniface and Sharman, 2001).

The first three mean that approaches employing rational choice mechanisms are static. This limits their ability to explain behavioral change. The fourth limits the questions that can be asked to address this drawback of the first three assumptions. However, perhaps most importantly, by making a priori assumptions about the motivations of economic actors they postulate a universal source of behavioral change. If firms are taking environmental concerns into account, it must be because it is in their interest to do so, with this interest defined in materialist, instrumental profit-seeking terms. Although such a clear causal path is intuitively appealing, the danger in simply constructing firms as instrumental profit-maximizers is that the range of possible explanations for them taking more environmentally-friendly courses of action is constrained. It must, by definition, be because it is profitable for them to do so. It must be that consumers' revealed preferences indicate that firms should take such a course of action, or regulations leave them no choice. The risk is what Katzenstein colorfully terms 'vulgar rationalism' as we 'infer the motives of actors from behaviorally revealed preferences'. Such over-simplification means the result may be tautological explanations that 'succeed in explaining everything and so explain nothing' (Katzenstein, 1996: 27).

While not necessarily rejecting the usefulness of simplifying abstractions per se, what is worrying about the liberal economic approach is that its use of a rational choice model based on a priori assumptions represents 'a curiously depoliticized form of the study of politics' (Crouch, 2005a: 447; see also Schmidt, 2002). Alternative institutional perspectives do not constrain explanations to the same extent. Their epistemological foundations are considered in the following section.

Institutional Perspectives

Institutional perspectives have been promoted by scholars such as North (1990), March and Olsen (1989 and 1998), Ruggie (1998a), and even

Goldstein and Keohane (1993).[21] The materialist, rational choice based approach has been modified (see, for example, Denzau and North, 1994) or attacked in the process (Blyth, 1997, 2003; Hay, 2002, 2004; Green and Shapiro, 1994). Institutional approaches do not assume actors are rational or, more accurately, they do not define actors' rationality in terms of a priori assumptions ascribing motivations. Instead, their starting point is that actors are motivated by norms that prescribe and proscribe appropriate action. That is to say, rationality is contingent on norms of behavior. When such norms become institutionalized, they have a 'taken-for-grantedness' about them such that behaving in a manner commensurate with them may be taken for rational behavior, but not in any a priori assumed sense.

The body of literature on institutional perspectives has now grown to the point where there are a variety of approaches embracing institutionalism, from those that emphasize the contextual or historically constructed nature of rationality (for example, rational choice institutionalism and historical institutionalism), to those that virtually discard rationality altogether to focus on cultural and identity aspects of actors (for example, normative/sociological institutionalism and constructivist institutionalism) (Hay, 2006b; Lowndes, 2002). Rational choice institutionalists such as North (1990: 3 and 14) define norms as 'shared common beliefs' that give rise to institutions as 'the rules of the game in a society or, more formally . . . the humanly devised constraints that shape interaction'. Constructivist institutionalists 'focus on the role of ideas, norms, knowledge, culture and argument in politics, stressing in particular the role of collectively held or "intersubjective" ideas and understandings of social life' and assert that: '(a) human interaction is shaped primarily by ideational factors, not simply material ones; (b) the most important ideational factors are widely shared or "intersubjective" beliefs, which are not reducible to individuals; and (c) these shared beliefs construct the interests and identities of purposive actors' (Finnemore and Sikkink, 2001: 393; see also Adler, 1997; Price and Reus-Smit, 1998; Ruggie, 1998b; Wendt, 1999). Somewhere in between, a broad working definition of the institutions to which norms give rise is provided by Hall and Soskice (2001a: 9) who say institutions are 'a set of rules, formal or informal, that actors generally follow, whether for normative, cognitive, or material reasons'.

Institutional perspectives thus challenge the rational choice mechanism in the liberal economic model by seeing the role of ideas, beliefs and the resulting norms of behavior as providing richer explanations of how decisions are made and institutions constructed. In short, they apply 'norm-driven logics of appropriateness (cultural logics)' (Hay, 2006b: 4). Liberal economic versus institutional perspectives are therefore delineated by the manner in which the rational choice mechanism is applied in the former versus the role of norms of behavior in the latter. Followers of the mainstream liberal economic perspective understand the world in terms of material interests, based on a logic of consequentialism (the outcomes of taking certain courses of action), whereas institutionalists accentuate the role of ideas and social behavior (i.e. norms) based on a logic of appropriateness (that there is an appropriate way to act not necessarily contingent on the outcome of such behavior) (March and Olsen, 1989, 1998).[22]

Taking an institutional approach means that seeking solutions to the problem of environmental externalities becomes more complex. For example, Paterson rejects the idea that states in a liberal international economic order can ever make the required interventions to effectively address environmental problems because 'existing political, social and economic structures are part of the problem' (Paterson, 2000: 254). Elsewhere he notes that the focus for analysis should be on the structural power of capital and how it relates to the state (Newell and Paterson, 1998: 680). Viewed this way, the liberal economic view is more an ideology, or the result of institutional embedding that says markets and governments must (or should) operate in certain ways.[23] Alternative and often more successful approaches for internalizing environmental externalities may be suggested. Indeed, they may be essential if one accepts the view that 'preventing situations such as global warming requires more than just market mechanisms that simply assign economic value to intangibles' (Karliner, 1997: 47). That is to say, behavioral change is not just a matter of changing material returns, it is about recognizing the normative basis of prevailing institutions.

A key implication is that rather than economic actors making rational decisions in the sense of operating purely on the basis of assumed instrumental profit maximizing goals, one must admit the possibility raised by Ostrom that individuals are 'fallible, boundedly rational, and norm-using. In complex settings, no one is able to do a complete analysis before actions are taken, but individuals learn from mistakes and are able to craft tools – including rules – to improve the structure of the repetitive situations they face' (Ostrom, 1999: 496). This does not mean that irrationality is the alternative, but that rationality is not defined by the a priori assumptions employed in the mainstream liberal economic model. Similarly, it does not mean that material interests are irrelevant, but simply that they may not be the issue. What is at issue is how these are perceived. Economic actors such as firms have material interests, but it is the normative aspects of how these interests are perceived that matter if we are to study motivations in respect of realizing them (see, for example, Hay, 2006a and b).

Perhaps the clearest outline of the normative aspects of how material

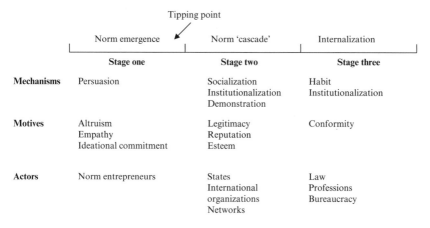

Source: Finnemore and Sikkink (1998: 896-898).

Figure 1.1   The norm lifecycle

interests are perceived is provided by Finnemore and Sikkink (1998). They conceptualize a norm lifecycle, shown in Figure 1.1. In stage one norm entrepreneurs, such as NGOs and often radical activists, advocate for a new approach to be taken that embraces a new norm. By raising the profile of the new norm, a tipping point is reached after which the norm is taken up in stage two by states, international organizations and other actors who intervene to promote the norm and construct rules flowing from its implementation. This leads to the new norm 'cascading' through other states and organizations. Finally, in the third stage norms are so habitual-ized that they become part of how actors in professions, the bureaucracy and the public at large behave, almost without them knowing that they are there. They become institutionalized (for example, few people today would recognize women having the vote or the abolition of slavery as issues worth discussing for their pros and cons). The norm lifecycle model therefore implies that institutionalized norms shape behavior and change over time, and in so doing form the basis of what is seen as rational.

What about the car industry? Institutional perspectives, including the above model, suggest that if firms are to change their behavior in respect of the environment, this will be a product of institutions that constrain certain types of behavior and enable others. This ultimately also produces institu-tional change. Livio de Simone, former chairman of the WBCSD, appears to suggest this has already happened in declaring that 'a paradigm shift has clearly taken place. Business used to be depicted as a primary source of the world's environmental problems. Today it is increasingly viewed as a vital contributor to solving those problems and securing a sustainable future for the planet' (Karliner, 1997: 31). However, whether or not a 'paradigm shift' has taken place necessitates an analysis that examines what political, economic and structural forces, and the institutionalized norms that inform their interpretation, are at work. In other words, it is necessary to tell an 'insider's story' to make sense of what events and actions mean (Wendt, 1998). A key part of so doing is recognizing the importance of firms' home states, for both material and institutional reasons.

THE MATERIAL AND INSTITUTIONAL IMPORTANCE OF FIRMS' HOME STATES

The picture painted earlier of the car industry as a global industry dominated by large MNCs was qualified by noting its national concentration, particularly in the three hubs of Germany (and the EU), the US and Japan. Therefore, there is a tension between conceiving the industry as truly global, versus the reality that it is comprised of companies with national bases that have international interests. This global/national tension reflects larger debates about the extent to which a shift in power has occurred from states to markets and the forces of transnational capital, versus the enduring relevance of states in international capitalist relations. The former global perspective is held by authors such as Strange (1996), Ohmae (1990), Friedman (1999) and adherents of the neoliberal view that markets are increasingly in command as a result of globalization, with states having diminished power to influence market outcomes.[24] The latter perspective is one that sits more comfortably with scholars of international relations who see commerce as based in national territories, with interaction between states and their major corporations occurring *internationally*. They include Pauly and Reich (1997), Doremus et al. (1999), Weiss (1998), Weiss and Hobson (1995), Vogel (2001), Boyer (1996), Wade (1996) and those who subscribe to the VOC approach such as those in Hall and Soskice (2001b).

In this section, the case is made for why, on the basis of both material and institutional factors, car firms' home states remain important. Therefore, whatever the theoretical perspective adopted, car firms' behavior is more a product of their national home bases than global markets. An international perspective in respect of the car industry, and thus an approach based on a comparative national analysis, is more appropriate. Furthermore, evidence will be presented that the industry's activities are concentrated in a handful of firms from each of these three territories that dominate their markets. From an institutional perspective, the relevance of the VOC approach for analysing the industry is then introduced.

Table 1.2   Transnationality measures for German, US and Japanese firms

	TNI (%)	Foreign sales as a proportion of total sales (%)
Volkswagen	56	72
DaimlerChrysler	29	39
BMW	67	73
German average	**51**	**62**
General Motors	34	31
Ford	49	42
US average	**41**	**36**
Toyota	49	60
Honda	69	77
Nissan	61	70
Japan average	**61**	**69**

Source: UNCTAD (2006).

The Material Importance of Firms' Home States

Although the car industry is characterized by global networks for production and distribution, the point was made earlier that its turnover, investment and production is actually concentrated in the three hubs of Germany/the EU, the US and Japan. Therefore, national/regional contexts for the industry and its firms remain important. This is the case for the geographical focus of firms' activities, their ownership, and the location of their key markets.

For geographical focus, Table 1.2 presents the transnationality index (TNI) for the major German, US and Japanese firms.[25] What is immediately apparent is that there is considerable variation in firms' TNIs. Japanese firms are the most transnational, but German and US firms' TNIs are around 50 per cent or less on average. The US firms, DaimlerChrysler and Toyota have TNIs of less than 50 per cent. In addition, the ratio of foreign to total sales is greater than the TNIs of the Japanese and German firms, whereas the converse is true for US firms. This suggests that not only are US firms less transnational than their German and Japanese counterparts, they are also the most focused on their home market. For the others, their transnationality is driven more by where they have their markets, rather than their operations.

Of course, there are other factors not considered here, such as the extent

Table 1.3   2006 passenger car production by the largest German, US and Japanese manufacturers

	Nationality (by ownership)	Car production (units)	Percentage of total
Toyota	Japan	6 800 228	13
Volkswagen	Germany	5 429 896	10
General Motors	US	5 708 038	11
Ford	US	3 800 633	7
Honda	Japan	3 549 787	7
Nissan	Japan	2 512 519	5
BMW	Germany	1 366 838	3
DaimlerChrysler	Germany	1 275 152	2
Total for firms shown here		30 443 091	59
World total		51 953 234	100

Source: OICA (2007).

to which firms are bi-national rather than transnational, or regional rather than global (Rugman, 2005; see also Dicken, 2003).[26] It suffices to say that even a cursory glance at the data demonstrates there is considerable variation in the extent to which these firms are global, and that the US firms, DaimlerChrysler and Toyota are not very global at all. The implication is that although firms should be concerned with international regulations and global market trends, those corresponding to their home state remain highly significant.[27]

Firms' transnationality, or rather their surprising lack of it, supports earlier data presented in Table 1.1 which demonstrated that turnover, investment and production are concentrated in Germany, the US and Japan where almost half or more of the industry's activity still takes place. In each of these territories, the industry has a magnified significance due to its concentration in them – e.g. five of the seven largest US industrial firms produce either cars or their fuel (Hawken et al., 1999: 23). Table 1.3 presents passenger car production by manufacturer for the eight largest manufacturers in these territories. It demonstrates that 59 per cent of total world production is concentrated in the hands of just these eight firms. This is a symptom of the increasing concentration of the industry generally, from 52 independent firms in 1964 to only 12 in 2004 as a result of takeovers and mergers between firms (Deutsche Bank, 2004: 13).[28] Therefore, these eight firms also represent two-thirds of the independent firms currently operating worldwide, so that the industry is not just concentrated on a state (and regional) basis, but also by the number of firms from each of these states.[29]

Turning to ownership, while cross-ownership may characterize the industry globally, some firms own others, or have a controlling stake in them, rather than being owned themselves. Smaller firms than the eight listed here are all in the latter category, making any determination of their nationality problematic. Of the top eight German, US and Japanese firms, General Motors and Ford are wholly US-owned; Toyota and Honda are wholly Japanese-owned; and Volkswagen and BMW are wholly German-owned, with Volkswagen also being the largest European firm (Deutsche Bank, 2004). Cross-ownership is a factor for DaimlerChrysler and Nissan. Even so, and this may be a controversial point, I would argue that they may be regarded as a German and Japanese firm respectively.

DaimlerChrysler was formed through the merger of Daimler-Benz (a German firm) and Chrysler (a US firm) in 1998 in what was supposed to be partnership of equals, but was really a takeover of Chrysler by its German partner. Although this meant it was culturally somewhat of a 'two-headed beast', with operations and a history that was half German and half US, the nature of the takeover and the subsequent setting of corporate policy and strategic direction in Germany meant it was in fact a German firm. Despite Chrysler's long history as a US company and its continuing operations there, the firm's Chrysler operations reported to a 'German-based parent' with the whole company being a 'German-controlled group' (Maxton and Wormald, 2004: 249–251; see also Deutsche Bank, 2004: 117–121). The arrangement never really worked, with the two halves of the company again going their separate ways in 2007. This demonstrates that German ownership of a US company was problematic, that control was *imposed* on the US half, and that the national distinctiveness of large MNCs such as those composing the car industry remains a reality.

Nissan has been part-owned by Renault since 1999 when Renault acquired a 37 per cent stake in the company, now increased to 44 per cent. Rather than a merger or takeover, as in the case of DaimlerChrysler, Renault acquired a substantial minority shareholding. The result is better characterized as a strategic alliance, because both brands have retained separate identities, separate operations and undertake separate reporting. Although it is certainly true that, from a Japanese perspective, radically different management practices were imposed on Nissan as a result of the alliance, it remains the case that a Japanese *culture* prevailed within the company because it was not actually taken over by Renault nor merged with it. Many commentators, such as Tiberghien (2007), would disagree with this. Yet, while there is undoubtedly a sharing of ideas and the fact of Renault's part ownership is inescapable, the cultural separation of the firms in practice is even more evident than for Daimle-Benz's takeover of Chrysler.[30] In short, both firms, in different ways, retained their respective national identities.

Observations on firms' ownership structures are important because they have implications for how strategic decisions are taken and implemented, in the sense that strategic decisions are more likely to be taken by firms that own others rather than ones that are themselves majority owned and controlled. And when the major firms that own or strategically control others are identified, it is clear that in addition to their economic activity, by the location of their headquarters and board membership the largest firms are all of European (mainly German), US or Japanese nationality. Their headquarters where strategic decisions are made remain in their home states, and the nationalities of their board members reflect their nationalities (Deutsche Bank, 2004).

In addition to the car industry's concentration in terms of economic activity and ownership, its production hubs of the US, Japan and the EU are also where its key markets are located. Seventy-five per cent of all cars are sold in these three territories, with Germany the largest market in Europe (Burns et al., 2002).[31] Despite growth in emerging markets such as China, it is still the case that only around 8 per cent of the world's population are car owners, and most of these remain in the industry's three traditional markets (Jain and Guiver, 2001). Furthermore, Table 1.4 demonstrates that firms continue to dominate their home markets where they have their headquarters. US and European brands hold a 63 per cent share of their home markets. In the case of European manufacturers, the German car industry is of critical importance because in addition to dominating their home market with a 71 per cent share, German firms hold nearly half the market for new car registrations in the EU. The only possible emerging exception to this rule is the Japanese industry whose firms' products penetrate markets outside Japan more than their EU or US counterparts, especially in the case of the US where they have taken a 28 per cent market share. Even so, they dominate their home market more than German and US firms do theirs with a 94 per cent share of registrations. The implication is that although firms should be concerned with global market trends and regulations, those corresponding to their own nationalities should be of critical importance because these are the markets they dominate and where they make most of their sales.

In summary, the car industry possesses both global and national attributes. It is an industry with globally networked operations in investment, production and distribution, but national strategic bases. These observations in respect of the car industry specifically, are reflected in more general observations by authors such as Wade (1996: 61) who stresses the

Table 1.4   2002 market shares for the major EU, US and Japanese firms

	Share of EU registrations (%)	Share of US registrations (%)	Share of Japanese registrations (%)
US brands	21	63	0.6
Asian brands	14	33	0.3
Specifically Japanese brands	11	28	94
European brands	63	6	5
Specifically German brands	46* (71 per cent share of German registrations)	6	4

Note: * German brands are the market leaders in Europe.

Sources: VDA (2003: 24, 33 and 45); JAMA (2003: 6-7); CCFA (2003: 13).

enduring importance of national differences in the world economy which remains 'more international than global. In the bigger economies, more than 80 per cent of production is for domestic consumption and more than 80 per cent of investment by domestic investors. Companies are rooted in national home bases with national regulatory regimes'.[32] Wade's comments have implications for states' differing institutional frameworks, a point made by authors such as Boyer (1996: 51) who notes that 'firms and sectors are clearly integrated within the international economy and, nevertheless, display very different institutional forms to cope with the same challenge of structural competitiveness. Even if the economic performances are quite similar, there is no one best way'. Therefore, a national comparative analysis on the basis of firms' home states is appropriate for a book focusing on the car industry's actions in respect of the environment, with potential implications beyond this to other industries. Hence the relevance of the VOC approach.

The Institutional Importance of Firms' Home States: the Varieties of Capitalism Approach

Dicken (1998: 196) observes that MNCs are 'produced through an intricate process of embedding in which the cognitive, cultural, social, political and economic characteristics of the national home base play a dominant part'. The evidence on the material importance of car firms' home states, despite their global operations, suggests that this perspective is especially relevant to them. Rather than placeless entities, they are likely to be institutionally embedded in their home states.

Although it would be an over-simplification to say that all MNCs from one home state are the same, firms from the same home state should share certain national characteristics. In this light, the VOC approach is a comparative institutional approach which holds that different capitalist states have different histories, cultures and structures that inform the nature of their capitalist relations, and that far from convergence on a liberal economic model globally, national differences persist. That is to say, the persistence of different institutional potentials gives rise to the persistence of different capitalisms.[33]

Given their different institutional potentials, the VOC approach sees capitalist states as either liberal market economies (LMEs) or coordinated market economies (CMEs). This is often presented in dichotomous terms, and those who do so are attacked by authors such as Crouch (2005a: 453) who say it amounts to designating mineral water as still or sparkling without bothering to consider a detailed chemical analysis of what is in the bottle. However, I prefer to think of the categorization more in terms of a continuum on one end of which are LME states such as the US, while at the other are CME states such as Germany and Japan. More problematic are states in between such as Spain, Portugal and Greece which occupy 'more ambiguous positions' (Hall and Soskice, 2001a: 21). But I agree with Pontusson (2005: 17) that 'we should not think of typologies as being right or wrong. Rather, we should think of them as heuristic devices – ways of organizing information – that may be more or less useful'. Without splitting hairs, the central point is this: while these are all capitalist countries, their institutions establish different 'rules of the game'. This has implications for how environmental problems are addressed, and indeed the success or otherwise of strategies for addressing them, because 'in any national economy, firms will gravitate towards the mode of coordination for which there is institutional support' (Hall and Soskice, 2001a: 8–9).[34]

Broadly speaking, firms in LMEs coordinate their activities via markets. In preferring market coordination of economic activity, they make their decisions based on market signals that define shorter-term profit levels. In regulatory terms, they therefore prefer deregulation over heavier state guidance and intervention. When they are subject to regulation, firms in LMEs will react more efficiently to clearly specified regulations, especially those aimed at altering market price signals.

Firms in CMEs are characterized by more non-market cooperative relationships to coordinate economic activity. It is not primarily the market and its price signals that determine their behavior, but relationships based on cooperative networks. Firms in CMEs tend more towards consensus decision-making between a greater range of stakeholders internal and external to the firm based on long-established networks. They will react more efficiently to regulations based on negotiated and agreed rules and standards.

Obviously, the division between firms favoring cooperative coordination in CMEs versus deregulated market competition in LMEs is very broad. Underlying this divide are a myriad of aspects. The ones most applicable to the analysis in this book are explained in detail in Chapter 2. The point at this stage is that, as the WBCSD (2004) notes, institutions determine how environmental issues are addressed in different states, the extent to which corporations take the lead in encouraging change and the type of action they take.

SO WHAT'S NEW HERE?

Cutler et al. (1999b: 4) say that 'in an era when the authority of the state appears to be challenged in so many ways, the existence of alternative sources of authority takes on great significance, especially when that authority is wielded internationally by profit-seeking entities'. If it is true that firms, as profit-seeking entities, increasingly exercise their power to affect social and environmental outcomes previously seen as the responsibility of states, then we should be looking at how they can take responsibility for their actions.[35] I am therefore sympathetic with Hall and Soskice's (2001a: 4, 6) desire 'to bring firms back into the centre of the analysis of comparative capitalism', in recognition that firms are 'the crucial actors in a capitalist economy',[36] rather than seeing actors surrounding them such as social movements and the state as the primary actors in addressing environmental degradation.

However, this does not mean that the state is irrelevant. After all, employing the insights of the VOC approach as the theoretical basis for analysis demonstrably leaves the state 'in' the analysis. This is because 'the basic institutional structures of MNCs may be influenced or even determined by the characteristics of states' through the laws they make, but also how they frame markets and relations of production with them (Pauly and Reich, 1997: 5; see also Crouch, 2005a: 450). The key point to stress is that the analysis here represents an attempt to move away from the traditional liberal economic model where the state and its intervention is the focus of analysis, to one which sees a *relational* approach, underpinned by national institutional variations in capitalist relations of production, as having greater explanatory power.[37]

Focusing on the car industry, with its track record or producing products that are a major cause of global environmental damage, the point is then that if such an industry can improve the environmental impact of its operations, *any* industry can. Its linkages with firms in other industries that supply components and parts also suggests the potential for a strong multiplier effect from any behavioral change it initiates.[38] Furthermore, given its visibility and the magnitude of its responsibility for environmental damage, any progress made in this industry is likely to have a strong demonstration effect in terms of bringing about cultural change in other less directly-related industries. In short, the centrality of the international car industry to the business/environment debate marks it out as a 'crucial case' and a 'least likely' case for environmental sustainability (Eckstein, 1975: 113–123; King et al.,1994: 208–212).

The VOC approach is one of 'talking about social embeddedness, path dependency and comparative institutional advantage' (Coates, 2005a: 4). Therefore, the analysis presented here represents an attempt to add to the institutionalist literature from an international perspective, rather than a global one. The insights of the VOC approach are used to support the empirical analysis conducted in respect of the car industry and the environment, but the converse is also true: the empirical analysis is used to support and extend the insights of the VOC approach. This is the case because in all the VOC literature, it is striking that there is little in-depth analysis of particular industry sectors or, as Hay (2005) notes, the relatively recent arrival on the scene of the VOC approach has not yet produced secondary literature that evaluates its core theoretical and substantive contributions. There is certainly no analysis that I am aware of from an environmental perspective. Related issue areas such as education and industrial relations feature, but not the environment.

Finally, given the two contrasting approaches to environmental externalities – one based on a rationalist material framework (the liberal economic model) and the other on a normative institutional one (the VOC approach) – the aim of this book is to assess whether the liberal economic model is universally applicable, and therefore sufficient to explain the behavior of firms, or whether it is a special case contingent on certain institutional foundations that may vary from state to state. The latter is shown to be the case. In taking a view that the nationality of firms matters, this book contributes to the VOC literature that promotes the perspective that rather than global isomorphism in the institutional foundations for economic affairs, national institutional differences persist. The new insights provided in this light are that the VOC of firms' home states impact on whether they are more or less disposed to take environmental initiatives, and the form these initiatives are likely to take. Thus, it will be shown that car firms' environmental initiatives are a product of the institutions of their home states' VOC.

CONCLUSION

The perspectives and issues outlined above give rise to three overarching, related questions. The first, and central question, is: what institutional factors are likely to motivate firms in the car industry to see environmental issues as central to their business interests? This is a more precise rendering of the question posed at the outset. The second question, related to the first one, is: are the motivators for firms embracing environmental improvements universal, or specific to firms based on their nationality or, possibly, individual cultures? Depending on the answers to the first two questions, the third is: why should the car industry be concerned about the environment, particularly given its global economic significance and resulting political power?

There is a dichotomy in how the questions are approached. On the one hand, the liberal economic perspective says that if environmental externalities are being internalized, this must be because firms are rationally responding to material exogenous factors: market forces and state regulation. On the other hand, the institutional perspective of the VOC approach says that institutional factors at the state level (i.e. the persistence of different Varieties of Capitalism) are relevant for how material factors are interpreted and their significance. The latter is preferred simply because it is not unreasonable to say that there is usually more than just 'rational' profit maximization going on because 'the world does not fit the Panglossian belief that firms always make optimal choices' (Porter and van der Linde, 1995a: 99). Indeed, *both* rational profit maximizing motivations and behavior based on institutionalized norms will be shown to explain the car industry's actions. Although the two are often presented in a way that makes them appear mutually exclusive, this need not necessarily be the case. To lean too much one way or another is to lean towards 'false extremes' (Hall, 1993: 43).

The working hypothesis adopted in this book may therefore be expressed as the following statement made by Haufler (1999: 201): 'corporate management obviously responds to market signals, as in the neoclassical model, but the character of that response is not equally obvious [because] corporate preferences are driven in part by norms about the appropriate approaches to business'. I similarly agree with the observation of Levy and Rothenberg (2002: 173) on the car industry in respect of climate change, that 'the formulation of strategy is generally treated as a rational process of matching corporate capabilities to market demands. But this does not always account well for the heterogeneity observed in corporate strategies towards complex environmental issues'. The point is this: while both material and institutional factors matter, the former is always predicated on the latter. To quote Levy and Rothenberg 2002: 173) again, 'market trends are themselves subject to institutional construction'. By employing the insights of the VOC approach, it will be shown that state-specific institutional variations in capitalist relations of production are crucial for understanding how firms of different nationalities approach the question of making environmental commitments given the material factors they face.

In Chapter 2, the insights of the VOC approach are outlined in greater detail as well as how the research will be operationalized by focusing on the environmental issue of climate change, and the car industry's contribution to it via the CO_2 emissions of passenger cars. Chapter 3 outlines the actual environmental product development initiatives being undertaken by the car industry in respect of the CO_2 emissions of passenger cars, and highlights the different emphasis placed on these initiatives by firms depending on their 'nationality'. This sets up the analysis to be conducted in the four empirical analysis chapters, Chapters 4 to 7. Chapters 4 and 5 examine the key material factors of state regulations and market forces. What is found is that the institutional insights of the VOC approach provide greater explanatory power than the rationalist perspective of the liberal economic model, and that the latter is sufficient only in the case of the US car industry because its LME attributes are themselves institutionally determined. The analysis then focuses on individual car firms in Chapters 6 and 7 by qualitatively examining their environmental reports and the results of interviews with key personnel. The analysis in these chapters encompasses institutional factors at the state level, but endogenous institutional factors emanating from within firms are also brought to bear. As such, not only do Chapters 6 and 7 present an analysis of firms' first-hand perspectives, they also serve to uncover the role played by such factors in greater detail that are not revealed by analysing exogenous state regulations or market forces alone. Chapter 8 presents the conclusions.

NOTES

1. The classic opinion piece that popularized this view is that of Friedman (1970). In it, he said 'there is one and only one social responsibility of business – to use is resources and engage in activities designed to increase its profits so long as it stays within the rules of the game'.

2. Perhaps the best overview of the VOC approach is provided by the contributions in Hall and Soskice (2001b).

3. Dicken (2003: 375–736) notes that all three major US producers have collaborative or cross-ownership links with Japanese and Korean firms, and the major European firms have joint research programs. A similar point is made by Koshiba et al. (2001). A comprehensive list of firms and their cross-ownership structures is provided by Deutsche Bank (2004: 13). For example, in 2004 General Motors owned 12 per cent of Isuzu, 20 per cent of Suzuki, 42 per cent of Daewoo, 20 per cent of Fuji Heavy Industries, 100 per cent of Saab and 100 per cent of Opel/Vauxhall.

4. This is calculated as follows. Paterson (2000) says that up to 85 per cent of transport-related CO_2 emissions are caused by passenger cars, and that transport in total accounts for 23 per cent of emissions in OECD countries. Therefore, this means that 19.55 per cent of OECD countries' CO_2 emissions are car-related (i.e. 85 per cent × 23 per cent). He goes on to say that these emissions are only around 60 per cent of emissions throughout the life of a car, the rest coming from other related activities. When one inflates the 19.55 per cent of OECD emissions to take account of this, the total is 32.6 per cent (i.e. 100/60 × 19.55 per cent). This corresponds reasonably closely with the figure of 30 per cent for the transport sector quoted in Deutsche Bank (2004: 58).

5. This is based on Germany and Japan's commitments to reduce their emissions by 7.4 and 8.5 per cent respectively. The US had made commitments to reduce its emissions by 7 per cent, but subsequently decided not to ratify the Kyoto Protocol.

6. Freund and Martin (1993: 17–19) point out that cars consume 35 per cent of the oil used in Japan and 63 per cent of the oil used in the US simply in their application (i.e. exclusive of related activities such as road building which also uses oil). In the US, car production consumes 13 per cent of all steel, 16 per cent of the aluminum, 69 per cent of the lead, 36 per cent of the platinum and 58 per cent of the rubber.

7. This is based on a conversion from 7 billion pounds.

8. For example, in his speech to the Fifth Annual Greenpeace Business Conference in 2000, Bill Ford, said his company had resigned its membership of the GCC because it 'felt that membership in that organization was an impediment to [its] ability to move forward credibly with [its] agenda on environmental responsibility' (Ford Motor Company, 2000; see also Source Watch, no date; Beder, 2002: 238–239).

9. In fact, light trucks such as SUVs accounted for around 75 per cent of DaimlerChrysler's US production over the period considered in this book. See also *The Economist*, 2002b, 2003.

10. This is the colloquial name for the United Nations Conference on Environment and Development (UNCED) held in Rio de Janeiro on 3–14 June 1992.

11. Australia, Kazakhstan, Croatia, Monaco and the US were the only non-ratifiers. With its change of government in 2007, Australia has now joined the rest of the world in signing up to the treaty.

12. See also Karliner (1997: 30) who discusses how corporate environmental departments and policies emerged within major corporations, along with senior executives coming to be in charge of environmental issues.

13. A similar viewpoint on the car industry is evident in Hawken et al. (1999).

14. This is an observation based on perusing firms' reporting since the late 1980s to the early 1990s. Many started with environmental reports, or environmental statements and guidelines, that have subsequently been incorporated in broader corporate citizenship or corporate social responsibility reports.

15. Ford and General Motors' first environmental reports were produced in 1989 and 1994 respectively.

16. This is based on a review of the environmental reports available from the major firms' websites, and/or discussion of them there. In addition, pdf files on firms' environmental initiatives downloaded from the website of the UNEP's Division of Technology, Industry and Economics were used to confirm firms' first year of publication of environmental reports (UNEP, no date).

17. There is a wide and well understood body of literature on environmental externalities and market failure. The classic articles are Hardin (1968) and Coase (1960). A basic explanation of many of the concepts may be found in almost any economics textbook, such as Boadway and Wildasin (1984: 55–62). For a more social and political perspective see Ostrom (1990, especially Chapter 1). For a discussion of the application of the concepts see Bürgenmeier (1997). In an international relations context see Greene (2005).

18. In the discipline of economics, the technical name given to the mainstream liberal economic perspective is, of course, neoclassical economics.

19. For an excellent description of classical liberalism see Crane and Amawi (1997). For a further introductory elaboration of the liberal economic perspective in a more contemporary sense see Dunne (2005) and Lamy (2005). For an analysis of economic liberalism from a critical perspective see Helleiner (2003). For an analysis, and criticism, of rationalism as a way of conceiving the actions of actors generally, see the now classic Green and Shapiro (1994).

20. This is also the view held by the WTO and UNEP. See UNEP and International Institute for Sustainable Development (2000), and Nordstrom and Vaughan (1999).

21. I accept that it might be mischievous to cast Goldstein and Keohane as staunch advocates of the institutional approach, but the importance of the approach is explicitly acknowledged and addressed by them.

22. For a more extended discussion of institutionalist perspectives and the role of ideas, beliefs and norms more broadly see also Risse (2000 and 2002), J. Hall (1993), P. Hall (1997), Wendt (1995, 1998) and Elster (1989).

23. For example, Karliner (1997: 2) sees the role of states and business in the environment debate as constrained by the rise of neoliberalism which opposes the notion of states intervening for the 'social good'.

24. Strange (1996) sees global capital's ability to transcend borders as resulting in states becoming powerless, with power having transferred to markets. Ohmae (1990) similarly sees the world as becoming 'borderless', with corporate strategies now characterized predominantly by a global perspective. In Friedman's (1999) view, states must adopt the 'golden straightjacket' approach to intervening in their economies, in the sense that any activist-style policies run the risk of capital flight. By way of contrast, though not necessarily contradiction, a more critical perspective is provided by Helleiner (2003). He identifies Margaret Thatcher's 'TINA Principle' ('There Is No Alternative' to neoliberal policies of minimum state intervention in markets due to the global interconnectedness of production and trade) as a *choice* taken by powerful industrialized states.

25. There are smaller firms such as Mitsubishi in Japan, but it is not a major producer in the sense that its car production is 26 per cent less than that of the smallest firm here, BMW. The disparity is, if anything, exacerbated if one considers that BMW is a niche prestige producer, whereas Mitsubishi is a volume producer (OICA, 2007). The TNI is used by the United Nations Conference on Trade and Environment (UNCTAD) and is a simple composite average of foreign assets, sales and employment to total assets, sales and employment.

26. For a general overview of the arguments, see also Hay (2006c).

27. This view coincides with that of Hirst and Thompson (1997: 346), who note that there are few truly transnational corporations and that 'most major manufacturing multinationals account for two thirds of their sales within their home region; moreover, there seems to be no tendency for this ratio to diminish'. More broadly, it agrees with authors such as Rugman (2005) who see the strategic impact of globalization as overstated because firms' nationalities, home markets and the regions in which they are located remain of crucial importance.

28. They are: Volkswagen, BMW, DaimlerChrysler, Porsche, PSA Peugeot Citroen, General Motors, Ford, Renault, Toyota, Honda, Hyundai and Rover.

29. Although, of course, this two-thirds only reflects the actual number of firms rather than their size and economic importance. For example, of the other four independent firms,

two are quite small: Rover has since gone into bankruptcy and Porsche is a niche producer of expensive high performance sports cars.

30. Maxton and Wormald (2004: 116 and 221–222) refer to Chrysler as having been 'bought by Daimler', but Nissan as having been 'subsumed (but nicely this time) into Renault'. There is therefore a qualitative difference in the associations of the companies involved in each case. Indeed, *The Economist* notes the following: 'Although Renault and Nissan have cross-shareholdings and a deep alliance, their relationship deliberately stops well short of outright merger. Perhaps that is why it has been so successful, avoiding the integration pain that has marred, for instance, Daimler-Benz's *takeover* of Chrysler. In his book, *Shift: Inside Nissan's Historic Revival*, published in English last month, Mr Ghosn (former President and CEO of Nissan) says that the strength of the alliance "can be found, on the one hand, in its respect for the identities of the two companies, and on the other, in the necessity for developing synergies"' (*The Economist*, 2005 with emphasis added). For a colorful description of the takeover of Chrysler by Daimler-Benz see Vlasic and Stertz (2001). For Renault's share in Nissan and the nature of the relationship between the two companies from Renault's perspective, see Renault (2001: 12–15). See also Deutsche Bank (2002 and 2004) for the cross-ownership percentages.

31. Data on German car sales were presented in Table 1.1 by value. For data on sales volume (i.e. units sold) which show that Germany is the largest market in Europe on this basis as well, see ACEA (no date a). For a historical time series showing this to be true for the time period covered in this book, see ACEA (no date b).

32. He also points out that the observations made here on national ownership and geographical location of operations are generalizable to MNCs more generally. Similar observations are made by Weiss (1998).

33. The literature in this vein continues to burgeon. In addition to Hall and Soskice (2001b), it includes contributions in other edited works such as Coates (2005b); Kitschelt et al. (1999b), Crouch and Streeck (1997); Hollingsworth and Boyer (1997); Berger and Dore (1996); and Clegg and Redding (1990). Contributions from these are cited in the following chapter.

34. The following is a brief summary of the points they make at pp. 21–33.

35. There are many authors who assert this, and it is a major part of the thinking that underpins the CSR literature. For example, Korten (quoted in Lawrence et al., 2005: 47) sees it as avoidable that business, as the 'most powerful institution on the planet' and therefore the 'dominant institution in society' must take the place of the state and 'take responsibility' for its actions in the face of receding state regulation.

36. A similar desire is expressed in Hall (1999: 147).

37. It is worth noting that such an approach is not at odds with that advocated by the OECD (2001a, b). Seiichi Kondo, former Deputy Secretary General of the OECD, is quoted as having said that 'international order and prosperity is no longer achieved through a traditional balance of power among states, nor through the hegemony of a superpower. In this new age of globalization, cooperation among four key actors – states, international organizations, civil society and markets – has become more essential than ever' (OECD, 2001b: 80).

38. It is estimated that one qualified job in the automotive industry indirectly creates up to ten qualified jobs in related industry sectors (UNEP, 2002: 24). Dicken (1998: 326) actually describes the car industry as an 'assembly industry' requiring hundreds of thousands of components mostly sourced from suppliers worldwide.

2. The Varieties of Capitalism approach

Standards for evaluating organizational performance and prevalent criteria for judging firms' strategic priorities vary significantly across institutional regimes and cannot be derived from a single universal market rationality.

(Whitley, 1999: 13)

Institutions are embedded in a culture in which their logic is symbolically grounded, organisationally structured, technically and materially constrained, politically defended, and historically shaped by specific rules and norms.

(Hollingsworth, 1997a: 266)

The key questions to be addressed in this book were posed in Chapter 1. The first, and central question, is: what institutional factors are likely to motivate firms in the car industry to see environmental issues as central to their business interests? The second, related, question is: are the motivators for firms embracing environmental improvements universal, or specific to firms based on their nationality or, possibly, individual cultures? Depending on the answers to these, the third question is: why should the car industry be concerned about the environment, particularly given its global economic significance and resulting political power?

In discussing how these questions will be answered, the significance of material versus normative factors was highlighted, and therefore rationalist versus institutional perspectives. The assertion was made that although material factors are important, norms and the institutions to which these give rise are crucial for explaining why firms of different nationalities approach making environmental commitments – that is internalizing environmental externalities – in different ways. In Chapter 1, the enduring importance of car firms' home states in terms of production and key markets, as well as ownership and headquarters, led to the identification of an institutional analysis on the basis of firms' home states via the Varieties of Capitalism (VOC) approach.

The VOC approach suggests insights into national variations in capitalist relations of production in industrialized states. It is therefore applicable to a comparative institutional analysis of the car industry's activities in its three hubs of Germany, the United States and Japan. The broad divide between liberal market economies, such as the US, and coordinated market economies, such as Germany and Japan, has been introduced. This chapter describes key aspects of the divide in greater detail. The aim here is to expand on some of the VOC approach's key insights in order to establish why national variations in capitalist relations of production have implications for whether, and how, firms of different nationalities address the environmental impact of their actions. As such, the chapter concludes with some inferences on how the VOC literature may be applied in a novel way to the environmental motivations of firms. The application is novel in the sense that rather than examining the competitive advantages of states' industrial bases, or the operation of their product and financial markets etc., what is shown is that a state's variety of capitalism has implications for traditionally less 'core' considerations such as the environment.

INSIGHTS OF THE VARIETIES OF CAPITALISM APPROACH

The VOC approach speaks to debates about whether the imperatives of global capitalism mean that all capitalist economies are inevitably converging on a neoliberal model characterized by privatization, deregulation and free markets. Those asserting this include early authors on globalization such as Ohmae (1990) and Strange (1996 and 1997), who see state power being transferred to markets, or more accurately, internationally mobile capital. This means states are increasingly 'merely the handmaidens of firms', with each state at best 'a kind of landlord for the enterprises inhabiting the national territory' (Strange 1997: 184).[1] However, such a view soon came to be seen as more 'globaloney' than reality (Hay and Marsh, 2000: 6),[2] with authors such as Weiss (1998), Weiss and Hobson (1995), Hirst and Thompson (1996), and (from a regulatory perspective) Vogel (1996) saying this misrepresents what is happening in reality. A recent excellent essay on the waves of theorizing on globalization by Martell (2007) puts such early views on globalization in their place.

Rather than throwing up their hands and declaring that 'states are now virtually powerless to make real policy choices' with all states 'forced to adopt similar fiscal, economic and social policy regimes' (Weiss, 1998: 188), most authors now argue that states still do have power. Even if they do not dismiss the idea of globalization altogether, they see a more complex picture in which states' power is not so much coercive as it is 'soft', or institutional (see, for example, Held et al., 1999). Furthermore, state sovereignty is often shared with private actors, especially MNCs. Haufler (2006: 89) makes a particularly profound point when noting that only with Adam Smith's *Wealth of Nations* 'does a separation between public and private economic affairs start to be widely discussed'. The reality is that industry associations and firms do have power in international affairs, but that they interact with states to share power in achieving their profit-motivated goals. It is also the case that states benefit from sharing their sovereignty with such private entities in achieving their goals. This means that regulatory governance is best seen neither in terms of the loss of state sovereignty to markets, nor in terms of its retention by states. It is neither private nor public. In this vein, the VOC approach says that because there are different Varieties of Capitalism that reflect the different institutional capacities of states, state power is exercised in different ways (see also Hall and Biersteker 2002; Cutler 2006).

A related debate regards the corporate strategies of multinational corporations. One perspective is that MNCs have incentives to standardize their products to reap economies of scale from their global investment, production and distribution networks. Alternatively, there is the view that MNCs use their international reach and information networks to tailor products for local markets (see, for example, Dicken, 2003; Dunning, 1993). The VOC approach walks a line between these two arguments by saying that while MNCs may operate both globally and tailor their products to satisfy local market conditions, there is another factor to be considered. This is that the products they offer in the first place are very much determined by the institutional framework of their home territories.

Fundamentally, the VOC approach therefore says that firms are institutionally embedded in their home states for economic, political, social, cultural and historic reasons, and that capitalist states possess historically institutionalized norms which endure over time. Rather than institutional isomorphism as a result of the forces of globalization, national institutional variations endure and produce different outcomes in terms of competitiveness, the types of goods and services produced and how these are produced. States' different capitalisms also suggest different propensities for change and how change occurs. The contention of this book is that this has implications for non-economic outcomes, such as addressing environmental externalities, because these are directly related to national variations in the institutional basis of capitalist relations of production.[3]

As noted in Chapter 1, in what Crouch (2005a: 442) dubs the 'emblematic citation' for the VOC approach, Hall and Soskice (2001a: 9) define institutions as 'a set of rules, formal or informal, that actors generally follow, whether for normative, cognitive, or material reasons'. Starting from this point, they see capitalist economies as shaped by the institutions that underpin them which provide different 'capacities for the exchange of information, monitoring, and the sanctioning of defections relevant to cooperative behavior among firms and other actors' (Hall and Soskice, 2001a: 10–11). This perspective leads to the categorization of states' capitalisms as tending more towards LMEs versus CMEs. It was noted that firms in LMEs coordinate their activities via market competition, whereas firms in CMEs are characterized by more non-market cooperative relationships to coordinate economic activity.

It was also noted that there are a myriad of aspects underlying the LME/CME divide. Those most applicable to the analysis in this book are: the nature of state–business relations; the role of product markets; the role of financial markets; the organizing principles of firms; the role of technology; the relationship between exogenous versus endogenous factors impacting on firms; and the centrality of historical context. This is not an exhaustive list, but one that would seem to describe the institutional relations most pertinent to the empirical analysis to follow.[4] They are discussed below, drawing on the work of scholars specifically identifying themselves as employing the VOC approach, as well as those in the broader comparative institutionalist vein. Some readers may find this problematic, but it seems to me that the VOC approach is embedded in a rich comparative institutionalist literature, and flows from it. The VOC approach is, of course, different in certain respects, especially its dichotomous LME versus CME categorization of states. However, taking a similar perspective to that of Pontusson (2005), my point is that to divorce it from this broader literature that informs it is to decontextualize it to such an extent that the risk is the creation of artificial, and unnecessary, theoretical boundaries.

State–Business Relations

A major divide between LMEs and CMEs is the extent to which the state and business cooperate to achieve mutual objectives. Firms in LMEs tend to pressure their governments for deregulation, whereas firms in CMEs expect the state to be an activist one and a partner in the market with them. LME-based firms prefer free markets that operate on laissez-faire principles unless there is a clear case for state intervention due to market failure, whereas CME-based forms are to a large extent also state coordinated (Hall and Soskice, 2001a: 57; see also Berger, 1996).

As the archetypal LME, the US has long had an ideology of non-intervention in markets. This means the US government has never had an effective industry policy. It has taken the more indirect approach of creating an *environment* for business to succeed in markets. The distinction is important. It means that when it comes to regulation, the US has taken the LME perspective that the state should only intervene to internalize market externalities. Of course, one should not caricature US industry as a paragon of self-reliance operating in some vacuum free from government intervention, assistance, or protection from time to time. However, there is certainly a strong ideology that this is virtuous, and there is the reality of less state coordination of business.[5]

In fact, there is considerable state–business antagonism, with 'the most characteristic, distinctive and persistent belief of American corporate executives (being) an underlying suspicion and mistrust of government' (Vogel quoted in Wilks, 1990: 143). The ideology underlying this belief is characterized by Wilks (1990: 143) as follows:

> The dominant value is an emphatically and sincerely articulated support for the 'free enterprise system' and associated with that is the practical norm of rejecting any action that inhibits management autonomy. More specific to government is a parallel value that wholeheartedly rejects the legitimacy of state intervention in the economy and a norm that is suspicious of the competence and the motives of public officials.

It follows that when market intervention does occur, including for environmental reasons, it does not occur in a coordinated manner, but is highly pluralistic in nature, occurring at many levels and with many 'voices' taking part. Consensus is hampered by competition for representation, and a tendency to reject compromise (Scruggs, 2003: 227–228; see also OECD, 1996; Kraft, 2002).[6] The result is an adversarial relationship between the state, industry and other stakeholders. Given such a relationship, state–business relations are often characterized more by industry lobbying and attempting to 'capture government agencies', rather than working with, or following the agenda set by, those agencies (Wilks, 1990: 131). Firms desire autonomy to pursue their profit-motivated interests, so individualism and market orientation in business is promoted over collectivism and national spirit.

In contrast, German state–business relations are generally conceived as more amicable and constructive. Germany is not a laissez-faire economy, but one in which there is a national approach to economic development with the state playing a 'passive, facilitative role' (Wilks, 1990: 138). Thus, the state's role is one of support for industry, working with firms and industry associations to further national objectives, and helping to coordinate firms' activities. The German state may be thought of as an 'enabling state' (Streeck, 1997: 38). While not necessarily command-and-control in character, the state does work to develop consensus between powerful business actors, both via laws as well as by way of constructive discourse between the state and business (see, for example, Schmidt, 2002).

State–business relations in Japan go further to exhibit an almost symbiotic relationship. An 'iron triangle' of business–bureaucracy–government relations means that a type of 'corporatism without labor' exists, in the context of a belief that 'capitalism needs the visible hand of the state' (Broadbent, 2002: 143). Though not a centrally planned economy, Japan can still be thought of as a *developmental state* where the government has a vision for the goals of the private sector, has a history of arranging preferential allocation of capital to targeted industry sectors and key firms, and has a bureaucratic architecture designed specifically to consult and work with firms and industry sectors – e.g. the Ministry for International Trade and Industry (MITI), now renamed the Ministry of Economy Trade and Industry (METI) (see Dicken, 1998; Dore, 2000a). This leads Broadbent (2002: 300) to label Japan a 'nationalist-paternalist capitalist state'.

This does not simply mean the Japanese government takes decisions and business implements them.[7] Instead, a more *organic* relationship, based on mutual understanding, is implied by Redding and Whitley (1990: 92) who characterize Japanese state–business relations as 'subtle but indirect strategic guidance and only limited use of open suggestion', or Wilks (1990) who emphasizes the Japanese preference for harmony and consensus via accommodation, consultation and conflict avoidance wherever possible that leads Japanese bureaucrats to be able to issue legally non-binding instructions. The result is 'reciprocal consent' between the state and business, such that industry groups are involved in developing policies with the state setting stringent yet flexibly implemented regulations that are constructed with industry consultation (Wilks, 1990: 143).

Whatever the nuances, in both Germany and Japan, the line between business and government interests is more blurred than in the US. This is not to say that the differing basis of state–business collective action between them is spurious,[8] but to stress that in both business and nationalism are to some extent conflated.[9] While US firms desire deregulation and hands-off laissez-faire market operations, German and Japanese firms operate more on the basis of consensus-oriented negotiation with the state. While business 'cooperation' with government has as its goal the capture of regulatory agencies in the US, the state is more an agenda-setter in Germany and Japan, coordinating firms or informally suggesting strategies. Instead of the lobbying-conflict US model, German and Japanese firms operate within a collaborative-consensus model through which business and government develop regulations, agree on targets to be met, and establish priorities and goals to be achieved.

The Role of Product Markets

Differences in the role of product markets (i.e. markets for goods and services) revolve around the priority accorded market forces. These are accorded higher priority for LME-based firms, while being one among a range of motivating factors in CMEs. Related to priority is the degree to which markets *drive* firm strategies in LMEs, as opposed to *reflect* them in CMEs. This is a question of causality, such that firm strategies reflect market forces more in LMEs, whereas market forces are more a reflection of firm strategies in CMEs.

Concomitant with an LME preference for a less interventionist state,[10] a market mentality comes to dominate firms' strategic thinking. Competition in markets is held to be of paramount importance, because it is seen as necessary for 'efficient' outcomes. Markets thus play a primary role in organizing economic activity and determining production strategy, with the goal being shorter-term profits via competition in them. As Hollingsworth notes of LMEs such as the US, 'a market mentality tends to become pervasive', the result being that 'the dominant institutional arrangements for coordinating a society's economy tend to be markets, corporate hierarchies, and a weakly structured regulatory state' (Hollingsworth, 1997a: 271). Thus, when the state does intervene in LMEs, Hall and Soskice (2001a: 49) find that governments 'should find it more feasible to implement market-incentive policies that do not put extensive demands on firms to form relational contracts with others, but rely on markets to coordinate their activities'.

Markets play less of a strategic organizing role in CMEs such as Germany and Japan. It is not that market forces are unimportant, but they are not the driving force they are in LMEs like the US. Instead, communitarian obligations (e.g. to the state and society) and higher levels of trust and coordination between economic actors, rather than competition, are more the norm. There tend to be institutional arrangements (both cultural and legal) that facilitate cooperation rather than competition. Rather than focusing on short-term profits in markets, this facilitates a longer-term view when it comes to strategic planning because if 'winning' is not the aim, but coordinated action with competitors and the state to be more competitive on a longer-term basis, then short-term financial gains are less important than longer-term market domination (see, for example, Wilks 1990; Hollingsworth, 1997a).

The difference in emphasis on the role of markets has direct implications for non-economic outcomes. In CMEs, concepts such as reputation and standing have heightened importance. In addition to market success there is the notion of firms possessing a social contract with society. By contrast, in LMEs strategies that do not clearly produce financial rewards in the short term are seen more as 'philanthropy' – i.e. an 'add-on' to the core purpose of making profits (a point implicit in *The Economist*, 2006). Speaking plainly, the division is between the firm serving society in CMEs and the firm serving itself in LMEs.

By way of illustration, Wilks (1990: 138) notes in the case of Germany that government support for industry's interests is reflected in private entrepreneurs seeing themselves as embodying principles of 'good citizenship', with public obligations as important as 'the private concerns of selfish individuals'. Thus, private enterprise sees itself as serving societal interests as well as amassing private wealth. In the case of Japan, he notes that the authority of the state is reflected in a broader desire to act for the greater good on the part of business: 'the fear of letting down the side, of breaking with consensus, of not meeting expected standards provides the main psychological drive for generating what must be the most impressive political and social power in Asia' (Pye and Pye, 1985 quoted in Wilks, 1990: 141).

The above observations have implications for inter-firm relations. In the US, market competition is enshrined by law. Anti-trust laws, for which there have been largely no historical equivalents in Germany or Japan,[11] work against oligopolistic competition (in theory, if not necessarily always in practice) to promote market competition between firms. Thus, reputation building is more market contingent than founded on close business networks or associations. Indeed, it is estimated that as little as 1 per cent of research and development funds spent in the US private sector is devoted to collaborative research (Boyer, 1996: 45; see also Hollingsworth, 1997b). For US firms, a predilection to avoid acting collectively, with legal sanctions against doing so, reflects an institutional framework that favors short-term, more competitive relations based on market forces (Soskice, 1999: 110–113).

Inter-firm relations in CMEs are seen less in competitive terms than the need for coordination through large, organized firm groupings. Such groups present views to government, but more than this they influence production strategies. In the case of Germany, competition is not so much seen in terms of competing with other firms, as a focus on product differentiation and niche production, given an overall goal of harmonious inter-firm relations (Hall and Soskice, 2001a: 26–27). In the case of Japan, Hampden-Turner and Trompenaars (1993) observe that markets are characterized by deep non-market relationships between firms, their customers and suppliers. Japanese firms are reluctant 'to break relationships with those particular partners who keep them supplied and informed', and cultivate 'deep relationships over time with clients [because] you do not switch customers or suppliers day by day on the basis of price calculations' (Hampden-Turner and Trompenaars, 1993: 25).[12]

On the whole, a preference for deregulated competition in product markets, and the primacy of competitive market forces as a strategic motivator are features of LMEs such as the US. By contrast, market forces are one factor among many for firms in CMEs such as Germany and Japan, with a preference for coordination, cooperation and longer-term relationships based on trust as organizers of economic activity.

The Role of Financial Markets

Mirroring differences in the role of product markets in LMEs versus CMEs, are differences in the role of financial markets (i.e. mechanisms for accessing investment finance). Reliance on stock markets and the interests of shareholders is a (or rather *the*) major focus for firms in LMEs, whereas a broader range of stakeholders are the focus for firms in CMEs. This is because the latter have historically relied more on debt than equity finance. As with differences in the role of product markets, this produces shorter-term market perspectives in LMEs versus longer-term relational perspectives in CMEs.

Dore (2000a) labels US capitalism as 'stockmarket capitalism' because of US firms' reliance on equity finance. Indeed, stock market capitalization is of a magnitude two to three times greater in the US and other LMEs by comparison to CMEs such as Germany and Japan (Hall and Soskice, 2001a: 18).[13] This means US firms' access to finance is contingent on shareholder approval, which in turn is contingent on assessments of publicly available financial data and payment of financial returns in the form of dividends. Shareholdings are volatile and often held by smaller portfolio investors, so market sentiment can lead to firms' ownership changing hands if the stock price falls. Firms are expected to pay dividends reflecting their profitability in the current period and are judged on their ability to do so. Shareholder value is the primary goal of the firm, because diversified portfolio investors seek higher short-term returns than stable institutional investors, meaning that firms must adopt a short-term, shareholder focused strategy or risk being starved of the capital they need to invest and survive (Vitols, 2001: 337–339). As such, US firms are encouraged to 'focus on the publicly assessable dimensions of their performance that affect share price, such as current profitability', meaning there is also a reliance on 'market modes of coordination in the financial sphere' (Hall and Soskice, 2001a: 29 and 18–19).

In Germany and Japan debt finance has been more the norm. Banks are often represented on the boards of major German companies, and are regarded as strategic industry partners rather than simply financiers (see, for example, Dore et al., 1999; Wilks 1990; Pauly and Reich, 1997). In Japan, the major financial groups are often attached to, or closely affiliated with, large corporations. It is common for large firms to rely on one bank for all their capital requirements (Hollingsworth, 1997a: 279). More than half the equity of Japanese firms is held by 'stable shareholders': banks, insurance companies and related companies with which the firm trades or has joint ventures (Dore, 2000b: 108).[14] Reciprocal trust between firms is also increased in the case of Japan where cross-firm stable shareholdings are the norm, and in Japan company boards tend to be appointed from management ranks, not outsiders (i.e. not the largest shareholders) (Redding and Whitley, 1990: 89; see also Hollingsworth 1997a). Therefore, rather than being monitored by shareholders on the basis of their short-term financial performance, firms in CMEs such as Germany and Japan rely more on trust and support from their stable shareholders and financial partners based on their reputation, and for strong financial performance in the longer term (Hall and Soskice, 2001a: 23).

This means that Japanese and German shareholders are investors, rather than controllers. Dividends paid by firms are less closely related to short-term profits because satisfying the immediate desires of shareholders is a lower priority. A 'stakeholder model' rather than a 'shareholder model' is often said to describe the difference because a wider variety of constituencies have 'voice' in the firm, including employees, suppliers and customers (Vitols, 2001: 337–339; see also Dore, 2000a).[15]

There are some differences in the stakeholder model between Germany and Japan though, particularly the location of key stakeholders. For Japanese firms, these are located within the 'enterprise community', largely within the firm. Therefore, concern for stakeholders beyond the firm is very much a function of how they affect the inner community of the firm itself. A large part of the reason for this is the long-term nature of employment in Japanese corporations and resulting strong feelings of belonging to the firm, as if to a family, traditionally for the whole of an employee's working life. Thus, for management 'decent treatment of customers and concern for suppliers affects the reputation of the firm in the society at large; hence it affects the "standing" which the manager himself has when he goes to seminars and meetings of his business federation, as somebody who is identified with, and identifies himself with, his firm'. German firms' key stakeholders are primarily located outside the firm. They have a strong sense of responsibility to society. Even if they are majority privately owned and operated, German firms are to some degree regarded as public institutions in their responsibility to society, certainly more so than in the case of Japanese firms. Thus, while Japanese firms look inwards to fulfill their responsibility to stakeholders, German firms look outwards to society as a whole (Dore, 2000a: 10–11 and 18; see also Streeck 1997).

Whatever the differences in the stakeholder model for Germany and Japan, their reliance on debt finance means they have a longer-term perspective because their major banks and other debt financers have a stake in the company's fortunes at a more strategic level. This means they are more 'immune' to short-run sharemarket fluctuations than LME-based US firms (Hollingsworth, 1997a: 280). They are more willing to focus on strategic goals such as increasing market share and postponing short-term profits to achieve this However, US firms *must* be more focused on short-term profit maximization because they are 'dependent for raising capital on liquid financial markets rather than on banks' and in so doing are 'dependent on the whims and strategies of stockholders' (Hollingsworth, 1997a: 293). They cannot afford the luxury of incurring the disapproval of equity investors for long.

Organizing Principles of Firms

A picture starts to emerge of what motivates LME versus CME-based firms. In LMEs the separation of the state from business, with a relationship between the two that is more adversarial than cooperative, reflects a belief in free markets with state intervention only in cases of market failure. Markets coordinate economic activity, and this is true for both product and financial markets. A shorter-term perspective is the result as firms seek profits on the basis of current market forces, with the imperative of paying dividends to shareholders on the basis of these profits. By contrast, CMEs are characterized by closer state–business relations for coordinating economic activity. Greater prominence is given to cooperative, relational factors, and this is true for both product and financial markets. The result is a longer-term perspective.

Authors in the VOC mold relate these observations to the organizing principles of firms. This is because firms' different perspectives on the role of the state, markets, and the strategic timeframe this produces have implications for how they organize themselves internally. Some key implications are summarized in Table 2.1.

On the shareholder (or market) versus stakeholder model divide between LMEs and CMEs, the point about mergers and acquisitions is largely the one already made. Differences in the role of financial markets mean that mergers and acquisitions are far more common in LMEs than CMEs. In addition, in the case of Japanese firms the enterprise community aspect of stakeholder concern is reflected in a view that firms possess individual cultures that cannot easily be merged (Dore, 2000b). More on this is said below, but for now the point is that this cultural aspect puts a 'brake' on mergers and acquisitions in addition to the different role played by financial markets.

Management objectives reflect differences in the role of markets, especially financial markets. In LMEs, managers are concerned with making

Table 2.1 Organizing principles of firms in LMEs versus CMEs

	LMEs (US)	CMEs (Germany and Japan)
Shareholder/market versus stakeholder model		
Mergers and acquisitions	Common, including hostile takeovers, and therefore a major preoccupation of top managers and the financial press.	Exceedingly rare, and of low concern to top managers and the press. Also inhibited (in the case of Japan) by a view of the firm as an entity with a specific culture that cannot easily be merged with another.
Management objectives	Delivering profits to shareholders, thereby enhancing personal claims on increased financial rewards, and maintaining the share price.	Working for the long-term prosperity of the firm, and their reputation within it. Other factors such as market share, sales margins, value added per employee, growth in all of these plus sales growth are important, as well as the share price.
Disciplinary constraints on managers: accountability	The share price, because a fall in it can lead to dismissal by shareholders at the annual general meting, or hostile takeover.	Managers are responsible to the firms' stakeholders: their bankers and *committed* shareholders; and peers and juniors within the firm. This is where managers' reputations lie.
Intra-firm relations		
Social perception of the firm and nature of the employment contract	The place where, at the moment, one earns a living. A legal entity to which one owes obligations under an employment contract. The firm can be conceived of as a web of contracts prescribing and prescribing behavior for individuals who work for it. Therefore,	For Japanese firms, a community of people that is slowly renewed as people retire and new employees are recruited. It has an identity that is greater than the sum of its parts. CEOs can talk about 'the future of our great firm' much as a nation's leader might talk about the state, without

41

Table 2.1 (continued)

	LMEs (US)	CMEs (Germany and Japan)
	the employment contract is for a certain salary/wage for a certain job function, with promotion through an internal labor market via bids for vacant posts.	being regarded cynically. For German firms, a public institution with social responsibilities, and relationships between managers and between managers and employees codified by law. The nature of the employment contract is more in the nature of a career contract. Shedding labor is rare/seen as extremely undesirable (Japan), or legally difficult (Germany).
Response to economic pressures: recession (short term cyclical) versus industry sector decline (long-term structural)	Recession: Strenuous efforts to maintain profitability to maintain dividend payments and the share price, mean that costs are quickly cut to match falls in sales. This often entails labor shedding. Industry sector decline: Rapid liquidation of loss-making divisions, usually by labor shedding.	Recession: Strenuous efforts to increase/maintain sales with the prime objective of maintaining employment and financial rewards to employees, even if this means a temporary drop in profitability and dividend payments. Industry sector decline: Gradual withdrawal and diversification to other areas to seek new markets and products in growth industries that can capitalize on the firm's existing technological skills or market expertise. Employees are internally transferred accordingly.

Wages and salaries	Clear distinction between wage and salary earners. For both, the 'market rate' for the job and 'equal pay for equal work' are key concepts. Large reward dispersion between managers and workers.	Little wage/salary distinction, with predictable pay-rise trajectories related to job functions, period of service and educational qualifications. Small reward dispersion between managers and workers.
Effort-inducing incentives	Mostly individual, in the form of cash, and short-term.	Rewards are less cash-based and more long-term through building up reputation for appointments over the next 20 years.
Workers' interests	Workers' interests are seen as antithetical to shareholders' interests. Unions seek to protect their members' wages and conditions.	Lower-ranking members of Japanese firms speak up to protect their rights against arbitrary managers and for their wage claims. In German firms, employees are represented on the board via state legislated co-determination laws.
Nature of authority relations	Relations between managers and workers are adversarial and based on contracts. The hierarchy of the firm is seen as more one of licence to command obedience than one based on technical competence.	For Japanese firms, a sense of membership of a community, with authority more on the basis of technical competence (e.g. there are more PhDs and engineers on German and Japanese boards than accountants). German managers are more collective in their relations with employees than their US counterparts, but slightly less so than the 'organic' form of management relations in Japanese firms.

Sources: Dore (2000a: 26-32); also see Vitols (2001); Pauly and Reich (1997); Doremus *et al.* (1999); Hampden-Turner and Trompenaars (1993)

43

profits and delivering these to shareholders via dividends in the short term, whereas in CMEs they are more concerned with the long-term prosperity of the firm and their reputation within it. Concomitant with this observation is the fact that share price as an indicator of firm performance is the main preoccupation of LME managers, but in CMEs the longer-term prospects of the firm in the broader sense of market share, sales margins, etc. are more to the fore. Thus, while managers in LMEs are accountable to shareholders via their firm's share price, managers in CMEs are accountable in a more holistic sense to stakeholders internal and external to the firm.

The imperatives of making profits and paying shareholders dividends in the short term mean US managers are held accountable for investment in new products on this basis. They need to possess evidence that such investment is likely to provide tangible returns in the near future. German and Japanese managers are more willing to 'take a bet' on products that might produce benefits 10–15 years down the track, because they can strategize more for long-term growth and market, rather than focusing on short-term profit. Hampden-Turner and Tompenaars (1993: 75) use the analogy of a 'train' to illustrate the point. US managers want to catch it before it leaves the station, whereas German and Japanese managers are more willing to invest in a process of learning and development for a train that may never come, but if it does they hope they will already be on board when it reaches the station. Thus, German and Japanese managers have much longer timeframes over which they are accountable than their US counterparts.

Of course, US managers are not solely driven by making profits and maximizing shareholder value, but this is their 'dominant touchstone objective' (Dore, 2000b: 103). They may also focus on employees, customers, suppliers and (by inference) the environmental impact of their firm's activities, but rarely at the expense of the bottom line, increased earnings and higher share prices. However, for CMEs, the quality of a firm's activity comes before the financial rewards it brings. Profits are the *means* of generating further activity rather than an end in themselves. CME-based managers are more prepared to focus on enduring, growing, gaining market share, and making an excellent product via a customer/stakeholder focus, rather than primarily the short-term demands of the market. The difference is between a customer/stakeholder focus to do with more intangible notions such as service, quality and timeliness, versus a market focus to do with profits and margins. Put simply, the divide is between value in production (CMEs) versus value in the market (LMEs).[16]

Turning to intra-firm relations means asking the question: what is a 'firm'? Given the LME shareholder/market focus, US firms are less characterized by close-knit cooperative networks. The firm is a legal entity, a place where one works for the moment, where hiring and firing occur in response to changed market (i.e. profitability) conditions, where management has the power to do this and is expected to, and where there is a large gap between managers and workers in terms of their rewards. Top management and the board tend to exert control over the firm, and in keeping with external relations, especially with regulators, relations between management and employees tend to be more adversarial. This leads to a willingness to shed labor for economic gains when the firm faces profitability pressures, resulting in LME-based firms being characterized by shorter job tenures and 'fluid labor markets' (Hall and Soskice, 2001a: 30).

By contrast, cooperation and collaboration are terms that apply more to CME firms. In the case of Germany, this leads to a 'structural bias towards consensus decision making' (Hall and Soskice, 2001a: 24), or what I would call *negotiated consensus*. This reflects the stakeholder basis for capitalist relations of production in German firms which reinforces the importance of supporting long-standing business networks, both internal and external to the firm, rather than focusing on short-term profitability. Long-term, cooperative product development and productivity growth are emphasized (see, for example, Fioretos, 2001: 220–221). In fact, cooperation and consensus-building are legislated: 'it is not so much convention as law . . . which governs the owner/manager/worker relationship', meaning that German firms *must* have union and worker representation on their boards (Dore, 2000a: 182; see also Streeck, 1997). The German Codetermination Act of 1976 mandates that all companies of more than 2000 employees must have supervisory boards with employee as well as shareholder representation on them. The result is that 48 per cent of the seats on the supervisory boards of the 100 largest German industrial corporations are held by union or employee representatives (Pauly and Reich, 1997: 12). All companies with more than five members must also have a Works Council through which managers are reminded on a daily basis about group morale and opinion on productivity and specific issues in the workplace. As a result, German managers are legally required to consult employees as well as shareholders in a cooperative fashion.

In Japanese firms, the point has been made by many commentators that an employee traditionally joins a Japanese firm for life. This means workers and management share a relationship closer to that of 'a soldier's sense of regimental loyalty', with a firm's top management closer to the status of 'elders' than 'agents of shareholder principals' (Dore, 2000b: 107). There is no external market for executives in Japan, or at least it is a very small one largely the preserve of foreign firms operating there. Japanese CEOs are appointed from within their firms, and the sense of enterprise community referred to earlier means there is a smaller distance between managers and their staff. In contrast to the US LME model where firms hire and fire employees in the face of economic pressures that threaten the share price, nobody really owns a Japanese firm but the firm itself (at least in the sense of who determines its destiny).[17] In times of economic trouble, the 'sense of responsibility for managing difficult processes of restructuring within tight traditional constraints is palpable' (Pauly and Reich, 1997: 11; see also Dore, 2000a: 24–26).

These observations on the social perception of the firm, the nature of the employment contract and how these are reflected in responses to economic pressures are reflected in empirical studies. In a survey of 15000 managers from European, American and Asian companies, 74 per cent of US managers saw a company as a system designed to perform functions and tasks efficiently, but only 41 per cent of German and 29 per cent of Japanese managers saw their companies in these terms. Instead, they saw a company as a group of people working together, dependent on social relations with others internal and external to it. Similarly, while 40 per cent of US managers saw the prime goal of a company as making profits, only 24 per cent of German managers and 8 per cent of Japanese managers saw their companies this way. Instead, they had a more holistic view in which a firm, besides making profits, is focused on the well-being of a wide range of stakeholders and endures on the basis of attending to their needs (Hampden-Turner and Trompenaars, 1993: 32).

The implications for wages and salaries, effort-inducing incentives and workers' interests flow from this. Japanese employees see achievement as deriving from commitment and length of service with their company, a view not so strongly favored by their German and US counterparts. While 99 per cent of US managers surveyed said they had a relationship of limited duration with their company, only 41 per cent of Japanese managers saw their relationship in such a short term. German managers were somewhere in between at 83 per cent (Hampden-Turner and Trompenaars, 1993: 60). Achievement as a concept thus requires qualification. In the case of the US it is strongly linked to individual achievement, with cash rewards for success, and winning through a competitive process, whereas in the case of Japan it comes from bonds of family, a cadre of juniors and seniors within a firm and a cooperative approach to success over a longer period of time. The result in the case of US managers is that they are far more mobile and footloose than their Japanese counterparts who tend to see their future as more tightly linked to that of their colleagues within the company for which they will work in the long term, as noted earlier, traditionally the duration of their working lives. Thus, achievement in the case of Japanese firms is more likely to be ascribed to teams and groups than the heroic individual.

The Japanese preference for achievement by teams and groups is reflected in an 'organic' ordering within Japanese companies that mirrors symbiotic cooperative relations with the state. Junior team members bring information to their seniors in the context of a goal of creating harmony within the organization, so that management vision is agreed/shared widely at all levels. It is not so much a matter of managers giving orders and employees carrying them out, as reaching a broadly agreed position within the entire company. Reflecting this, Akio Morita of Sony has said:

> Our encouragement of long-range plans from up-and-coming employees is a big advantage for our system, despite all the meetings. . . . It enables us to create and maintain something that is rare in the West, a company philosophy. . . . Even if a new executive takes over, he cannot change that. In Japan, the long-range planning system and the junior management proposal system guarantees that the relationship between top management and junior management remains very close. (Hampden-Turner and Trompenaars, 1993: 158)

Thus, a system that is based not on the individual but the communitarian whole, is more likely to produce a long-term and enduring company vision than in a US firm.

Something similar happens in German firms, but reflecting their legally mandated negotiated consensus approach to coordination, rather than the organic ordering in Japanese firms, even if initiation comes from top management, '*formally* structured mutualities between suppliers, industries, unions and customers' are the basis on which this initiation is made real (Hampden-Turner and Trompenaars, 1993: 97–99, with emphasis added).[18]

In the US, top management tends to make decisions more unilaterally. It is then the responsibility of employees to implement these decisions. Key senior managers are very much in the 'drivers' seat' in developing and promoting a company vision. This is regarded as entirely appropriate given a business culture that is more a function of the individual driven by profits, and the need to ensure shareholder value to retain a position of power.

Finally, this brings us to the nature of authority relations within firms. Commensurate with the idea of a firm as a network of contracts, relations between managers and workers in US firms are generally more adversarial than in German or Japanese firms. Managers have more distance from their employees and more power to act unilaterally. By contrast, CME firms are more communitarian, in the Japanese case, and more collective, in the German case. Japanese firms turn to the informal bonds of the enterprise community, and German firms have formal (legally mandated) systems for coordinating internal collective action. One might say German firms are *well-oiled machines* (that is, all the parts are put together formally to form the whole efficiently operating machine),[19] Japanese firms are *organisms* (that is, they operate on the basis of communitarian obligations and understandings as much as rules and regulations)[20] and US firms are *mechanisms* (that is, they are designed on a contractual basis to produce certain outcomes).[21]

The difference in firms' organizing principles between Germany and Japan is summarized by Soskice (1999: 106–110) as one of 'industry coordination' for European CMEs versus 'group coordination' for Japan. The divide is between the extent to which coordination occurs at an industry level (i.e. across firms) for German firms, versus across the company group for Japanese firms. Thus, while unions tend to be industry-based in Germany, they are company-based in Japan. While technical standard setting occurs at an industry level in Europe and Germany, it occurs at a company level in Japan. German firms are likely to be more outward looking in their strategic vision, whereas Japanese firms are likely to be more inward looking, to be more focused on the company group and the community of the firm, in developing strategies (see also Kitschelt et al., 1999).

Whatever the differences, what Germany and Japan share as CMEs is summarized by Dore (2000b: 106) thus:

> They remain economies in which the stock market plays a much less central role, and the state a larger one; in which the financial sector is less dominant; and manufacturing industry correspondingly more important; in which engineers tend to have the edge over accountants; and the doctrine of the supremacy of shareholder value is still a much weaker element in determining company goals.

Although their differences are not irrelevant, it is their common CME institutional framework that should be stressed more in contrast to that of the LME institutional framework of the US.

The Role of Technology

The roles of state–business relations, product and financial markets, and the organizing principles of firms have been discussed above. General points have been made in respect of each. However, when discussing improvements in firms' environmental performance, one is often implicitly discussing something quite specific: technological improvements. Although it is not impossible to imagine car firms encouraging alternatives to the car (e.g. more bicycle use), they are more likely to develop technological solutions to reduce the environmental impacts of the products they sell. Based on the factors already discussed above, the VOC approach observes that LME firms tend towards radical technological innovation, whereas CME firms tend to innovate more incrementally. Empirically, this is supported by the observation that patents in LMEs tend to cite scientific sources, whereas those in CMEs tend to cite previous patents or non-scientific sources. This suggests the former are groundbreaking, while the latter are more incremental technological innovations (Margarita et al., 2001: 174–175).

The institutional framework of LMEs supports radical, rapid change and innovation because firms have a short-term market focus, can buy and sell subsidiaries without concern about long-term stable shareholdings, and top management possesses greater unilateral power to make and implement decisions, including the ability to hire and fire labor. These characteristics mean that LME-based firms rapidly embrace new ideas and opportunities in order to exploit new market opportunities. Being less 'weighed down' by long-term networks based on mutual cooperation, they are more able to adjust rapidly and act opportunistically (Hall and Soskice, 2001a: 35–40; Soskice, 1999: 117–118; Hollingsworth, 1997a: 296).[22]

CMEs are better at supporting incremental innovation over the longer term by virtue of denser corporate networks that facilitate a more gradual, less market-focused, diffusion of new technologies. They focus better on more traditional, well-developed markets in consultation with suppliers, workers and other stakeholders. Thus, Soskice (1999: 114) notes the following of German firms' predisposition to incremental technological change: 'Germany is the undisputed leader in improving and upgrading technology in fields in which its industry is established, but there are weaknesses in newer fields' (see also Hall and Soskice, 2001a: 41). In a similar vein, Hollingsworth (1997a: 289) notes that 'Germans have placed less emphasis on developing entirely new technologies and industries than in applying the latest technologies to the production of more traditional products' (see also Streeck, 1997: 41).

Japanese firms share these characteristics, but there is an added dimension to state–business relations in Japan that amounts to a shared overarching goal of economic independence (Wilks, 1990). This manifests itself in a national drive to develop the latest technology and thereby have a competitive edge in so doing. This is labeled 'technonationalism' by Pauly and Reich (1997). In keeping with the technonationalist version of Japan's CME, Japanese firms in aggregate spend a higher percentage of their resources on research and development than in any other country (Hollingsworth, 1997a: 291). Their aim is to be at the technological forefront in every industrial sector in which they participate.

The discussion in the preceding paragraphs on Germany and Japan seems to confound any clear distinction regarding the role of technology in LMEs versus CMEs, or at least between the three territories considered in this book. But perhaps Vitols (2001) offers a clue to a key distinction when he notes that LME firms are radical in their innovation and entry into *new* industry sectors, but behave more conservatively in established ones where they compete more on the basis of market price. By contrast, CME firms compete more via non-price competition through incremental innovation.[23] Therefore, the distinction is one that revolves around the role of price competition in established versus emerging industries. For established industries, such as the car industry, the implication is that CME firms will compete more through non-price product innovation than LME firms. The latter will tend to place greater emphasis on price competition in markets. For Germany, competition via non-price product innovation in mature industries is likely to be more incremental. For Japan, competition via non-price product innovation means technological innovation with the goal of always leading competitors and pushing technological frontiers. This may produce radical innovation even in established industries.

Exogenous versus Endogenous Factors

The preceding discussion also has implications for the role of exogenous versus endogenous factors that, while not explicitly addressed by the VOC approach, are nevertheless implied.[24] Exogenous factors are those factors external to firms that impact on their activities. They are exogenous in the sense that they derive from outside firms and impact on them. They may be conceived as material factors, such as market forces and state regulations, but also the institutional context of these as illuminated by the VOC approach that affects how market forces and regulations are constructed in terms of both their creation and importance. Endogenous factors arising from within firms affect how exogenous factors are interpreted and addressed. These include the actual material facts of the situation in which individual firms find themselves, such as their product line-ups and the competencies these represent, but also normative questions about internal company strategies such as corporate policies and leaders' visions.[25]

How does the intersection of exogenous and endogenous factors relate to the VOC approach? The following observation made by Dicken (1998: 197) is a good starting point:

> As US companies, Ford and GM are quite distinctive from Toyota, Volkswagen, Fiat or Renault. But they are also different from each other. Similarly, Toyota and Nissan are distinctive, but not identical, Japanese automotive firms; the

same point can be made about the French auto producers and so on. However, there are generally greater similarities than differences between firms from the same national base.

The point is that while it is an over-simplification to say that firms of the same nationality are identical, national characteristics are nevertheless predominant. Therefore, although Hall and Soskice (2001a: 15) raise the caveat that the 'point is that institutional structure conditions corporate strategy, not that it fully determines it', firms of the same nationality are still more similar overall than firms of different nationalities. Hence, 'organizational forms tend to become remarkably uniform within societies dominated by particular institutional conventions' (Whitley, 1999: 13). The value of the VOC approach, in terms of facilitating comparative analysis, is that it allows us to concentrate on these broad differences in organizational forms between states' capitalist institutions.

Given the broad national differences, the VOC approach suggests some national variations in the importance of exogenous versus endogenous factors. For US LME-based firms, a preference for market forces and responding to government regulations with material goals in mind, suggests they should be more exogenously motivated. However, the distance between management and workers, the ability of managers to act more unilaterally and hire and fire labor also suggest that the vision of a firm's leader may carry considerable weight from an endogenous perspective. Of course, even then, environmental concerns are likely to be seen in more materialist terms along the lines of making profits to satisfy shareholder demands, while addressing imposed regulatory requirements.

As the VOC of German and Japanese firms leads them to be less profit-motivated, less market driven and more long-term in their perspective, a greater role for endogenously derived strategies is suggested. This is especially the case for Japanese firms because their focus on the enterprise community suggests a very strong role for internal strategies as a motivator for action, rather than exogenous forces. German firms occupy the middle ground, operating on the basis of negotiated consensus with a range of stakeholders both exogenous and endogenous to the firm, with an eye to their social responsibilities by both convention and law.

Historical Context

Finally, it should be stressed that the insights of the VOC approach, including the implications in terms of the role of technology and exogenous versus endogenous factors, are the result of historical processes.

After all, 'institutions are embedded in a culture in which their logic is symbolically grounded, organisationally structured, technically and materially constrained, politically defended, and historically shaped by specific rules and norms' (Hollingsworth, 1997a: 266). For example, Japanese technonationalism has its roots in the Meiji Restoration. The industrial conglomerates that this spawned, along with the drive for education and skills development, industrialization and the competitive drive for market share were then further (re)interpreted through the lens of the aftermath of the Second World War. Similarly, the Prussian state's desire to unite Germany, the impact of Nazism and the aftermath of the Second World War helped to shape its variety of capitalism, including the cartelization of industry, the role of unions on company boards, the role of banks in financing growth and the incremental, inclusive, consensus-approach to decision-making. For the US, the establishment of the stockmarket as a prime driver of perceptions of company worth and endurance was already evident in the 1920s when the separation of management from ownership of major corporations was entrenched (Dore et al., 1999; Hollingsworth (1997a).[26]

There are many implications from recognizing the importance of historical context. One is that the mainstream liberal economic approach, which stresses market forces and the central role of the state in addressing environmental externalities, is a particularly LME one derived from historical specificities. This 'suits' the US, but Germany and Japan's different histories have produced institutions that 'deviate from the prescriptions of neoclassical textbooks' (Dore et al., 1999: 102). Another implication is that a degree of path dependence is built into the institutions and norms that underpin national capitalist relations of production. Although commentators like Hall and Soskice (2001a) point to economic actors gravitating to modes of action and coordination that are most efficient given particular institutional environments, this should not in any way imply that the institutions and norms of individual states' capitalisms are necessarily efficient of themselves, or qualitatively 'better'.[27] They are the results of historical processes and so are 'sticky' – i.e. they possess an 'inertia' once in place and tend to endure, rather than being 'plastic' or 'open to opportunistic adoption and combination' on the whims of either policy-makers or firms (Berger, 1996: 22; Boyer, 1996: 56).[28] Yet, in opposition to this observation, because they are the product of history, norms and institutions can change over time. As Dore et al. (1999) note, it would be naive to believe that a certain state will possess the same institutions forever, or that the institutions it has at present are the same as those pertaining in the past. Even so, institutional change is constrained and enabled by what has gone before, and by current institutional arrangements.

CONCLUSION

At the core of the VOC approach is a belief that there is no universal rationality that describes firms' strategic priorities. Individual states have developed particular institutions over time that underpin different Varieties of Capitalism. As such, 'standards for evaluating organizational performance and prevalent criteria for judging firms' strategic priorities vary significantly across institutional regimes and cannot be derived from a single universal market rationality' (Whitley, 1999: 13; see also Redding and Whitley, 1990). Firms gravitate to those modes of behavior and action that have institutional support and are therefore most efficient.

Universal prescriptions for the 'best' institutional foundations miss the point. Different cultures within firms and the states where they are located mean that similar actions produce different ramifications. If anti-trust laws were removed in the US would this lead to greater cooperation and collaboration to the benefit of society as is the case in Germany and Japan? The answer is surely no, because LME capitalist relations of production in the US would likely increase the propensity for exploitation of the market to the detriment rather than the benefit of consumers. Should the US adopt the legally mandated consultative requirements between workers and managers as exists in Germany? Again that answer is no, as this would surely tie the US system up in more disputation and litigation than exists already, and potentially rob the US of its key advantage over the Japanese and Germans: the ability to act rapidly to respond to market challenges. Therefore, value judgments as to whether LMEs/CMEs are 'good' or 'bad' are largely pointless. The institutional features of these states are what they are, and recognizing this is a good starting point. Rather than declaring which variety of capitalism is better, the point is to tease out the implications of national institutional differences.

From the above discussion it is possible to distil five, key linked drivers of firms' strategic priorities in LMEs versus CMEs:

1. Closer state–business relations in CMEs versus a separation of the state and markets in LMEs. For Germany, a coordinating role for the state is the case, while for Japan a more organic, symbiotic relationship is suggested based on mutual understanding.
2. A resulting priority for markets as organizers of economic activity in LMEs, in both the product and financial spheres, versus markets as one among a variety of mechanisms for organizing economic activity in CMEs on a more relational, cooperative basis. In the case of Germany, the role of society and a feeling of responsibility towards it is particularly important, as well as negotiated consensus between a

range of stakeholders often prescribed by law. For Japan, the enterprise community, and the relationship between stakeholders within it,
plays a stronger role.

3.   LME-based firms may be conceived of as networks of contracts with
significant power invested in management. They act on market signals
to make profits in the short term and pay dividends to shareholders. A CME-based firm is best conceived as a collective (Germany)
or community (Japan) that acts to enhance its reputation through
close relational ties with stakeholders. US firms are mechanisms (of
profit), German firms are well-oiled machines and Japanese firms are
organisms.

4.   US firms are likely to be more focused on exogenous material factors,
but with more power in the hands of management to act unilaterally
in devising strategies to respond to these. Because Japanese firms are
more internally driven strategically, endogenous factors have greater
prominence. German firms are somewhere in between, but with prominence given to (exogenous) social responsibilities.

5.   A preference for non-price competition via product innovation in
established industries in CMEs via incremental technological change,
versus price competition in established industries in LMEs. Radical
technological change is favored in new industries in LMEs, however
Japanese technonationalism may produce quite radical technological
advances even in established industries.

Taken together, these drivers of firm strategies imply a shorter-term perspective for LMEs versus a longer-term perspective for CMEs. This is
because in the latter there is less focus on markets, profits, paying shareholders dividends, and competing in established industries on the basis of
price. A clear preference for materialist perspectives on the part of LME-
based firms is also implied. This is the result of the institutional basis for
capitalist relations in LMEs, whereas institutions in CMEs lead firms to
focus more on responsibility to society rather than shareholders, responsibility to fellow employees rather than economic pressures, market share
and influence rather than short-term profit.

Of course, national institutional differences, while enduring, may change
over time. Whether, and how they do, is hard to predict, and this leads
commentators such as Crouch (2005a and b) and Hay (2005) to highlight
the inability of the VOC approach, and indeed that of comparative institutionalist approaches generally, to explain institutional change. Coupled
with this, they point to the overly blunt dichotomy asserted by the VOC
approach. Some commentators have tried to address these deficiencies,
such as Thatcher (2007). While accepting that they exist, such deficiencies

are not addressed here. Although attacks may be warranted on theoretical grounds, nevertheless some form of categorization is always necessary for comparative analysis. Without it, we are simply left saying everything is important, as indeed it always is, but this does not help us to get out of the analytical 'starting blocks' (see, for example, Sartori, 1970; Collier and Mahon, 1993; Collier and Adcock, 1999; Adcock and Collier, 2001).

With the limitations in mind, the intention in the following chapters is to apply the insights of the VOC approach in a novel way to the environmental motivations of car firms. The application is novel in the sense that rather than examining the competitive advantages of states' industrial bases, or the operation of their product and financial markets, etc., what is shown is that a state's variety of capitalism has implications for 'non-economic' considerations such as the environment. As environmental questions increase in importance for business, the point is that institutional differences in capitalist relations between states have implications for whether, and how, firms from different states address the environmental impact of their operations.

For the US, we should expect concern for the environment to be expressed more in material terms of market forces, profits and the imperatives of competition. If firms take environmental action, we should expect to see the rationale for this expressed in terms of what consumer demand dictates and state regulations require. These must be addressed in the short term in order to maintain market position, profits and shareholder value.

We should expect to see an incremental approach to environmental concerns from German firms that is based on consensual cooperation with regulators, while mindful of the concerns of a variety of stakeholders, especially societal stakeholders. The aim of firms will be to balance competing views and interests via gradual/incremental measures aimed at ensuring ongoing consensus and cooperative coordination, while at the same time maintaining profits. Furthermore, we should see firms exhibit a belief that the maintenance of constructive stakeholder relationships contributes to their material business outcomes – i.e. the maintenance of a well-oiled machine.

We should expect to see similar drivers for Japanese firms, but with a more radical technologically-driven approach to environmental concerns, in concert with the state and guided by technonationalist imperatives. There should be less of a role for organized civil society, but more for society and the nation as an 'organic' whole of which the firm is a part. A longer-term internally-driven strategic view based on future benefits and market leadership should be key drivers behind environmental initiatives.

Therefore, the key perspective taken by this book is that car firms' environmental initiatives are, to a significant degree, a consequence of different capitalisms pertaining in their home states. Rather than convergence on a single way of addressing environmental concerns, their divergent approaches reflect different institutional frameworks for capitalist relations of production in the states where they are headquartered, and in which they are economically, politically, socially and historically embedded.

NOTES

1. She also declares that the problem with authors who take a comparative approach to the political economy of modern capitalism is that they do not 'see the wood for the trees [and] overlook the common problems while concentrating on the individual differences' (Strange, 1997: 184).
2. They in turn point out that it is a term that has entered common usage to the point where the identity of the person who first coined it is unclear.
3. I recognize that environmental externalities are, of course, not strictly non-economic considerations. As noted in Chapter 1, they represent market failure in economic terms as much as anything else, and therefore are said to require intervention to internalize their value in market transactions. However, the point here is more that the environmental implications of institutional differences in capitalist relations between states are not usually addressed in the VOC literature, yet that literature has clear implications for whether, and how, the environmental impact of economic activity is addressed.
4. It does so in the sense that it covers the role of the state and markets, their impact on firms' operations, the nature of technical advances in product development firms are likely to take, and how all these factors are evolving over time. Of course, the VOC literature says much about other aspects of the LME/CME divide such as differences in the education, training and vocational skills of workers, and there is some extensive literature on the nature of union power and bargaining. However, these are only relevant to the research here in as much as they describe the organizing principles of firms, and so have been grouped under this umbrella rather than treated separately.
5. Weiss and Hobson (1995) note that 'the state was not the principal driving force in industrialisation' (p.219), and follow this statement with 'American political economy subsequently developed in an anti-statist direction, leaving economic coordination to the business organisation' (p.220). The result is said to be 'a regulatory rather than developmental central state' (p.221). A similar point is made in Dicken (1998: 119–121). In respect of environmental externalities specifically, see also von Moltke and Rahman (1996).
6. These authors focus on the adversarial, competitive nature of reaching consensus on environmental issues specifically.
7. This may be relevant for other East Asian states in their post-war development such as South Korea though.
8. Crouch (2005a and b) in particular, warns against brushing over such differences.
9. Associated with this is the view that business must to some extent be altruistic and principled in its behavior, looking beyond its own 'selfish' concerns to that of society and the state. This point is made by authors such as Wilks (1990), and expanded on further in the following section on the role of product markets.
10. As discussed above, being interventionist means the state playing a more coordinating role in the case of Germany, and having a more organic, symbiotic relationship with business in the case of Japan.
11. Japan has recently introduced such laws and the European Commission has responsibility for such matters in Europe now, but this statement remains true for much of Germany and Japan's post-Second World War economic development.

12. See also R. Dore (1997: 23), who notes that 'a list of the sixty-odd members of Toyota's first-line suppliers' club in 1990 has only two or three names not present in 1970, and only two or three of the names which figured in the earlier list have now disappeared'.

13. This is despite GDP per capita being comparable between LMEs and CMEs on average – i.e. the magnitude of stock market capitalization in the US versus CMEs such as Germany and Japan is not a function of the different magnitudes of their economies.

14. See also Pauly and Reich (1997: 10) who point out that cross-shareholdings in Japanese firms have barely changed in the past decade.

15. However, it should be noted that this may be more accurate for the earlier portion of the period covered by this book than the later portion. For example, Tiberghien (2007) demonstrates that after 1998 the stability of cross-shareholdings began to break down in Japan.

16. This is a theme of Hampden-Turner and Trompenaars (1993). For example, they note that managers of US firms believe that 'if they are profitable, then everything else must be all right' (p.44). However, 'for Germans, value must be deeply imbedded in products of solidity and worth [because] they do not like it when money and its enjoyment becomes separated from worthwhile artifacts' (p.213). Indeed, 'for German managers, money is a means, not an end; a lubricant of industrialization, not a potion in itself; of value in furthering work, but dangerous in itself' (p.218).

17. By way of illustration, Dore (1997: 20) notes that a US company chairman is likely to address a meeting of shareholders by talking about 'your firm', whereas a Japanese company chairman will talk about 'our firm'.

18. It may be noted that the negotiated consensus aspects of German corporate governance versus the more organic ordering in Japanese firms has been noted by others and given a variety of similar terms. For example, Jacoby (2005: 1) refers to European 'statutory stakeholder governance' versus Japanese and East Asian 'voluntarist stakeholder governance'.

19. This because the 'values that Germans bring to their processes of wealth creation is [*sic*] manifested in a highly codified economic system' (Hampden-Turner and Trompenaars, 1993: 198).

20. In fact, the Japanese themselves appear to believe that 'the company resembles an organism that grows and develops, even more, it is a family with deep and affectionate bonds' (Hampden-Turner and Trompenaars, 1993: 132).

21. A US firm may be thought of as a 'perfectly tuned machine' as well, but it is one in the sense of being designed for 'responding to a market mechanism' (Hampden-Turner and Trompenaars, 1993: 73). Therefore, the emphasis is most appropriately on the latter rather than the former – i.e. it is a mechanism for responding to material market signals.

22. Whether or not this is an advantage of US capitalism is hotly debated, because while an ability to act rapidly and embrace radical technological change would seem to confer competitive advantages, some commentators say that the US's lack of ability to embrace incremental technological change is resulting in its firms losing the competitive edge they once possessed. They are increasingly in a position of always having to play 'catch-up' with technological advances made by firms in Japan and other East Asian states, and possibly Europe too. For example, see Weiss (1998) and Weiss and Hobson (1995).

23. He makes this distinction by comparing the competitive strategies of UK LME-based firms versus German CME-based firms (see Vitols (2001: 339).

24. Statisticians, accustomed to analysing exogenous and endogenous factors in their models, will be unhappy with the following discussion. This is because the terms are defined in a less technical manner than is usually the case in analyses employing statistical methods. I accept this criticism, but in my defence, point out that this book does not fundamentally apply statistical techniques, and that there is a broader definition of the terms outside statistical studies. Also, as shall become clear, I wish to differentiate internal company strategies from factors deriving from within the firm (i.e. factors internal

to firms that give rise to internal strategies). This is why the term 'endogenous' is used to describe such factors for how they impact on internal strategies, rather than risking conflating the two.

25. For example, because Ford is more dependent on the production of light trucks than Toyota, this might explain why Toyota introduced a medium-sized petrol-electric hybrid passenger car in the form of the Prius, while Ford chose to introduce a hybrid version of its SUV Escape. But this does not answer the question of why each firm decided to introduce a hybrid at all, especially in the case of Ford as it is the first US company to do so. For firms' different production profiles, see the relevant sections on each firm in Deutsche Bank (2004). The timing and nature of the firms' introduction of petrol-electric hybrids is discussed in their environmental reports, and outlined in greater detail in the following chapter.

26. Such historical processes are also at the heart of the analysis in Doremus et al. (1999) and Pauly and Reich (1997: 3) who note that 'the institutional legacies of distinctive national histories continue significantly to shape the core operations of multinational forms based in Germany, Japan and the United States'.

27. Although Dore (2000a: 219) confesses to 'an underlying evaluative bias' against LMEs because he believes that 'the processes of marketization and financialization are a bad thing'.

28. The point about the path dependence of institutions in specific societies is widely made. For further examples, see also Hall (1999), Hollingsworth (1997a) and Weiss (2003).

3. The car industry and climate change

> The strategies of the major automobile producers are more diverse than is often realized, a fact not unrelated to their national origins.
>
> (Dicken, 2003: 397)

So far, the case has been made for an institutional analysis based on the Varieties of Capitalism approach. However, the car industry itself has only been touched on briefly. The point made in Chapter 1 was that while it is global in its reach, its productive assets, production, employment and even sales are concentrated in a handful of states. The dominant ones are the industry's three hubs of Germany (and the EU which German firms dominate), the United States and Japan. In addition to geographical concentration, it was also shown that production is concentrated in a handful of firms hailing from these states. This allows us to focus on these three states, and the major firms based in them, in order to answer the central questions posed.

The aim of this chapter is to expand on the features of the car industry highlighted so far, focusing on the key environmental initiatives it is undertaking to reduce its environmental impacts. Some sobering statistics were quoted in Chapter 1 to highlight the magnitude of the environmental impacts wrought on the world by the industry. But how are we to analyse these impacts? The problems are too complex and multifaceted. If the car industry is a crucial case for addressing environmental sustainability, what crucial aspect of the problem illustrates the whole? The case is made for why the primary environmental impact considered is carbon dioxide emissions because of their prominent contribution to cars' environmental damage in use, plus their contribution to perhaps the most pressing global environmental issue of our time, climate change.

Given the focus on climate change, and specifically CO_2 emissions, the next question asked is what is the industry doing to address the problem? The industry's main environmental product development initiatives affecting the impact of passenger cars in use on climate change are briefly summarized. The intention is not to embark on a detailed study of the engineering possibilities, but to highlight some key aspects based on a selection of authoritative literature that does this in more detail. The initiatives identified are classified as incremental technologies; petrol and diesel-electric hybrid drivetrains; hydrogen fuel cell vehicles and alternative fuels.

The summary of these product development initiatives is followed by a comparative analysis of those that individual firms chose to highlight in their 2003/04 environmental reports. These reports present the views of firms themselves at the end of the period over which environmental issues were mainstreamed, but before the material imperatives of the escalation in oil prices became an unavoidable reality. Similarly, this conforms to the historical snapshot taken by the analysis in this book. It is shown that far from a universal strategic approach, there are distinct national differences. This supports the view that firms' home states matter, that a study on the basis of national institutional differences is relevant, and therefore that the VOC approach is pertinent for explaining national differences in firms' product development strategies.

The insights of the VOC approach are shown to be pertinent in the following ways. First, US firms clearly place the highest priority on market forces and market potential for new products in their development process. By contrast, Japanese firms seem more internally driven for the initiatives they are undertaking, and German firms are developing a range of solutions based on their technological competencies. This highlights the role of market forces for liberal market economy-based US firms, versus other non-market drivers for coordinated market economy-based German and Japanese firms. Second, and related, the timing variations between firms for the development and introduction of environmental attributes further illustrates the LME/ CME divide, especially in terms of the importance of markets. Japanese firms are internally driven to be first on the market with the latest technologies (therefore, the point about Japanese technonationalism appears relevant), whereas German firms aim to have environmental technological solutions ready when the moment is right, although not necessarily for market reasons. US firms are investigating a range of product development alternatives but are driven by markets for their introduction and the aim of selling the most vehicles, rather than being first on the market with them.

By the end of this chapter, the product development initiatives of car firms aimed at reducing the CO_2 emissions of passenger cars in use will have been outlined. More importantly though, it will be shown that there are clear national differences in the initiatives being undertaken. This suggests that firms' nationalities matter, and hence that institutional factors pertaining in firms' home states affect their strategies, the environmental initiatives they choose to stress, and how they do so. Prior to detailed empirical analysis in Chapters 4–7, reasons for the national differences are shown to be suggested by the VOC approach that are further explored in these following chapters.

ADDRESSING ENVIRONMENTAL CONCERNS: CLIMATE CHANGE, CO_2 EMISSIONS AND FUEL ECONOMY

While the concept of the environment itself is obvious, 'environmental issues' and 'concern about the environment' are less clear. Inevitably, one ends up discussing sustainability, a somewhat murky concept because 'everyone knows what this word means; it's just that no one knows exactly what it looks like in practice' (Suzuki and Dressel, 2002: 16; see also Harrison, 2000). Perhaps it is best not to get too caught up in absolute definitions. It is more helpful to take a relativist approach. Recognizing the distinction between the two, the Organization for Economic Cooperation and Development (OECD, 2000: 8) highlights the difference between absolute indicators *of* sustainability, versus relativist indicators of movement *towards* sustainability.

I take a relativist approach in the sense of considering action aimed at moving in the 'right' direction. The question is therefore one of whether there is a real shift in attitude, and general motivations for environmental action as opposed to 'greenwashing'.[1] The question is not one of what the appropriate *level* of environmental protection/action/technologies, etc. should be, in the sense of some destination to be reached that embodies sustainable practices that are definable and achievable. Instead, the question is whether firms are *proactively* disposed to action and taking it, how they are doing so and why. Thus, and hopefully this is clear by now, environmental issues and concern about the environment are defined in terms of the *actions* taken by the international car industry and the *motivators* for them.

Environmental issues are complex. This makes it difficult to analyse them holistically. It may be possible to speak of attitudes to the environment, but in terms of action and data in respect of such attitudes, something more tangible is necessary. For the sake of manageable analysis, the focus is primarily on climate change and the fuel economy of passenger cars in use. There are three main reasons for this: the growing international visibility of the climate change issue from the 1990s onwards; the relationship of fuel economy to CO_2 emissions; and the resulting visibility of the issue to consumers of the industry's products. The reason for considering passenger cars in use is that this is the stage at which most environmental damage is done, as opposed to other stages in a car's lifecycle such as manufacturing.

With the rise in environmental concern generally from the 1990s onwards has come concern for the issue of climate change. I would assert that it is uncontroversial to say this is unequivocally *the* most visible global environmental issue. The profile of climate change and how to address it has been growing since it was first brought to the attention of corporations, governments and civil society through the crucial event of the United Nations Conference on Environment and Development in Rio do Janeiro in 1992 (Levy and Rothenberg, 2002; Paterson 1996; Luterbacher and Sprinz, 2001; Schreurs, 2002; Porter and Brown, 1996; Barrett, 2003).[2] The subsequent Kyoto Protocol, signed in 1997 by over 180 states and ratified by all industrialized nations with the exception of the US,[3] has been described as 'the most conspicuous policy step' in terms of environmental regulation impacting on the car industry (Deutsche Bank, 2004: 58). The result is that policy-makers, the general public and business are widely aware of the issue and the need to address it.

The major greenhouse gas contributing to climate change, CO_2, is also the major greenhouse gas produced by industrialized states, and is responsible for the majority of their contribution to climate change. For example, it is responsible for 94 per cent of Japan's greenhouse gas emissions (OECD, 2002a: 218). In addition to the general figures as to the CO_2 emissions from cars in OECD countries presented in Chapter 1, car CO_2 emissions conservatively account for up to 20 per cent of all CO_2 emissions in the European Union, US and Japan specifically.[4] Reducing CO_2 emissions critically depends on the actions of the car industry in respect of the products it develops. In addition, the International Energy Agency (IEA, 1997: 9) finds that the transport sector must make a greater contribution to reducing CO_2 emissions than the proportion for which it is accountable:

> Whilst over a quarter of total carbon dioxide emissions in the group of IEA countries comes from transportation, it is too simplistic to argue that roughly one quarter of abatement ought necessarily to occur in this sector. Transport is today implicated at the core of many social and environmental problems. There is intense pressure within the policy process in many IEA countries for radical changes in transportation.

As such, while the issue of climate change is the global environmental issue of the 21st century in general, it brings pressure to bear on the car industry in particular.

The problem for car firms is that virtually all the emissions from a car's exhaust are CO_2. This is also unavoidable, because CO_2 is produced in a fixed proportion to the fossil fuel combusted in any internal combustion engine. For example, a typical petrol engine that uses a liter of petrol will combine 635g of carbon from the petrol with 1702g of oxygen from the air to produce 2337g of CO_2. Thus, CO_2 emissions expressed in grams per kilometre (g/km) have commensurate fuel economy measures in litres per hundred kilometres (l/100km): the lower the l/100km measure of fuel economy, the lower the g/km of CO_2 emitted (Bradsher 2002: 246 and 451; Austin et al., 2003: 20 and 74).

Given the growth in the fleet of vehicles worldwide, it is projected that the contribution of CO_2 emissions from cars will also grow significantly, at around 2 per cent per annum in absolute terms (Deutsche Bank, 2004: 58; OECD, 2004: 7). In OECD countries alone, if no action is taken, transport sector CO_2 emissions were projected to increase by 30 per cent over the decade to 2010 (IEA, 1997: 19–20).[5] Therefore, dramatic improvements in fuel economy are needed if the contribution of cars to CO_2 emissions is to remain constant, let alone be reduced. For the industry to stabilize CO_2 emissions at current levels, based on current conditions and trends, fuel economy improvements of around 32 per cent will be required for the whole fleet of cars in use by 2020 (OECD, 2004: 18). It therefore is a major focus not just for the car industry, but also regulatory authorities in the industrialized states where its major firms are headquartered.[6]

Fuel economy is arguably the most visible aspect of a car's environmental performance. Consumers are not only informed of fuel economy figures by manufacturers and regulatory authorities, they are also made aware of their car's fuel consumption every time they refuel. Some consumers will know that fuel economy is related to CO_2 emissions, but all will know that a fuel efficient car is more environmentally-friendly than a 'gas guzzler'. While improvements in manufacturing processes and in reporting environmental activities are important, it is cars' actual fuel economy that governments and consumers are most aware of, and therefore this is a 'spotlight' environmental issue for the car industry above all others.[7]

Given the acute relevance of the issue of climate change, and the direct relationship between CO_2 emissions and fuel economy, the focus for analysis is passenger cars in use. The reason is that around 75 per cent of CO_2 emissions over the lifecycle of a car occur in use. This dwarfs CO_2 emissions at all other stages – for example the assembly of a vehicle in the manufacturing process accounts for only 2 per cent of total lifecycle CO_2 emissions (Deutsche Bank, 2004: 58). Therefore, industry initiatives that reduce the CO_2 emissions/improve the fuel economy of cars in use are most significant.

Overall, the issue of climate change is one that has global significance, and particular significance to the industrialized states where the major car firms are headquartered. It is of direct relevance to the car industry because of its contribution to the problem and the nature of its product, it is of concern to states as they must legislate to address the problem, and it is the most visible environmental attribute of passenger cars' environmental performance in use because of its relation to fuel economy, making it especially visible to consumers. With these aspects in mind, we now turn to what the industry is doing about it.

ENVIRONMENTAL PRODUCT DEVELOPMENT INITIATIVES

Given the crucial environmental issue of climate change, and the direct relationship between CO_2 emissions and fuel economy, the major areas in which the car industry is taking initiatives aimed at reducing the CO_2 emissions of its passenger cars in use are incremental technologies; petrol and diesel-electric hybrid drivetrains; hydrogen fuel cell vehicles (FCVs); and alternative fuels. The literature on these is extensive. The following summary is drawn from recent reliable sources that summarize the trends (OECD, 2004; UNEP and ACEA, 2002; Deutsche Bank, 2004; Austin et al., 2003; Maxton and Wormald, 2004).

Incremental Technologies

Incremental technologies refer to advances in the design of the conventional product of the car industry. They involve advances in vehicle design, such as the use of lighter materials, reduction of a car's rolling resistance and improved aerodynamics (all of which mean less fuel needs to be used to propel the vehicle). Transmission advances, such as the introduction of six-speed manuals, advanced intelligent automatics, and continuously variable transmissions, have also improved the performance that can be accessed from conventional drivetrains. For example, continuously variable transmissions reduce fuel consumption by around 4–8 per cent (Deutsche Bank, 2004: 61). Therefore, the combined effects of these advances can amount to significant fuel economy savings.

Engine advances, such as cars that can deactivate some of the engine's cylinders when not required in order to reduce fuel consumption, are now available. But most significant are advances in the design of conventional petrol and diesel internal combustion engines. Since 1996, improvements to conventional petrol engines have resulted in estimated CO_2 emission reductions of around 35 per cent (Deutsche Bank, 2004: 60). These have been achieved through the development and commercial introduction of engine technologies such as electronic fuel injection systems, multi-valve engines and variable cam timing that result in efficiency improvements in engine operation as well as increased power.

For diesel engines, remarkable technological advances have been made through the introduction of advanced high pressure direct injection engines, particularly by European firms. Diesel is denser than petrol and so burning a liter of diesel produces about 2636g of CO_2 (by comparison to 2337g of CO_2 for petrol). However, diesel engines are inherently more fuel efficient than petrol engines. A diesel vehicle tends to be 20 to 40 percent more fuel efficient than a comparable petrol vehicle, so it emits 10 to 30 per cent fewer CO_2 emissions per kilometer travelled (Austin *et. al.*, 2003: 20; Bradsher, 2002: 246). Therefore, not only are advanced diesel engines more efficient than the conventional diesels they replace, they are more efficient than equivalent advanced petrol engines. By running cleaner than older diesel engines they also produce fewer noxious emissions,[8] often less than equivalent petrol engines. Sales of diesel cars now account for up to half of all new car sales in major European markets (Deutsche Bank, 2004: 61; ACEA, no date c).

Petrol and Diesel-electric Hybrid Drivetrains

Petrol-electric and diesel-electric hybrid drivetrains use two sources of power instead of one. They consist of a normal internal combustion engine mated to an electric engine. Mild hybrids deactivate the internal combustion engine when the car is idling, while full hybrids can operate on either power source or a combination of both. Japanese firms were the first to introduce full petrol-electric hybrids in the 1990s with models such as the Toyota Prius and Honda Insight. Toyota passed the 500 000 sales mark for its Prius in mid-2006, with Japan and the US being its biggest markets. Both companies are now expanding the range of models offered in hybrid form (Dowling, 2006; Maxton and Wormald, 2004: 80; Green Car Congress, 2006). Ford was the first non-Japanese firm to release a full petrol-electric hybrid vehicle with the release of a hybrid version of its Ford Escape sports utility vehicle. Other US firms have had plans to release mild hybrids, although General Motors has just released a full hybrid version of its Yukon SUV (Dowling, 2008). At the time of publication, no diesel-electric hybrid vehicles had been commercially released.

Hydrogen Fuel Cell Vehicles

Hydrogen FCVs are the long-term goal of the car industry. Fuel cells are 'electrochemical devices that convert a fuel's energy directly into electrical energy' (Deutsche Bank, 2004: 63). FCVs fueled by hydrogen only emit water vapor as their exhaust gas. They produce no CO_2 emissions at all. Hydrogen internal combustion engines have also been developed by many firms, such as BMW, that similarly emit only water vapor, but use a more conventional drivetrain. The main problem with the technology is that it is currently more expensive than petrol and diesel internal combustion engines to produce, and little refueling infrastructure for hydrogen exists. To date, research into hydrogen technologies has only resulted in proto-types rather than vehicles for commercial sale.

Alternative Fuels

Vehicles that run on alternative fuels, or dual fuel vehicles that are capable of running on conventional petrol/diesel as well as alternative fuels, have been commercially available for some time. The alternative fuels they can run on include liquefied petroleum gas (LPG), compressed natural gas (CNG), ethanol and methanol. These have CO_2 emission advantages over petrol engines, but not necessarily over diesel engines. Methanol is not widely used any more because of its corrosiveness and toxicity. In addition to these, new biofuels are now being trialed that are sourced from biomass stocks that can be used in conventional diesel engines, as well as advanced synthetic fuels. These have the potential to deliver CO_2 emission benefits in the order of 30–60 per cent less than petrol or diesel cars, while also reducing noxious emissions and reliance on non-renewable fossil fuels (OECD, 2004: 14).

What about Fully Electric Vehicles?

Fully electric vehicles were once seen as the way to minimize the environmental impact of cars, because they produce no emissions in use at all. All car firms have had electric vehicle research and development programs, and some still mention them in their environmental reports.[9] However, the commercial impact of such vehicles has been minimal. They may be resurrected one day as a commercial alternative, but as things stand they have not been widely offered by firms, nor embraced by consumers, in the way that advanced diesels or petrol-electric hybrids have been. In terms of impacting on the overall CO_2 emissions of the industry and future developments in this regard their impact has been, and is likely to continue to be, minimal. At the time of writing this book, it was hard to find a reference in which fully electric vehicles were cited as a central strategy for addressing the challenge of climate change by either the industry or commentators on it.[10]

CONVERGENT OR DIVERGENT STRATEGIES?

The environmental product development initiatives that impact on climate change that the major firms from each state chose to highlight in their 2003/04 environmental reports are summarized below.[11] The critical reader will be concerned that much has been left out in such a radical distillation. Firms' activities are more complex than this summary, and their environmental reports are dense documents with a great deal of more information. However, the purpose here is to distil the essence of their activities for the purpose of comparative analysis, and to show the broad brushstrokes in terms of the most evident initiatives that firms report they are taking that impact on CO_2 emissions/fuel economy.

It must also be conceded that not all firms' investment in product developments that produce positive environmental outcomes is necessarily undertaken out of concern for the environment. For example, developments in engine technology may result in engines with greater efficiency that use less fuel and emit less CO_2, but they also deliver greater power and performance. The purpose here is not to judge the extent to which such developments were initially undertaken for environmental reasons, but to highlight the key product development initiatives that *firms themselves* choose to highlight in their environmental reports as having such benefits. Having identified these, some associations may be drawn between the national differences and the insights of the VOC approach, the upshot of which is that 'the strategies of the major automobile producers are more diverse than is often realized, a fact not unrelated to their national origins' (Dicken, 2003: 397).

What Major German, US and Japanese Firms Say in their Environmental Reports

All firms stress their concern for fuel economy and CO_2 emission reductions, and highlight technology-driven solutions with conventional engines. They all mention the product development initiatives already identified to one degree or another. The main point of difference is the degree to which German firms stress their advances in diesel. For them, the promotion of clean, small diesel engines is seen as a key way to reduce fuel consumption and meet required EU CO_2 emission reductions. There even seems to be something *German* about their diesel commitments. For example, DaimlerChrysler (2004: 33) notes the following:

> In 1936 came the highly acclaimed debut of the first diesel-engined car: the Mercedes-Benz 260D – soon the vehicle of choice for every German taxi driver. . . .Today, diesels are top-notch high-tech machines, with only a fraction of the emissions of their ancestors.

German firms are developing an existing technology, one that they invented and have experience in producing, to its furthest point.

Recognizing diesel cars' potential in the European market, US firms mention them in relation to their European operations. However, outside Europe they see limited opportunities for diesels. For example, General Motors (2004: 6.30) says:

Diesel usage in the US will depend on how diesel-equipped vehicles will comply with future emissions requirements, customer acceptance, and the price of diesel fuel. We see advanced diesel engines as complementary to gasoline-powered engines. Concerns over emissions regulations, market acceptance, taxation based on engine displacement, fuel consumption, and the price of fuel largely dictate in which markets diesels are popular today.

Fundamentally, General Motors sees diesel's acceptance outside Europe in regulatory and market acceptance terms, and limited as a result of these. Ford (2004: 17) takes a similar view in noting that 'when it comes to perception of diesel engines, Europe and North America seem to be more than an ocean apart'.

Japanese firms might be expected to take a similar view for their European operations, but do not. Despite the increasing market share of diesels in Europe, they barely mention diesel technologies at all. In conventional engines, Japanese firms remain focused on advanced petrol engines. But what distinguishes the Japanese firms is the centrality of hybrid vehicles in their environmental strategies. They see hybrids as the next step in the mass production of highly fuel-efficient small cars, and not necessarily an interim step in advance of hydrogen FCVs. Not only do they have research and development programs, but in the case of Honda and Toyota, have been selling hybrids commercially since the 1990s. Toyota is licencing its hybrid technology to US firms and Nissan (for example for the Ford Escape SUV and the Nissan Altima hybrids). Nissan identifies the development of petrol-electric hybrid cars as a priority.

The US firms also see hybrids as important enough to warrant the recent/imminent release of a range of models. However, there are qualitative differences. The first hybrid released by a US firm is the Ford Escape, an SUV. This is mirrored in General Motors' plans to release hybrid SUV models, as well as that of DaimlerChrysler for the US side of its operations. While Japanese firms are producing small, efficient cars using hybrid technologies, US firms see hybrids as a way of making their big, powerful, light trucks more fuel efficient.

The German firms are not at all focused on hybrids to the same extent. Volkswagen has been producing prototypes since 1986, which is possibly even earlier than Toyota, yet has not commercially released any hybrid models. It is committed to continued research. BMW sees FCVs and hydrogen powered drivetrains as the next step without any reference to hybrids in the interim.[12] DaimlerChrysler (2004) sees hybrids as 'an important interim stage' yet dismisses them as inferior to diesels because they do not clearly use less fuel and do not generate lower CO_2 emissions than a modern diesel engine.

FCVs are seen as the future by all firms, and all are investing in FCV technologies. However, the future is varying distances away depending on firms' nationality. US and German firms see the commercial introduction of hydrogen FCVs as 10–20 years away, whereas Japanese firms see them as a more imminent prospect. German firms report that they continue to undertake development work with the aim of having excellent prototypes that perform well, so they can be introduced when the time is right. Thus, DaimlerChrysler's goal is to sell FCVs commercially by 2010, while agreeing with Volkswagen that real commercialization is at least 20 years away. BMW sees them as the most promising long-term solution. Both General Motors and Ford see FCVs as a long-term goal, the former aiming to make them commercially viable by 2010, but the latter having no clear timeframe and suggesting commercial viability is highly contingent on a range of factors the results of which will not be clear until 2015. By contrast, Toyota (2004: 14) wants to introduce FCVs 'early', while Honda proudly announces that it is the first company in the world to have an FCV approved for commercial sale. Nissan sees 2005 as the year it develops FCVs to a level where they are suitable for practical use.

The approach to the introduction of FCVs is therefore qualitatively different between the Japanese, US and German firms. The Japanese firms want to be the first with products on the market, rather in the vein of hybrids. Indeed, Toyota sees the possibility of hybrid FCVs, so that rather than hybrids representing an interim technology, they may be incorporated in FCVs. This first-on-the-market approach may be contrasted with that of General Motors. Rather than being the first to sell hydrogen FCVs, General Motors wants to be first to sell the most of them: its goal is to be the first company to sell one million FCVs. Ford wants the market to mature enough and the refueling infrastructure to be in place before it makes clear commitments to releasing FCVs, and likewise German firms simply see them as a technology solution whose day will eventually come. Therefore, US and German firms are focused more on market conditions, whereas Japanese firms are keen to make the technology commercially available and shape the market for them. While US firms are waiting for the market to mature and German firms have the technology ready for when the moment is right, Japanese firms are releasing their products in the hope that markets will catch up with their advanced, commercially available products.

Alternative fuels barely rate a mention in Japanese firms' environmental reports. Their focus is much more on radical new technologies involving alternative drivetrains, particularly hybrids and FCVs. It is US and German manufacturers who focus most on alternative fuels. However, once again there are qualitative differences. The US manufacturers stress that they are already producing dual-fuel vehicles and vehicles that can run on alternative fuels such as ethanol. Again, this is primarily for their light trucks in the US, versus 'normal' cars in the EU.[13] Of the German manufacturers, BMW makes no mention of alternative fuels at all, again focusing on hydrogen as the most effective fuel of the future. However, Volkswagen and DaimlerChrysler stress the potential for, and their investment in, synthetic alternative fuels and fuels derived from biomass that may be used in their current diesel engines. They are working together in a cooperative partnership with a range of other companies and organizations to develop such fuels which Volkswagen (2003: 46) describes as 'an ideal interim stage between the hydrocarbon and hydrogen economies'. Such biofuels, mentioned in passing in Ford's report, are a centerpiece of Volkswagen and DaimlerChrysler's environmental strategies.

In summary, all the major firms identify strategies in respect of all the environmental product developments identified, regardless of their nationality. What they have in common is that while research and development continues on hydrogen FCVs, these are seen as a distant prospect. They are all also working on incremental technologies and introducing them to vehicles that they have on the market. However, beyond this there are three major differences. First, in Germany (and Europe) there have been strong moves towards diesel cars and alternative fuels that can be used with them (ACEA, 2004a and no date c). Second, hybrid vehicles are very much a Japanese initiative, and even though Ford has introduced a petrol-electric hybrid model it has done so licencing the technology from Toyota. Hybrids are thus the key strategy for Japanese firms while being gradually introduced by the US industry and considered by German firms.[14] Third, for the US no clear strategy is evident, except possibly dual-fuel vehicles, and vehicles that operate on alternative fuels generally. These are mostly stressed for larger vehicles such as SUVs. The relative emphasis and qualitative differences in the way these technologies are viewed are expanded on and related to the insights of the VOC approach below.

National Differences and the Varieties of Capitalism Approach

The national differences evident from firms' treatment of CO_2 emissions and fuel economy in their environmental reports reflect the institutional differences highlighted by the VOC approach. These are considered on a territory-by-territory basis in the following sections.

German firms
German firms are largely focused on diesels and alternative fuels. They were the pioneers in the former, and the latter is complementary in that

such fuels allow them to advance conventional technologies, particularly diesel, without needing to turn to more radical drivetrains. Volkswagen's approach is typical. The impression conveyed is of a company not taking radical steps, but focused on what can be done now in order to be a market leader in diesels with cleaner emissions, based on more environmentally-friendly fuels. Where investment is being undertaken in more radical technologies, such advances are being done experimentally rather than in the market. In short, German firms are advancing conventional technologies in the market and developing radical technologies for when conditions emerge that permit these to be implemented. As such, more radical solutions such as hydrogen drivetrains, particularly in the form of FCVs, are seen as a long-term environmental solution. Even if portrayed as *the* environmental solution, as in the case of BMW, it is one that is at least 20 years away.

There are two caveats to this. First, generalizing on the German firms is to some extent difficult because of BMW and DaimlerChrysler. Being more a prestige car maker, BMW's strategic focus is somewhat different to the others for whom the prestige market is one segment among others in which they compete. Because BMW's focus is narrower, the scope of its activities is also more limited. No activity is reported on hybrids and no mention is made of alternative fuels other than hydrogen as the long-term final solution. However, what it does have in common with the other German firms is a focus on more traditional technologies and developing these to advanced levels. Therefore, BMW fits the German model in the *nature* of its activities, even if the *scope* of them is more limited.

DaimlerChrysler's mixed heritage makes categorizing its activities more problematic. Sometimes it looks like a German firm, while at others it looks like a US firm. For example, it is focused more on diesel technologies than hybrids as a way of reducing CO_2 emissions and improving fuel economy, like Volkswagen and BMW. Like the other German firms, it stresses its implementation of advanced diesel technologies in small efficient cars like its 'Smart' range, and in advances in conventional engines generally. However, it sees potential in melding diesel and hybrid technologies and putting such engines in its larger SUVs and pickup trucks, in a similar manner to Ford and General Motors. It sees FCVs as a long-term alternative, like the other German firms, yet wishes to introduce them within the next 20 years subject to market conditions in the manner of General Motors' and Ford's indicative timeframes. It stresses the potential for alternative biofuels in the manner of Volkswagen, and CNG for its European models, but does not mention ethanol as an alternative fuel for its US models at all.

Clear conclusions on DaimlerChrysler are therefore problematic, but the German side of its operations does square with what is evident from Volkswagen and BMW's reporting. DaimlerChrysler's diesel focus fits with the observation that German firms prefer an incremental approach based on refining and advancing existing, proven technology. Overall then, German firms demonstrate a conventional technology strategy. This is not to say that significant investment in new technologies is not the case, but that those brought to the market *now* are based on a platform of diesel engines and knowledge of them. German firms' embrace of advanced diesel technologies, especially in smaller cars, is the centerpiece of their product environmental strategies.[15]

These observations are commensurate with the incremental approach to technological improvements characterizing Germany's CME style of capitalism. The German firms are taking an incremental approach with the aim of balancing competing interests via gradual/incremental measures – that is, technological environmental advances while maintaining profits. They have developed advanced diesel technologies, in which they have a history of expertise, are examining alternative fuels, and are introducing new products to the market in a considered and measured manner. CME-style, it is also not so much a matter of responding to market forces, as having the appropriate vehicles for the overall environment as and when this may be appropriate, and developing technologies on the basis of their histories of expertise in particular technologies (i.e. firms' expertise dictates their actions rather than market forces).

Japanese firms
Japanese firms have the most radical technological approach. Although fuel economy is seen as a priority in all vehicles, along with emission reductions, and the goals set by firms involve optimization of conventional technologies, more radical drive technologies are embraced and highlighted. FCVs are not seen so much as a distant possibility as one that is imminent. Hybrid petrol-electric vehicles are seen as a viable alternative *now* and being brought to the market. Diesel technologies are not so much dismissed, but if mentioned at all they are certainly in the background. Alternative fuels for conventional engines are similarly in the background by comparison to US firms, Volkswagen and DaimlerChysler. Thus, Japanese firms have, or intend to have, radical technological solutions in the market before anyone else, while improving the environmental performance of conventional drivetrains.

The more radical technology-driven, first-to-market approach of Japanese firms suggests they are motivated more by internal strategies than reacting to market forces. They are not waiting until the moment is right, in the vein of German firms, but are developing and marketing new technologies regardless of whether a market exists for them yet, and without waiting for markets to mature. This fits with the technonationalist version of Japan's CME-style of capitalism, as well as the point that markets are less of a driver for action in CMEs generally – that is, like German firms, what they have a history of expertise in internally motivates them, in the sense that the German firms are diesel experts, whereas the Japanese firms are petrol and advanced technology experts.

US firms

Rather than being focused on a single clear strategy, one gets the impression that US firms are doing *everything*. Of course, the German and Japanese firms operate in the same way to some extent, but they are more strategically focused on one type of technological solution. Yet, US firms' lack of focus also seems a conscious strategic decision. Ford (2004: 64) explicitly acknowledges this in noting that 'benefits can be gained by exploring these technologies simultaneously and in combination, rather than trying to select one "winner"'. This is not to say that German and Japanese firms do not recognize this too, it's just that their reports do not demonstrate it so clearly.

Therefore, US firms are not random in their approach, so much as they are mindful that the development of new technologies is contingent on their market potential.[16] For example, hybrids are seen as a solution for light trucks in the US market, while diesels are seen as the solution for Europe. Such a market-driven approach suggests less a market leading or market defining role for US firms, and more one in which market conditions must be recognized and *reacted* to. So, as German firms define their strategy in terms of where their expertise lies, and Japanese firms focus on a radical technology approach that may shape what the market evolves to, US firms look first to market conditions existing *now* and tailor their products accordingly. Their environmental solutions are less radical than those of the Japanese firms, and although they exhibit a German stance in terms of focusing more on conventional technologies they do this more overtly in terms of maintaining their position in markets and competing in them.

Overall, for the US firms what is evident is a 'horses-for-courses' approach, with different solutions for different markets, such as environmental initiatives for large SUVs which dominate the US market, rather than new vehicles in the mould of Toyota's Prius. They focus on market success expressed in terms of sales targets, rather than on being first in the market per se. This suggests a more LME-style materialist perspective in which reaction to, and tailoring products to fit, market conditions is more to the fore. In offering new environmentally-friendly products, they stress reacting to different market situations and providing the products they see as most suitable to market conditions, rather than attempting to lead the market with new innovations.

CONCLUSION

Climate change is a crucial environmental issue. Its profile among policy-makers, civil society and business as a result of international events such as UNCED and agreements such as the Kyoto Protocol, mark it as the global environmental issue of the 1990s. It remains so going into the 21st century. It is of particular relevance to the car industry, in terms of moving towards greater environmental sustainability and ensuring the industry's survival given the nature of its product. The industry's contribution to CO_2 emissions, the major greenhouse gas responsible for climate change, and the relationship of CO_2 emissions to fuel economy, arguably the most visible environmental aspect of passenger cars in use, make this a crucial environmental issue for the industry as much as for the world. This leads to an analysis of environmental product developments because it is the industry's products in use that are responsible for 75 per cent of CO_2 emissions in the lifecycle of a typical vehicle.

Four key areas in which the car industry is taking initiatives aimed at reducing the CO_2 emissions of its passenger cars in use have been identified: incremental technologies; petrol and diesel-electric hybrids; hydrogen FCVs and alternative fuels. Although all firms have strategies in respect of all of these, their relative emphasis depends on their nationality. Japanese firms are focused on hybrids, while German firms are focused on diesels. German and US firms are focused on alternative fuels, but in different ways: for US firms this is a strategy for addressing the fuel consumption of their larger light trucks, for German firms it is an across-the-board strategy. Alternative fuels are not such a high priority for Japanese firms. While FCVs are a relatively distant prospect, Japanese firms want to introduce them as soon as possible, whereas German and US firms want to be ready to introduce them when the environment for them is appropriate. There is clearly a stronger emphasis on reacting to market forces and developing products to suit different markets for US firms. Such market motivations are less prevalent for German and Japanese firms whose strategies seem more internally-driven – e.g. on the basis of technological expertise for German firms, and an embrace of radical new technologies by Japanese firms.

These observations have implications in a VOC context for three reasons. First, the technonationalist version of the Japanese CME appears manifested in Japanese firms' more radical embrace of hybrid technologies, and radical leading-edge technological advances generally. The focus is then on being first on the market with such technologies. Second, LME-style, US firms appear to be more driven by market forces than CME-based Japanese and German firms for whom non-price, internally-driven innovation strategies seem more the case. Third, the time frame for the introduction of these technologies is commensurate with the divide between short-term profit motivated LME-based US firms, versus longer-term perspectives of CME-based German and Japanese firms that are less dictated by market forces.

However, these are simply observations at this stage, more in the nature of suggested implications of the activities that firms are undertaking. The story 'fits', but is not the result of rigorous analysis. This is the task at hand for the next four chapters in which firms' product development initiatives are examined in the light of state regulations, market forces, and the rationales offered by firms themselves in their environmental reports and interviews with key personnel.

NOTES

1. 'Greenwashing' is a term used by environmentalists to describe well publicized commitments to environmental concerns that do not translate into action. They therefore amount to cynical public relations exercises. See for example *Scientific American* (2002).
2. Levy and Rothenberg (2002) actually identify it as such for the car industry specifically.
3. Australia also shared the dubious distinction of being a non-ratifier with the US until a change of government led to belated ratification in 2008.
4. The calculation done for this in Chapter 1, note 4, is for all OECD countries. The figure used here for the EU, US and Japan specifically is based on estimates in OECD (2003), OECD (2002a and b), Austin et al., (2003), JAMA (2003), ECMT (2001), and Harrington and McConnell (2003).
5. As an indicator of the contribution of passenger cars to these figures, approximately 80 per cent of emissions from transport in Europe are accounted for by road transport, and of this two-thirds is accounted for by passenger cars (ECMT, 1997: 10).
6. Indeed, Deutsche Bank (2004: 58) believes that that 'fuel economy and CO_2 emissions standards offer the best prospect for reducing vehicles' contribution to climate change'. The IEA (1993) has also long held that improving fuel economy, such as via switching to alternative fuels, is *the* way for the industry to reduce the CO_2 emissions of cars.
7. It could be argued that another is noxious emissions for the smog they cause at a primarily local, rather than global, level. However, there is no doubt that climate change and CO_2 emissions are *the* global environmental issue of the last decade, and one of primary concern to the car industry.
8. This is especially the case for emissions of nitrogen oxides and particulate matter.
9. For example, Volkswagen (2003: 15) notes that it has been researching and developing electric concept vehicles since the 1970s.
10. The OECD (2004: 12–13) concurs with this perspective.
11. This is based on Volkswagen (2003), DaimlerChrysler (2004), BMW Group (2003a), Toyota Motor Corporation (2004), Honda Motor Company (2002, 2004), Nissan

Motor Company (2004a and b), Ford Motor Company (2004) and General Motors Corporation (2004). There are smaller firms such as Mitsubishi in Japan, but it is not a major producer in the sense that its car production is 26 per cent less than that of the smallest firm here, BMW (OICA, 2007). The disparity is, if anything, exacerbated if one considers that BMW is a niche prestige producer, whereas Mitsubishi is a volume producer. Mitsubishi is also partially owned by DaimlerChrysler (Deutsche Bank, 2004).

12. The word 'hybrid' is not even mentioned in BMW's report.
13. Although Ford also notes that it is discontinuing vehicles that can run on LPG and CNG in the US.
14. Whatever the hybrid programs of the industry in general, Toyota and Honda were the first on the market with such products.
15. It is also, as we shall see in the following chapter, largely responsible for the success of the German, and indeed entire EU car industry, in reducing CO_2 emissions. Not only have they developed more technologically advanced diesel engines, but the commercialization of them on a large scale and the uptake of them by consumers has had very beneficial results (see ECMT, 2003: 7).
16. In the sense that they are dictated by market forces and consumer demand, this squares with the strategic rationale for product developments outlined in AAM (no date b and c).

4. How rules are made: state regulations in the European Union, US and Japan

> The differences voiced in the climate change negotiations speak to larger differences that have developed among these countries in terms of the roles they feel that government and markets should play in environmental protection and where responsibility for taking action lies.
>
> (Schreurs, 2002: 10)

Changing the behavior of economic actors to internalize environmental externalities is unlikely without effective regulation. The liberal economic argument is that economic actors responsible for environmental damage will not voluntarily face the costs they impose on society. They must be forced to do so. Traditionally, the degree to which environmental regulations are effective is therefore seen in material terms: when regulations are introduced, their stringency, effective monitoring of those subject to them, penalties for non-compliance and the like. There is no doubt that regulation is necessary and alters firms' behavior. However, from an institutional perspective, understanding the way regulations are developed – i.e. how rules are made – is necessary to explain the extent of compliance with them, and therefore their degree of effectiveness. The proposition in this chapter is that the institutional basis for developing regulations explains their effect and the level of compliance with them *more* than the material facts of the regulations themselves. Specifically, when the institutional basis of state–firm relations encourages cooperation, consensus and a longer-term view rather than short-term gains, as in coordinated market economies, the effect of regulations and compliance with them is greater. The converse is the case in liberal market economies.

First, the institutional basis of state–firm relations suggested by the Varieties of Capitalism approach is related specifically to environmental regulations in the European Union, United States and Japan. Second, given the focus on climate change, actual regulations to reduce carbon dioxide emissions by passenger cars in use up to 2004 are outlined in each of the territories. Third, empirical evidence for the effect of these regulations is presented. What is shown is that the toughest and longest-standing regulations do not necessarily produce the lowest CO_2 emissions. Therefore, while there are differences in the timing and stringency of regulations in the EU, US and Japan, a model is presented that suggests why such material differences are less important than the institutional basis of the relationship between business and government that informs the way in which regulations are developed. At the heart of this relationship is a question of causality: whether regulations affect firm behavior, or whether they are in fact a reflection of firm strategies. The greater the extent to which environmental regulations have been developed on a co- to self-regulatory basis, rather than imposed by regulators, the greater the compliance with them, the greater the effect of them, and thus the more environmental externalities are internalized.

The conclusion reached is that institutional aspects of the way rules are made are more important than the material facts of them. Specifically, the insights of the VOC approach in general apply specifically to the manner in which CO_2 emission regulations have been developed in each of the three territories. The CME nature of EU and Japanese firms' home states results in co- to self-regulation. Therefore, EU and Japanese firms are more likely to proactively suggest and implement initiatives to reduce CO_2 emissions than their LME-based US counterparts. Importantly, it is also shown that this has ramifications beyond the borders of firms' home states, because car firms 'export' the institutional features of their home states' regulations in the products they sell – i.e. the products they offer for sale beyond their borders reflect the institutional effectiveness (or otherwise) of their home states' regulations. The result is that US firms trail EU and Japanese firms when it comes to addressing the CO_2 emissions of the passenger cars they sell not just in their home territory, but internationally.

THE VARIETIES OF CAPITALISM APPROACH AND ENVIRONMENTAL REGULATIONS

Chapter 2 outlined the insights of the VOC approach in respect of state–business relations in LMEs versus CMEs. Briefly, in LMEs a separation of states and markets is preferred, versus closer state–business relations in CMEs. This is reflected in markets as the primary organizers of economic activity in LMEs, versus greater state coordination of economic activity, and state involvement in markets, in CMEs. A greater focus on the material imperatives of markets produces a shorter-term perspective for LME-based firms, whereas a longer-term perspective not dictated as strongly by the short-term material imperatives of market forces is the case for firms in CMEs. Firms in LMEs are happier making decisions based on market signals that define shorter-term profit levels, and will usually prefer deregulation over heavier state guidance and intervention. Firms in CMEs tend more towards consensus decision-making, including with regulators, based on long-established networks. In regulatory terms, firms in LMEs should therefore react more efficiently to regulations that alter price signals in the market, whereas firms in CMEs will react more efficiently to regulations based on (agreed) rules and standards.

The following expands on the institutional basis of state–business relations in the EU, US and Japan by introducing some key observations on what this means for environmental regulations.

The European Union

Germany and Japan are CMEs, while the US is an LME. Hall and Soskice (2001) incorporate these three states in their overall categorization of OECD countries which includes the UK, Australia, Canada, New Zealand and Ireland along with the US in the list of LMEs. For reasons of their common heritage, these are often referred to as the Anglo-Saxon economies (see, for example, Dore, 2000a). Switzerland, the Netherlands, Belgium, Sweden, Norway, Denmark, Finland and Austria are grouped with Germany and Japan in the list of CMEs. States that fall somewhere in between include France, Italy, Spain, Portugal, Greece and Turkey. As such, in addition to Germany and Japan being CMEs, most European countries fall into the CME category, or somewhere between the two (Hall and Soskice, 2001a: 19–21). This is important because the focus in this chapter is on EU rather than German regulations. The reason is that 'the regulations of the European Union have become almost as important as national policies' (Hall and Soskice, 2001a: 52). Indeed, for all intents and purposes, EU environmental policies *are* national policies given their applicability to all EU member states. The 1991 Treaty on European Unity (the Maastricht Treaty) represented 'the most extensive abdication of national sovereignty in modern times' (Fioretos, 2001: 213), and resulted in a good deal of what were previously national policies being transferred to the European Commission.[1]

Can it be said that there is an EU variety of capitalism though? This is more problematic for at least three reasons. First, there are methodological problems in doing so as the VOC approach is fundamentally one about states, not regions.[2] Second, there are practical reasons, to the extent that within the time period considered the EU expanded from 15 to 25 member states. Therefore, the EU itself has undergone a compositional change. Third, there are problems even generalizing among its key, founding members. As Schmidt (2002) so clearly demonstrates using the cases of

Germany, France and the UK, it is hard to say these member states share a single European variety of capitalism. Instead, she finds that national variations mean they have at least three distinct Varieties of Capitalism.[3] What is true in general for EU member states is also shown to be the case in respect of environmental policy and regulations by authors such as Scruggs (2003) and Leveque (1996).[4]

It may seem anathema to the VOC approach to ascribe one type of capitalism to an entire region. Nevertheless, authors such as Esping-Andersen (1990) and Crouch (2005a) see Germany as *representative* of a continental European model. Pauly and Reich (1997: 6) explain the centrality of Germany in Europe in the following terms:

> We view the German base as distinctive enough and regionally dominant enough to be the central analog to the American and Japanese cases. Of Europe's top one hundred firms, twenty seven are German. They account for the largest share of European industrial production and sales, and, across key technology-intensive sectors, German firms hold a much larger – and rising – share of world production than firms based in any other European country.

Therefore, there is a blurred line between Germany as a state and Europe as a region. Furthermore (and conversely), EU regulations effectively are the basis for German environmental regulations, in reality as well as for the purpose of analysis. What is true for Germany is also true for other EU member states. Furthermore, when speaking about the German car industry, given its dominance of the EU market we are to a large extent speaking about a European, as much as German, industry.[5] Clearly drawing the boundaries between what is a German versus a European firm, or industry, and German versus European regulations is a somewhat futile exercise because the boundaries cannot be clearly defined. Crossing them is somewhat inevitable, certainly in regulatory terms.

I would contend that for analytical purposes there are at least four reasons why the EU overall may be said to be CME-*like* in setting environmental regulations specifically. First, Leveque argues that the EU has increasingly performed a centralizing role for environmental policy-making that includes industry and peak bodies in what may be best thought of as a coordinated regulatory 'game'. Since the Act of Political Union, environmental protection has been established as an explicit action of the EU with decisions made on the basis of qualified majority voting. This has created 'a harmonized environmental policy and regulatory system among the member states' (Desai, 2002a: 17; see also Haigh, 1996; Macroy and Hession, 1996). It has increased the impetus for coordination between member states and harmonization of their rules.

Second, the existence of a regional market provides impetus for firms to coordinate their actions through peak bodies in order to influence the outcome of regulatory processes, and indeed to be proactive in so doing. This allows them to avoid the complexities and additional costs that arise from the existence of different regulations in individual member states. Firms influence EU-wide environmental policy-making via inter-firm coalitions, meaning that 'the regulator is confronted with a dominant source of information instead of obtaining contrasted data from competing industry interest groups' (Leveque, 1996: 22; see also Schnitter, 1997). Industry peak bodies suggest environmental targets and regulations to be adopted in order to provide greater regulatory clarity and certainty, and thus voluntary agreements with industry are being increasingly employed. Thus, there is a regional partnership approach between firms and regulators.

Third, Directives are the main legal instrument of EU environmental policy, proposed by the EC and approved by the Council of Ministers. Because the EU has increasingly gone down the path of voluntary industry agreements, Directives often confirm as legally binding regulations initiatives that were initially proposed by industry. Once in effect Directives are binding on all member states. Therefore, the EU is CME-like in the sense that Directives on environmental regulations are often proposed voluntarily by industry peak bodies, negotiated with the EC and, subsequent to their acceptance, generalized to the whole of the EU. Firms, who were instrumental in their proposal, have a stake in their implementation in concert with relevant state authorities (see, for example, Leveque, 1996: especially 3–5, 9 and 48–49; Haigh, 1996; Macroy and Hession, 1996).

Fourth, there is a wealth of (often quite critical) literature on the EU that points to the way in which the EU moves in slow, bureaucratic, incremental steps in the development and implementation of regulations.[6] This is characterized by an iterative process involving rounds of negotiations, compromise, and consensus-building. Understanding the process, let alone the outcome, of these processes is so problematic that to view them as merely the state imposing regulations (LME-style), rather than the result of close business–regulatory relations and a complex negotiation process, would be to completely miss the point. At the end of the day, rather than a model based on business lobbying as in the US, the relationship between firms and regulators in the EU is better understood as one of 'dialogue, private meetings, and corridor lobbying' (Newell and Levy, 2006: 168).

The US

State–business ties in the US have historically been institutionally weak. The adversarial relationship between state and business highlighted in

Chapter 2 means that rather than being based more on voluntary commitment and consensus, as in the EU, US environmental regulations have primarily been of a command-and-control nature. They have been imposed by government with stiff penalties for non-compliance (see, for example, Kraft, 2002). Coupled with this, or because of it, high levels of litigation have been employed to challenge environmental measures. Litigation is frequently used both before and after regulations are introduced. In fact, the outcome of litigation is generally built into environmental regulations to ensure their acceptance by both non-government organizations (NGOs) and firms, and thereby formalize their implementation.[7]

Litigation exists in tandem with a pluralistic multi-tiered federal system of government and bureaucracy that sees many levels of environmental regulation possible, and existing simultaneously, in a context of shared authority that the OECD (1996: 122) characterizes as follows:

> The complexity of federal–state–tribal–local government relationships, and of procedures regulating pollutant emissions, has meant that the process of implementation of regulatory policies has involved high transaction costs to regulatory agencies at all levels of government and to the regulated industries.

A reflection of the 'many voices' aspect of state–business relations in the US, many layers of lobbying go on all the time through many and varied highly organized NGOs and industry groups. This, plus the fracturing of the implementation of national rules through a federal system coupled with high litigation levels, means that the legal enforcement capacity of the state is actually quite weak. This concurs with the idea of firms in LMEs competing in markets, and preferring competition and conflict over coordinating their activity through relational cooperation.

Japan

Along with Japan being characterized by a strong partnership between government and industry, it is generally true that environmental regulations have not been as tough as in the EU or US (Braithwaite and Drahos, 2000: 271). Although stiff penalties may exist for breaking environmental regulations, in reality litigation is very much a last resort because environmental policy is based on a consensus approach between industry and government. Implementation is more a case of moving forward slowly so that consensus is more likely. Negotiated (often legally non-binding) agreements between industry and government are common for achieving environmental targets. Targets may be suggested by the government in the form of vague guidelines initially, industry has time to digest them and incorporate them in business plans, and government–industry consultation is ongoing throughout. The result is that when legally binding targets are set they are attainable by firms, and the rationale for them accepted (Schreurs, 2002; OECD, 2002a). Given the blurred line between government and business interests in Japan, Scruggs (2003) notes that the two cooperate closely on environmental issues in a conscious attempt to shift the economy out of high environmental impact modes to ones with lower environmental impacts.

This reflects the more organic nature of state–business relations in Japan discussed in Chapter 2, in the sense that rather than regulations being the result of collectively negotiated agreements, and a drawn out process of negotiated consensus-building à la the EU/Germany, Japanese environmental regulations are more the result of a common position reached behind closed doors. This is typical of the Japanese CME blurred line between government and business interests, as opposed to the drawn-out bureaucratic process of reaching a common position that characterizes the EU.

Comparing the EU, US and Japan

Clear points of difference in how regulations are made emerge from the preceding discussion. These lead commentators such as Schreurs (2002: 10) to observe that varying levels of support for the Kyoto Protocol are directly related to national variations in capitalist relations of production:

> The differences voiced in the climate change negotiations speak to larger differences that have developed among these countries in terms of the roles they feel that government and markets should play in environmental protection and where responsibility for taking action lies. They further reflect differences in the relationships that have emerged among governments, business, and environmental NGOs in the policy-making process.

The US sees addressing climate change in terms of an LME preoccupation with market efficiency and competition, with a minimal role for government. A more arm's-length and at times litigious relationship between NGOs, business and government based on pluralism and a lack of consensus has helped to foster such a view. By comparison, a more coordinated/partnership approach is taken in the EU and Japan where firms and regulators are more likely to cooperate in developing regulatory strategies. This does not mean that firms in the EU and Japan are eager to be regulated while those in the US are not. While firms in both are keen to avoid regulation, in the EU and Japan they are more likely to work closely with regulators to find regulatory solutions in a spirit of consultative decision-making rather than confrontation (see, for example, Schreurs, 2002: 11; Desai, 2002a: 11–14, 2002b: 357).

What are the implications? Firms in the EU and Japan are more likely to cooperate with government in setting regulations on a more voluntaristic basis than in the US. They will be more willing to accept regulations, on which they have had considerable input, rather than push for the idea of 'free' competition in markets. They will be more inclined to consensus-driven regulation rather than regulations that have been imposed as a result of a multi-stakeholder 'fight', the outcome of which may have been decided through acrimonious litigation. They are therefore more likely to feel comfortable with, and committed to, the aims of regulation and comply with its requirements more willingly.

We now turn to actual CO_2 emission regulations in each of the three territories before seeing how the empirical evidence bears out the points made by the institutional perspective outlined so far.

CO_2 EMISSION REGULATIONS IN THE EU, US AND JAPAN

The close and fixed relationship between fuel economy and CO_2 emissions means there are only three ways to reduce CO_2 emissions for cars powered by the combustion of fossil fuels: reduce car use; improve fuel economy; or switch to alternative fuels/propulsion systems (Harrington and McConnell, 2003: 52). While the first is less applicable to car manufacturers (because it is hard to imagine they would desire reduced car use) it nevertheless has been the focus of governments, particularly through the market mechanism of point-of-sale fuel taxes. These should make vehicles with higher CO_2 emissions more expensive to run, and indirectly alter firms' behavior as they will switch to the production of vehicles with lower CO_2 emissions that are cheaper to run and thus regarded more favorably by consumers. The latter two sit very much with car manufacturers and command-and-control regulations put in place by regulators, more simply referred to here as 'standards'. Standards that focus on CO_2 emissions and fuel economy are considered.

Market Mechanisms

Point-of-sale fuel taxes have been imposed in the EU, US and Japan for a considerable period of time. There have been a variety of rationales for them other than reducing CO_2 emissions or improving fuel economy (one example being funding road construction). They have also been implemented in a rather uncoordinated way with national, regional and local taxes levied by a variety of authorities. But regardless of their rationale they should indirectly affect manufacturers' strategic decisions by changing price signals for consumers who should initially attempt to reduce their car use, and then demand cars with greater fuel efficiency. Table 4.1 presents fuel prices and the total of all taxes as a percentage of fuel prices in the EU, US and Japan in 1980, 1990 and 2000.

Clearly, the EU and Japan have substantial fuel taxes. With the exception of diesel in 2000 when Japan had higher taxes, the EU has always had the highest taxes followed by Japan, with the US a distant third. In terms of tax increases as a share of price, these were much greater over 1980–1990 than 1990–2000. In fact, increases in the 1990s were modest, with the exception of Japan where the tax share of diesel prices increased by 54 per cent and that of petrol by 17 per cent. Conversely, the US actually reduced taxes on petrol in the 1990s.

For the EU and Japan the magnitude of state-imposed taxes clearly encourages consumers to use less fuel, or buy cars that are more fuel efficient. In the case of Japan, the impetus for doing so has been strengthened through substantial tax increases over the entire 1980–2000 period, but unlike the EU where the tax on diesel is lower than that for petrol, by 2000 there was no difference in Japanese taxes on diesel and petrol. While the EU's taxes therefore encourage the greater uptake of diesel over petrol cars to encourage lower fuel consumption, Japanese taxes signal a desire for greater fuel efficiency across the board. Low US taxes, and falls or only modest increases in them over the 1990s, encourage comparatively higher fuel consumption.

While the tax share in price indicates state intervention in the market, it is fuel prices that actually impact on consumers' purchasing decisions. Obviously, there are more factors that affect the price of fuel than taxes. Prices in all territories fell over 1980–90 as world oil prices stabilized after the shocks of the 1970s. What is interesting though, are price movements after 1990. Given tax levels in the EU, it is unsurprising to find that it has both the highest petrol and diesel prices, but that diesel is cheaper thereby encouraging its uptake over petrol. The EU's petrol and diesel prices both rose over 1990–2000. The US, with the lowest taxes (falling in the 1990s in the case of petrol) also has the lowest fuel prices.[8] But unlike the EU, fuel prices in the US went down and stayed down in the 1990s. For Japan, despite a large rise in petrol taxes and a huge rise in diesel taxes in the 1990s, petrol and diesel prices actually fell by 13 and 11 per cent respectively. In other words, fuel prices came down and went down further to the extent that by 2000, petrol in Japan was cheaper than diesel in the EU, and diesel was cheaper than petrol in the US.

Table 4.1 Fuel prices and taxes in real terms at 1995 prices adjusted for purchasing power parity

	Unleaded petrol						Diesel					
	1980 ($US/ litre)	1990 ($US/ litre)	2000 ($US/ litre)	1980 tax (%price)	1990 tax (%price)	2000 tax (% price)	1980 ($US/ litre)	1990 ($US/ litre)	2000 ($US/ litre)	1980 tax (%price)	1990 tax (%price)	2000 tax (% price)
USA	0.61	0.40	0.41	–	27	23	0.46	0.35	0.36	15	28	30
Japan	1.11	0.75	0.65	37	47	55	0.77	0.44	0.39	24	36	55
EU15 average	1.21	0.91	1.01	49	62	63	0.68	0.58	0.70	25	45	48

Source: OECD (2002c: 23). Prices and taxes are for unleaded petrol except that 1980 prices and taxes for European countries are for leaded petrol, and 1990 prices and taxes for Spain and Sweden included in the average for EU15 are for leaded petrol. US data are not available for 1980 unleaded petrol taxes.

Only the EU has clear price signals to encourage the use of less fuel, thereby encouraging the production of more efficient vehicles. While fuel prices in Japan have been on the whole higher than in the US, continuing falls in price have reduced incentives for fuel efficiency although, like the EU, price incentives exist for favoring diesel over petrol in Japan. In the US there have been, and remain, no strong price incentives for fuel efficiency.

Standards

Although market mechanisms may have played an indirect role in changing car industry strategies, regulations in the EU, US and Japan have also been based on standards that target firms directly. These have been introduced at different times and in different ways.

Although the EU has had an environment policy since 1973, greater harmonization of environmental regulations in the 1990s occurred subsequent to the Act of Political Union, and in vehicle emission standards specifically (ADB, no date; Leveque, 1996).[9] With respect to car CO_2 emissions, in 1995 the EU car industry's peak body, the Association des Constructeurs Européens d'Automobiles (ACEA), was invited to make voluntary commitments to reduce new car CO_2 emissions for cars sold in the EU through a Joint Declaration with the European Conference of Ministers of Transport (ECMT). These commitments were submitted to the European Commission in July 1998, and subsequently made a Directive. If achieved, more than 15 per cent of the total CO_2 emission savings being sought under the EU's Kyoto Protocol obligations will be met (ACEA, 2002; ECMT, 2003). The targets set are shown in Table 4.2. Individual car models were to be made available with CO_2 emissions of 120g/km or less by 2000, with the fleet average for all new cars to be 140g/km by 2008 and 120g/km by 2012. An interim 2003 target of 165–170g/km was also set. The target of 140g/km equates to average fuel economy of 5.8l/100km for petrol cars and 5.25l/100km for diesels, representing a

Table 4.2   EU industry commitments on CO_2 emission reductions

Category	Date effective	g/km
Some new cars	2000	120
All new cars	2003	165–170 fleet average
All new cars	2008	140 fleet average
All new cars	2012	120 fleet average

Source: Official Journal of the European Communities (1999).

25 per cent reduction on 1995 levels. These voluntary commitments are described by the ECMT (2001: 2–3) as 'ambitious, both technically and economically'.

The US introduced fuel economy standards in the 1970s via its corporate average fuel economy (CAFE) program. CAFE was launched through the 1975 Energy Policy Conservation Act with standards coming into force in 1978. It applies to all cars manufactured for sale in the US, whether produced domestically or imported, and is a sales weighted average fuel economy of a manufacturer's passenger car fleet in any given model year. Unlike the EU's voluntary industry commitments, CAFE standards have always been state-mandated with stiff penalties for non-compliance.[10] In fact, for most of the 1990s, the US was the only industrialized state with mandatory fuel economy standards (IEA, 1991). Table 4.3 presents the CAFE standards for passenger cars and light trucks since the program commenced. Light truck standards are included because a separate category exists for them, and because light trucks, mostly in the form of pickup trucks and four-wheel drive sports utility vehicles, now account for approximately 50 per cent of the new car market in the US. In recognition of this 50:50 split, a derived average standard combining the individual standards for passenger cars and light trucks is also presented.[11]

Despite consistent strengthening of US standards up to the mid-1980s, there was no change in the CAFE standard for passenger cars after 1990, nor for light trucks after 1996. Before this the standard actually regulated for *worsening* fuel economy in the late 1980s for passenger cars before being strengthened again in 1989. The result is that the 2004 fuel economy standard for passenger cars is actually the same as it was in 1985. For light trucks, there is a similar story with the standard little changed from 1987 levels. It is also at significantly weaker levels than for normal passenger cars. Given the 50:50 sales split between passenger cars and light trucks, the effective standard is really best thought of as the average for the two categories at around 10 l/100km since the mid-1980s. It should be pointed out that at a subnational level the state of California has always had much stricter regulations for non-CO_2 emissions that have foreshadowed national regulations. Given such a track record, in 2002 California passed a law requiring 'maximum feasible reductions' in greenhouse gas emissions from cars and light trucks. However, given that no specific standards are mandated under this law and manufacturers are not required to take any action to reduce emissions until 2009, plus the fact that it was subject to litigation via a court challenge in 2004, this may effectively be ruled out in terms of the comparison over the time period being undertaken here (Austin et al., 2003: 6; OECD, 2004: 110–112).

In Japan, fuel economy targets were introduced in the 1970s under the

Table 4.3   US CAFE standards

Model year	Passenger cars (l/100km)	Combined average for 2WD and 4WD light trucks (l/100km)[a]	Derived average standard – passenger cars plus light trucks (l/100km)[b]
1978	13.07		
1979	12.38	14.28	13.65
1980	11.76	15.75	14.42
1981	10.69	14.88	13.49
1982	9.80	13.44	11.62
1983	9.05	12.38	10.71
1984	8.71	11.76	10.24
1985	8.55	12.06	10.31
1986	9.05	11.76	10.40
1987	9.05	11.47	10.26
1988	9.05	11.47	10.26
1989	8.88	11.47	10.17
1990	8.55	11.76	10.16
1991	8.55	11.64	10.10
1992	8.55	11.64	10.10
1993	8.55	11.53	10.04
1994	8.55	11.47	10.01
1995	8.55	11.42	9.99
1996–2004	8.55	11.36	9.96

Notes:
a. From 1982, manufacturers could comply with separate standards for two-wheel drive and four-wheel drive light trucks, or a combined standard. Since 1992 there has only been the combined standard. Only the combined standard is shown here, and before 1982 it is derived as the average of the two-wheel drive and four-wheel drive standards.
b. This is a simple average of the standards: (2WD light trucks+4WD light trucks + passenger cars)/3 prior to 1992; (light trucks + passenger cars)/2 for 1992 onwards.

Sources: ECMT (2001: 4).

Energy Conservation Act. They were first set in 1979 for 1985 targets under the Law Concerning the Rational Use of Energy, and revised in 1998 by the Ministry of International Trade and Industry and the Ministry of Transport to accommodate Japan's Kyoto Protocol commitments. The 1998 revisions mean that petrol passenger cars must achieve average fuel economy improvements of 22.8 per cent on 1995 levels by 2010, and diesel passenger cars must achieve increases of 14.9 per cent by 2005. Car manufacturers which do not meet these standards are to be penalized, but penalties are less likely to be imposed than in the US because since 1998 targets have been set on the basis of the 'top runner method'. Rather than setting ambitious targets for firms to achieve, this method sets standards based on the most efficient model in a given weight class, and then all manufacturers are given time to match it (OECD, 2002a: 79–80; JAMA, 2003: 24; ECMT, 2001: 37 and p. 81; Stempeck, 2003; Arima, 2000).

Table 4.4 presents Japan's passenger car fuel economy targets for 1985, 2000, 2005 (diesel) and 2010. As can be seen, targets are set for nine weight classes and have been progressively tightened since they were first set for 1985. For the sake of comparison with the EU and US, average fuel economy standards for cars under and over 2015kg have been calculated on the basis that most passenger cars weigh under 2015kg, while light trucks tend to be heavier.[12] An average value for the 2010 target calculated on the basis of the fuel economy of cars in their respective weight classes sold in 1995 is also shown. For petrol cars, the derived 2000 average fuel economy target for cars under 2015kg was 7.9l/100 km for 2000, and 7.19 l/100km for 2010. Cars over 2015kg have significantly weaker standards, in fact much weaker than for US light trucks. The targets for diesel cars are less stringent than for petrol vehicles but must be met five years earlier. Whatever the mix of heavy and lighter vehicles sold, on the basis of 1995 weight class sales this equates to an overall target of 6.62 l/100km for 2010.

In summary, Japan had fuel economy regulations for passenger cars well before the EU, and the US was the first of the three with targets set for 1978. It must be conceded that the EU's Act of Political Union is largely responsible for the timing of its standards, and that significant steps taken by individual member states prior to the 1990s are omitted here. Even so, for Europe as a whole the timing is accurate in the sense that regional regulations have been in place for a shorter period of time than the US or Japan. In addition, there is evidence that the voluntary approach to regulation exhibited in the setting of these standards is a phenomenon that only came to the fore in the 1990s throughout the EU. This is because while it is true that variations between EU member states make it difficult to reach sweeping conclusions about policies and their implications before the 1990s, even for states such as the Netherlands and Germany where two-thirds of voluntary environmental agreements originated prior to 1990, the majority of these were concluded after 1990 (Mol et al., 2000a and b; Liefferink et al., 2000).

The US has clearly had the weakest standards for passenger cars since 1990, and the use of light trucks as passenger cars further reduces its effective fuel economy targets. Japan has significantly tougher standards for passenger cars less than 2015kg than the US, but it is worth noting that

Table 4.4 *Japanese fuel economy standards for passenger cars*

Weight (kg)	1985 petrol target (l/100km)	1985 average petrol target (l/100km)	2000 petrol target (l/100km)	2000 average petrol target (l/100km)	2010 petrol target (l/100km)	2010 average petrol target (l/100km)	2005 diesel target (l/100km)	2005 average diesel target (l/100km)	2010 average target based on 1995 weight class sales (l/100km)
<703	5.56		5.21		4.72				
703-827	5.85		5.49		5.32				
828-1015	6.58		6.13		5.59				
1016-1265	9.01		8.26		6.25		6.17		
1266-1515	9.01		8.26		7.69		7.58		6.62
1516-1765	12.05		10.99		9.52		8.40		
1766-2015	12.05	8.59	10.99	7.9	11.24	7.19	9.26	7.85	
2016-2265	19.23		17.24		12.82		10.20		
>2265	19.23	19.23	17.24	17.24	15.63	14.23	11.49	10.85	

Sources: OECD (2002a: 79), except diesel targets which are from ECMT (2001: 82). The 2010 target based on 1995 weight class sales is from JAMA (2004a: 41).

fuel economy targets for vehicles over 2015kg are far more lax than those in the US for light trucks. The Japanese standard for diesel cars over 2015kg, while not as lax as that for petrol, is also reasonably close to the US equivalent. However, the average 2010 target on the basis of actual weight class sales is perhaps the most accurate reflection of the effective Japanese target and it is clearly tougher than the US standard. While the EU is the latest starter it has easily the most stringent standards of the three.

COMPARING REGULATIONS WITH ACTUAL CO_2 EMISSIONS/FUEL ECONOMY

The question of whether tougher regulations result in lower CO_2 emissions may now be considered. Table 4.5 presents average CO_2 emissions and equivalent fuel economy for vehicles produced by firms by nationality and territory based on 2002 sales. What is clearly demonstrated is that in each territory, US firms sell the least fuel efficient vehicles that produce the most CO_2. EU and Japanese firms always sell more fuel efficient vehicles that produce less CO_2. This correlates with higher fuel prices and tougher standards in the EU and Japan, so what is interesting about this result is that firms appear to be exporting the regulatory requirements of their home territories to others in which their products are sold. Tougher regulations at home also result in better environmental performance not just within the borders where regulations apply but also abroad. As a counter

Table 4.5 Average CO_2 emissions and fuel economy by nationality and territory based on 2002 sales

Manufacturer nationality	Territory where cars are sold					
	US		EU		Japan	
	g/km	l/100 km	g/km	l/100 km	g/km	l/100 km
Average of EU manufacturers	237.67	10.13	177.00	7.55	185.00	7.89
Average of US manufacturers	290.00	12.36	203.67	8.66	195.00	8.31
Average of Japanese manufacturers	233.67	9.96	171.00	7.27	186.33	7.95
Average per territory	253.78	10.82	183.89	7.83	188.78	8.05

Source: Austin *et al.* (2003: 31).

argument to this it must be conceded that Japanese and EU firms' products in the US are less fuel efficient than those they sell at home, so local conditions do have an effect. Even so, their products are still significantly more fuel efficient than the US industry's products. Similarly, while US cars sold in either Japan or the EU are far more fuel efficient than the ones they sell at home, they remain less fuel efficient than EU or Japanese firms' cars.

The end result is very much an 'us' (EU and Japan) versus 'them' (US) market profile. Stronger regulations in the EU and Japan via higher fuel taxes and prices, combined with more stringent standards, correlate with the production and sale of more fuel efficient cars that produce fewer CO_2 emissions, regardless of the territory in which they are sold. It seems like a simple enough correlation. However, a more detailed examination of each territory sheds more light on this finding that raises questions for drawing simple conclusions on material factors alone. Indeed, such an examination casts doubt on whether the material facts of regulations, on their own, significantly change industry behavior at all in some cases.

The Effect of Market Mechanisms

If market mechanisms are to indirectly affect firms' decisions, they must first directly affect consumers' behavior in a way that leads them to demand cars with better fuel economy. Two observable changes should be possible: using less fuel and driving shorter distances. Figure 4.1 shows total distance travelled by passenger vehicles and Figure 4.2 shows total consumption of road fuels. In order to adjust for the number of cars in use average distance travelled per passenger vehicle is shown in Figure 4.3 and average fuel consumption per vehicle is shown in Figure 4.4.[13]

What is striking about Figures 4.1–4.4 is that comparing distance travelled and fuel consumption with movements in taxes and prices (see Table 4.1) reveals *no obvious relationship*. Higher taxes and prices are not necessarily associated with less car usage. The fact that fuel has been taxed in all three territories over the entire period (i.e. this policy is not new) does not seem to matter either.

For distance travelled, unambiguously higher prices and taxes in the EU are associated with increases in total distance travelled over the entire period, rather than decreases as one might expect. The best that can be said is that distance travelled per vehicle plateaued somewhat in the 1990s. For the US, falling prices in the 1980s are associated with increases in total distance travelled and in distance travelled per vehicle. However, after this, continued low prices are associated not with increased car usage as one might expect, but instead with a fall in total distance travelled in the

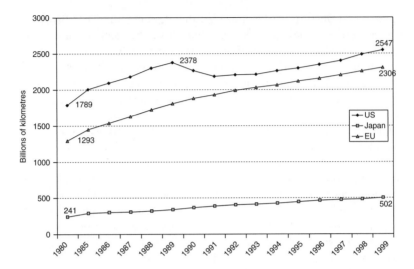

Source: OECD (2002c: 15).

Figure 4.1   Total distance travelled by passenger vehicles

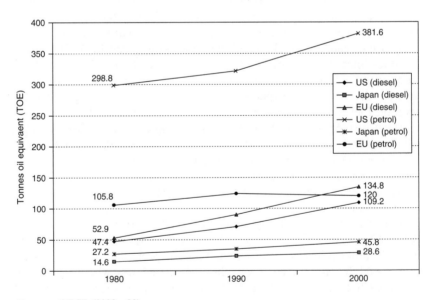

Source: OECD (2002c: 22).

Figure 4.2   Total consumption of road fuels

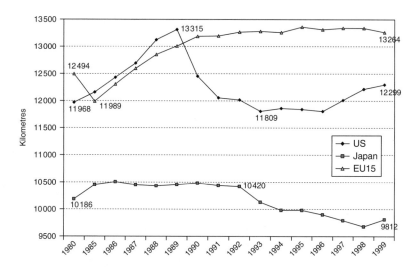

Source: OECD (2002c: 11 and 15).

Figure 4.3   Average distance travelled per passenger vehicle

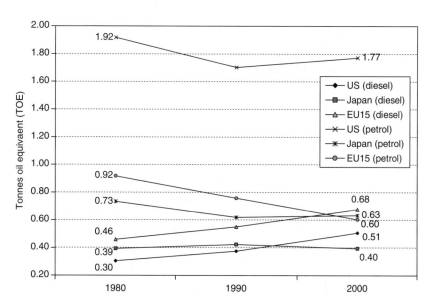

Source: OECD (2002c: 10 and 22). The calculation for 2000 for the EU and US uses 1999
vehicle stock data as OECD tables do not provide data for 2000.

Figure 4.4   Average fuel consumption per vehicle

early 1990s, and in the case of distance travelled per vehicle a sustained fall from a peak of 13 315km in 1989 to a distance of around 12 000km per annum for most of the 1990s. Even more incongruously, falls in fuel prices in Japan are not reflected in any more dramatic increases in total distance travelled per annum than are seen in either the EU or US. In fact, the average distance travelled per passenger vehicle actually fell in the 1990s despite fuel continuing to become cheaper.

For fuel consumption, the EU's tax policies and the price differential between diesel and petrol appear reflected in a clear increase in diesel use. Dramatic increases in total EU diesel consumption are mirrored in increases in diesel use on a per vehicle basis, while the opposite is true for petrol. But whatever the relative shifts in EU diesel and petrol consumption, high and increasing taxes and prices have not led to a fall in fuel consumption overall. This has still increased. For the US, petrol and diesel consumption has indeed increased as one would expect from its low taxes and falling fuel prices, but this cannot explain why petrol consumption per vehicle has fallen by around 8 per cent. Although falling fuel prices in Japan are also associated with increased fuel usage, petrol consumed per vehicle has fallen by even more than in the US, and diesel use per vehicle has remained static despite a similar price differential to the EU.

How can these equivocal and often counter-intuitive observations be explained? The answer is quite simple: fuel taxes and prices alone are not a determining factor in car use. Why should this be so? First, practical reasons associated with implementation mean that the effects of market mechanisms are less predictable because of the large number of individuals owning and driving cars which are the source of emissions. They have different preferences and face different situations that are not easily generalized. Second, while making fuel more expensive may initially make consumers use their cars less then desire more efficient cars, once these cars are made available they can drive further for the same price and the amount of CO_2 produced as a result of these longer trips will counteract the initial effects. Third, the effect of higher prices depends on the price elasticity of demand for fuel. There is evidence that fuel purchase decisions are price inelastic in both the short and long term and that other factors, such as income levels, are more important – e.g. estimates for the UK suggest that prices would have to rise more than incomes to affect fuel purchasing decisions, and that even if one holds income constant a substantial 10 per cent rise in the price of fuel produces only a 3 per cent fall in fuel consumption. Fourth, the availability of alternative travel modes is a factor. In the US, 90 per cent of travel is by motor vehicle, so higher fuel prices only serve to increase costs faced by people on lower incomes who have little choice but to rely on car travel anyway (OECD, 1996: 157; IEA, 1997; Graham and Glaister, 2002, 2004; Harrington and McConnell, 2003: 53).

In short, market mechanisms are unpredictable in the effects to which they give rise. There is simply too much going on besides them to isolate their effect. Only mandating better fuel economy/reduced CO_2 emissions from new cars through standards clearly impacts on the problem and on the industry itself.

The Effect of Standards

Turning to standards, and starting with the EU, Figure 4.5 shows average actual CO_2 emissions of ACEA new cars from 1995 to 2004. What is shown is an unbroken downwards trend in CO_2 emissions with the 2003 target of 165–170g/km reached in 2000, three years ahead of schedule. In fact, already in 2001 2.8 million cars with CO_2 emissions of 140g/km or less were sold, representing 23 per cent of all sales and an increase of 970 per

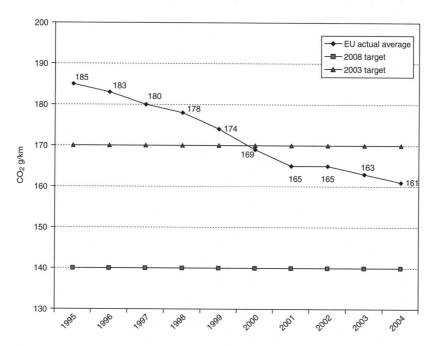

Source: Commission of the European Communities (2006: 9).

Figure 4.5 Average actual emissions of ACEA new cars weighted by registrations

cent on 1995 figures (ECMT, 2003: 7–8)! Whether the 2008 target of 140g/ km is achievable is more problematic. The latest European Commission reports cast doubt on this, yet what they do highlight is that 'the impact of labeling and fiscal measures has been negligible, while the voluntary commitments delivered the bulk of the reductions' (Commission of the European Communities, 2007a: 2). Therefore, it is the voluntaristic aspects of the regulations which have delivered the emission reductions, rather than tough regulatory measures or market intervention. Second, and related to this first point, the reductions have largely been achieved by incremental technologies – i.e. advances made by firms in conventional engine performance, particularly through the development and sale of technologically advanced diesels. The EU now accounts for 90 per cent of global passenger car diesel sales (ECMT, 2003; Austin et al., 2003: 20; Commission of the European Communities, 2006a).

For the US, the increasing popularity of light trucks as passenger cars goes a long way to explaining the worsening fuel economy of all cars since 1990, or at least little change since 1994 after which it is stuck at around 9.5l/100km. But even leaving light trucks aside and focusing on passenger cars, Figure 4.6 shows that there is only limited evidence for the standard improving fuel efficiency. Despite the 2004 CAFE standard being the same as in 1985, and unchanged at 8.55 l/100km from 1990 onwards, US firms did not manage to meet it until 1993. While they did meet it after this, the overall downward trend in fuel consumption was not unbroken, with worsening fuel economy in 1992, 1994, 1997, 1999 and 2001. Furthermore, until 2000 imported vehicles were consistently more fuel efficient. The reason for their variable fuel economy performance thereafter, as we shall see below, lies with the structure of CAFE standards themselves. Overall, it is clear that state-imposed standards in the US have played a far less consistent role in bringing about fuel economy improvements for domestically produced vehicles. Not only are the regulations weaker, but US firms have not met them as well as their European counterparts meet EU standards, nor with an unbroken downward trend in fuel consumption.

For light trucks the situation is worse. Although long-standing weaker standards for light trucks may have encouraged US manufacturers to build SUVs as passenger vehicles, Figure 4.7 shows they have increasingly had trouble meeting the standard. In fact, they were unable to meet it after 1994. Imported light trucks have consistently out-performed them, with improvements in fuel economy after 1995. Despite the fact that light trucks are most popular in the US, it would appear that a culture of making more fuel efficient vehicles in this class exists to a far greater degree elsewhere. Indeed, one might surmise that the only reason why the actual average fuel economy for all light trucks has remained around 11 l/100km

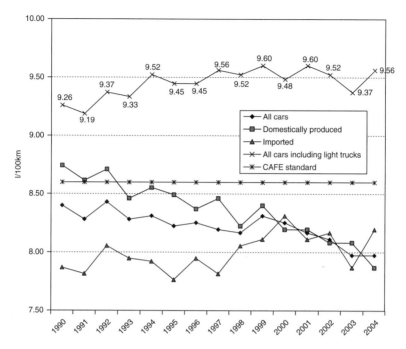

Figure 4.6   *US new passenger car actual average fuel economy as measured under CAFE regulations*

after 1998 is because of improvements in the fuel economy of imported vehicles. This is hard to prove though, because the US National Highway Traffic and Safety Administration (NHTSA, 2005), which is responsible for administering the CAFE standards, decided to cease classifying light trucks as domestically produced versus imported after 1998.

While the observation has been made that the US has preferred to impose what, by comparison to the EU and Japan, are weaker fuel economy standards, and that the US industry has had trouble meeting them, it is also true that there are ways for firms to distort their fuel economy results. One way is by carrying forward the amount they exceed the CAFE standard in one model year into future model years to offset failures to meet the CAFE standard in the latter (NHTSA, no date). In the case of passenger cars this has put US manufacturers at a disadvantage on their home territory due to keen competition from more fuel efficient Japanese brands which have increased their market share. As Crandall (2003) notes:

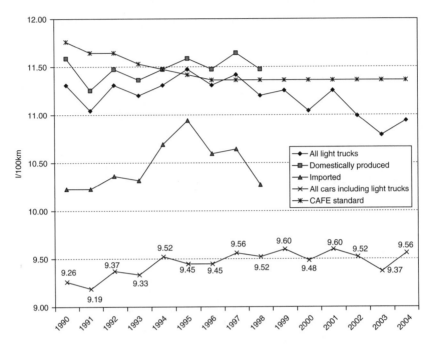

Source: NHTSA (2005: 20).

Figure 4.7   *US new light truck actual average fuel economy as measured under CAFE regulations*

Japanese companies have large carry-forward credits, while GM and Ford have deficits to make up from future surpluses. This situation has encouraged the Japanese companies to compete in the US market for large cars, because US manufacturers have to compromise on their large car designs in order to meet and even exceed CAFE, while the Japanese do not even have to meet the standard for three years because of their accumulated credits.

Similarly, the NHTSA (2003: 22) notes that for passenger cars 'the disparity between the average CAFEs of the import and domestic manufacturers has declined in recent years as domestic manufacturers have maintained relatively stable CAFE values and vehicle offerings, while the import manufacturers have introduced new vehicle offerings that feature larger passenger cars and light trucks to the market'. The decline in imported passenger cars' fuel economy supports these observations. It suggests that Japanese firms in particular recognize that in the US it is feasible to sell small import runs of gas guzzlers with little concern about overshooting CAFE standards due to the greater average efficiency of their passenger car fleets in previous years.

Another way that CAFE fuel economy figures are distorted is through concessions from the sale of alternative fuel vehicles. For example, a dual fuel vehicle that can run on petrol or ethanol has its fuel economy calculated as the average of the fuel economy on each fuel (NHTSA, no date). But the reality is that dual fuel vehicles almost never run on alternative fuels because even if their owners know this is possible, such fuels are very hard to buy and more expensive. In 2002, alternative fuel accounted for less than 0.2 per cent of all transport fuels used in the US (Austin et al., 2003: 14; see also Harrington and McConnell, 2003: 14; Bradhser, 2002).[14]

It does indeed seem likely that CAFE standards have been largely responsible for fuel economy improvements in the US, such as they are,[15] because despite the stability of the standards over the last decade the industry is still having trouble meeting them. One wonders what US firms' fuel economy would be like without them, because even with them the US Environment Protection Agency (EPA) finds that in reality the fuel economy of cars and light trucks in 2002 was at its worst for two decades, at 9.64 l/100km and 13.60 l/100km respectively. The best year for all passenger vehicles was actually 1988 (Hellman and Heavenrich, 2003a: iii-vi). One reason for this is that growing sales of the most fuel inefficient vehicles such as Ford's Excursion and General Motors' Hummer, which weigh over 3855kg, are not counted in CAFE figures because they are so big and heavy that they do not fit the definition of *any* vehicle under CAFE regulations (Harrington and McConnell, 2003: 54).

In stark contrast, Japan presents a dramatic case of easily exceeding standards. Figure 4.8 demonstrates that Japanese firms have not just met targets early, they have always been well ahead of them. The overall derived average targets are so much higher than the actual average fuel economy of new cars sold as to be almost meaningless for comparative purposes here. If one compares actual average fuel economy with the derived under 2015kg average targets, they met the 2000 target three years ahead of schedule and the 2010 target 10 years ahead of schedule. Therefore, the 2010 target had already virtually been reached in 2000, the target date that preceded it. The most 'realistic' comparison is probably that of actual average fuel economy with the 2010 average target based on 1995 weight class sales. In this case, the target was met in 2003, seven years ahead of schedule. The industry appears to continuously improve the fuel economy of its cars even in the absence of increasingly strict government regulation. In a sense, it has barely been regulated by standards because fuel economy has always been better than the standard required. In fact, given that 6.7 l/100km is approximately equivalent to 164 g/km of CO_2 emissions,[16] Figure 4.8 indicates the average fuel economy of Japanese cars matched that of those sold by EU firms in 2001 (see Figure 4.5) and

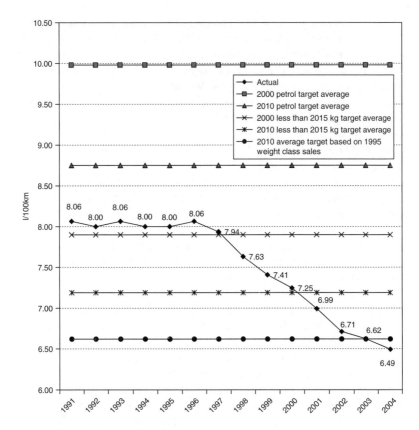

Sources: JAMA (2003: 24); JAMA (2007b: 26).

Figure 4.8 Average actual fuel economy for Japanese petrol cars

exceeded them thereafter. This is despite Japanese targets being weaker and fuel prices lower than in the EU. Fuel economy improvements have also not been met via a shift to diesel cars as in the EU, even though a similar price differential should (theoretically) encourage this, nor through what amounts to the 'creative accounting' permitted by CAFE standards. Nearly 100 per cent of Japanese cars sold are petrol-powered (JAMA, 2004b: 12).

Material Factors?

The evidence suggests that more stringent regulations explain differences in the industry's CO_2 emissions/fuel economy performance to some extent.

EU and Japanese firms, which face stronger market mechanisms in the form of higher fuel taxes and prices plus stronger standards, perform better than US firms. Furthermore, they do so in each of the three territories, suggesting that regulations have ramifications beyond the borders of their home states. Thus, the empirical evidence demonstrates that the regulatory environment of firms' home bases is more important than local market conditions. Even if less fuel efficient cars are sold in the US and more fuel efficient cars are sold in the EU and Japan, the relative efficiencies of EU versus US versus Japanese brands tends to be the same in each. Thus, firms' adherence to their home territories' regulations are to a large extent 'exported' to others in which their products are sold, further supporting the point made in the introduction that car firms are strongly affected by their home countries' environments.

Yet, things are not that straightforward. The evidence on the effect of market mechanisms is inconclusive. These do not appear to be a determining factor in car use. They therefore cannot be said to be a determining factor in changing firm strategies. Furthermore the Japanese industry, facing weaker standards than those of the EU and falling fuel prices, has performed as well if not better than the European industry. In fact, the Japanese industry is up to a decade ahead of the standards it faces, as opposed to the industry in the EU which is approaching targets set by its standards more modestly. Based on the evidence presented, the length of time regulations have been in place seems largely irrelevant, strikingly so in the case of the US for light trucks where its firms are having increasing trouble meeting the longest-standing, and weakest, standards of the three territories. The institutional implications of these observations are discussed further in the following section.

INSTITUTIONAL EXPLANATIONS

The US has primarily employed a command-and-control approach via CAFE standards rather than market mechanisms. The results are less effective by comparison to the EU and Japan. Tougher standards have proved politically intractable and regulators have caved in to industry lobbying and relaxed the standard at times. In general, 'the US Congress has repeatedly rejected bills proposing higher fuel economy standards and has shown no willingness to take action on climate change' (Austin et al., 2003: 6).

This is to be expected somewhat because, as an LME, market forces and competition are the main drivers in the US and so this should favor regulation based on market mechanisms. Yet we have seen that market mechanisms in the form of fuel taxes are generally less successful as a means of reducing car CO_2 emissions due to a range of factors that make them a blunter instrument. This puts the US at a real disadvantage because, being an LME and more favorably disposed to market mechanisms, in this case even if they could be used more, their effect would be less predictable and efficient than standards.

The result is that there has been far less internalization of environmental externalities through regulation in the US than in the EU or Japan. Rather than being involved in a cooperative way in the setting of regulations, the car industry in the US has instead played more of a LME-style lobbying role and, in the face of regulations it has not liked, resorted to bitter challenge through litigation. US government signals have not been consistent either. In addition to not toughening CAFE standards for over a decade, Ford and General Motors successfully lobbied for a relaxation of the standards in the 1980s. The industry does not comply easily with CAFE standards, fails to meet them in many instances and has used the loopholes available to avoid complying with the spirit of them in favor of the letter (see, for example, Crandall, 2003).

A large part of the problem may lie with the original rationale for CAFE standards. Although in place since 1978, their aim was not originally environmental. Instead, their aim was the protection of the US economy against vulnerability to rising fuel prices after the OPEC oil shocks of the 1970s. Unlike EU and Japanese standards, no norm of environmental protection, let alone CO_2 emission reductions, was intended by them. As the US has declined to ratify the Kyoto Protocol, one cannot even say that such standards are now a mechanism for meeting its targets, as is the case for EU and Japanese standards.[17] In the absence of an oil shock over 1990–2004, the US industry simply viewed these standards as an unfair burden. It contended, LME-style, that consumer demand should be the key determinant of fuel economy rather than such regulations (Crandall, 2003; AAM, no date b and c).

Although primarily comprised of CMEs, the EU has relied on market mechanisms via fuel taxes more heavily than either Japan or the US. The EU has used the price difference between diesel and petrol to encourage the use of diesel cars as a way of reducing CO_2 emissions due to their greater efficiency. This is certainly working. Even so, the lack of correlation between high fuel prices and car usage, plus the steady level of taxes in the EU as a proportion of fuel prices in the 1990s, cannot explain why firms committed to 25 per cent reductions in CO_2 emissions on 1995 levels. These were proposed by the industry itself, not imposed by the EC. Instead, in keeping with the CME nature of EU institutions for environmental regulation, a better explanation is that EU states and firms prefer a cooperative approach to car CO_2 emission standards, based on voluntary agreements between industry and regulators. Indeed, this is increasingly the case in other aspects of environmental regulation for which there are now over 300 voluntary agreements (Volpi and Singer, 2000: 3).

Voluntary agreements are not uncontroversial due to the absence of coercion through sanctions for non-compliance.[18] While this concern is valid, it is still the case that the conditions underpinning the EU industry's commitments are very much those one would expect of a CME, namely: a strong industry association that represents a large share of the market, higher levels of trust between government and industry, and a willingness to cooperate on setting regulations (Volpi and Singer, 2000: 10). The industry has coordinated its actions to head off competitive bargaining by presenting a united front to cooperate with public regulatory bodies in a manner that has not occurred in the US. In addition, commitment to the imperative of reducing CO_2 emissions is stronger because only the EU specifically targets CO_2 reductions in g/km, rather than focusing on fuel economy. In other words, while fuel economy and CO_2 emissions are linked and regulations for either largely serve the same purpose, the focus for the EU is *specifically* on climate change.

The Japanese industry is acting well in advance of imposed standards, and these standards to a large degree reflect rather than lead changes in firms' behavior. Fuel taxes provide less of an imperative than in the EU, but in any case falling fuel prices are associated with highly fuel efficient cars. Therefore, it is in the institutional framework for setting standards that answers are to be found. In this regard, the top runner method of setting fuel efficiency/CO_2 emission standards effectively enshrines competition on the basis of fuel efficiency *within* the Japanese industry. This is because the top runner method sets standards based on manufacturers who are producers of the most efficient vehicles. Less efficient firms must catch up with them, so those who are in the lead effectively set the regulatory pace. Rather than imposing an ambitious target on firms, the Japanese approach is based on what is already attainable by the most efficient producers. The industry has therefore internalized fuel efficiency as part of doing business because of the institutional structure of government–business relations, and the reflection of this in the manner in which standards are set.

The observation that the institutional framework of Japanese standard setting means that firms are asked to do no more than meet what is already industry best practice is consistent with the general observation of the CME-nature of Japanese regulation: the government rarely imposes unattainable targets and rarely resorts to coercion. In turn, business rarely resorts to litigation or other forms of direct confrontation to avoid regulations. Instead, the approach taken is one characterized by the state suggesting the strategic direction, to which industry responds as a challenge. The following observation by Arima (2000: 3) is worth noting:

> If a certain manufacturer or importer cannot comply with the target by the target year, the MITI Minister will issue [*sic*] recommendation to it, and if it fails to abide by the recommendation, its name will be made public or [*sic*] administrative order will be issued. This provides a very strong incentive for manufacturers and importers to comply with the Top Runner targets.

In other words, rather than stressing legal or financial penalties for non-compliance, the Japanese system focuses on reputation and relationships. As one would expect of a CME, these are highly important, and damage to them is a major concern of the industry.

THE INSTITUTIONAL BASIS FOR INTERNALIZING ENVIRONMENTAL EXTERNALITIES

If one was to summarize the effect of state–business relations in causal terms, it would look something like Figure 4.9. Three levels are proposed: state-regulation (US), co-regulation (EU) and co-regulation where firms have to some extent taken the lead (Japan). These speak to the relationship

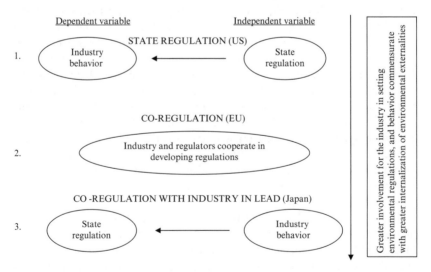

Figure 4.9   Regulation in terms of dependent and independent variables

between the state and business in terms of dependent and independent variables, in the sense of where environmental improvements are likely to be initiated. The implications are that firms in the EU and Japan are more likely to not just comply with regulations, but go beyond compliance to internalize environmental externalities to a greater degree than their counterparts in the US.

The EU and Japan both take an approach based on co-regulation. The industry proposes solutions that are then backed with regulatory standards. In the EU, a strong coalition of car manufacturers represented by the ACEA made commitments that were subsequently adopted as a Directive. Although negotiations on the commitments were tough and have been subject to criticism, the end result is a cooperative agreement on standards described by the ACEA (2002: 11) as reflecting a 'partnership based on mutual trust'. In other words, there is a shared norm between the industry and the EC for reducing CO_2 emissions based on consensus and cooperation. What exists is not so much a case of self-regulation by the industry, but co-regulation between its peak body and the EC: 'a hybrid form between self and public regulation for, like self-regulation, the set of measures to achieve the environmental target is set by the industry whereas, like public regulation, the environmental objectives continue to be set by public authorities' (Leveque, 1996: 48). The result is that firms' collective action is more likely, plus the chance of free riding is reduced because of regulatory involvement by authorities as well as the industry itself. The ACEA and the EC are working together in a relationship that is *structural*, rather than just a matter of good communications or lobbying by industry to government.

Japan tends to articulate targets or put policies 'out there': to signal to industry what is expected on the basis of current best practice with the industry responding before strong targets are set. In the case of CO_2 emissions, this amounts to fuel economy targets with long lead times (Energy Conservation Centre, no date). This regulatory culture, enhanced by the top runner method of setting standards, has entrenched a norm of continuous improvement in fuel economy as part of doing business. In this vein, the point was made earlier that sustained fuel economy improvements commenced the year before the introduction of the top runner method of setting standards in 1998. This suggests that the *foreshadowing* of the introduction of the 2010 target on this basis, as well as its *actual* introduction, impacted on industry strategies. The Japan Automobile Manufacturers Association (JAMA) proclaims the Japanese industry's successes and leadership in producing the cleanest and most efficient vehicles in the world. The organization says that the Japanese car industry sees its challenge as producing the world's cleanest vehicles (JAMA, no date b). On CO_2 emissions specifically, JAMA (no date c) says that 'Japan's automobile manufacturers consider increased fuel economy a top-priority issue and are therefore committed to, and actively engaged in, research and development aimed at the achievement of this goal'. JAMA (2003: 24) proudly reports that regardless of fuel economy targets set by government, 'greater cuts in CO_2 emissions are on the way for the transport sector overall and the automobile industry is responding by voluntarily making a number of bold moves'. Clearly, there is an attitude present that the environmentally-friendly nature of the industry's products is a competitive strength to be emphasized, not a millstone around its neck. As such, Japanese firms seek to meet standards ahead of the target year as a way of improving their corporate image (Arima, 2000).

For the US, there is no discernable norm of increasing fuel economy/ reducing CO_2 emissions. The government neither taxes fuel sufficiently, nor is proactive enough in demanding effective fuel economy improvements. The industry does not recommend improvements in its product's efficiency, but instead the relationship between state and industry is adversarial with the industry continuing to oppose CAFE regulations. The industry's peak body, the Alliance of Automobile Manufacturers (AAM) is not supportive in its position statements on CAFE, and sees market forces as a more natural determinant of what cars should be offered for sale. It asserts that US consumers demand less efficient cars, so the industry cannot be held responsible for worsening fuel economy. Therefore, it declares the following: 'the only way to control carbon dioxide emissions is to reduce fuel combustion, which requires making the vehicle smaller, lighter and less powerful. . . . We make more than 30 different models that get 30 miles per gallon or better. Very few consumers buy them' (Newton-Small, 2003). Rather than seeing fuel economy as its responsibility, the industry believes the US government should provide subsidies to consumers for the purchase of 'advanced technology vehicles' (AAM, no date b and c). What is left in the absence of cooperation is instead a battle between regulators and the industry. If the industry seeks to do anything other than what is required by government, it is a matter of avoiding or weakening what already amount to comparatively weaker regulations. For the US the result is that CO_2 emission reductions are not taken as seriously or proactively in business strategies as in the EU or Japan.

Looking forward, EU and Japanese firms are now in the position of having more environmentally-friendly products and facing lower adjustment costs in meeting any future regulations than US firms. The car industry's behavior is becoming the independent variable that affects the dependent variable of government policy in the EU and Japan, so that the need for strong government leadership on regulations is less necessary than in the US. Regulators in the EU and Japan are now following the industry in legislating for emission reductions rather than the other way around. This suggests greater internalization of environmental externalities by the industry, and therefore a normative change in attitude about how business is to be conducted rather than just a change in behavior in reaction to regulations.

CONCLUSION

It is easy to assume that the strictest and most enduring regulations must explain firm behavior when considering environmental problems. Therefore, one is always tempted to ask who has the toughest standards, the highest prices, the strongest enforcement measures, and the toughest penalties for non-compliance? However, only asking such material questions does not illuminate the degree to which industry complies with regulations, its support for them, and whether it is leading or following such regulations. These are questions that go beyond material interests to qualitative aspects of how well they comply, whether they are likely to continue doing so, and whether they are likely to lead change in future or only respond to what is demanded of them.

The evidence presented demonstrates that although the timing of regulatory standards is less important than their stringency, even the latter is not necessarily a determining factor in firms' behavior (e.g. Japan's weaker regulations produce at least as strong results as the EU's). The argument that market mechanisms in the form of point-of-sale fuel taxes and higher fuel prices change consumer, and ultimately firms' behavior, has also been shown to be false. The different institutional factors underpinning regulation in the EU, US and Japan better explain the car industry's approach to, and thence outcome of, regulations. The more CME institutional framework of the EU and Japan results in a co- to self-regulatory relationship between business and regulators. The result is greater internalization of environmental externalities via CO_2 emission/fuel economy improvements because, causally, firms' commitments are increasingly the independent variable, rather than being dependent on regulatory intervention. By contrast, state regulation remains very much the independent variable for the LME-based US industry. This has produced significantly less acceptance of the need to reduce CO_2 emissions/increase fuel economy.

Even in an age of supposed globalization, different national institutional settings have ramifications beyond the borders of states. While investment and production are increasingly international and trade freer, the importance of the regulatory environment in car firm's home states has been shown to override any notions of the 'stateless' corporation. The institutional features of firms' home territories remain important in their behavior. Car firms then 'export' the results of these institutional features in the products they sell. In all the territories in which they operate Japanese and European firms are more likely to sell cars that are more fuel efficient and produce less CO_2 emissions than US firms. The implications of these results may go beyond environmental concerns alone. It may also be true that US firms are at a disadvantage in a competitive sense if consumer demand is increasingly informed by environmental performance, or if one accepts the view that there is a positive relationship between environmental protection and economic prosperity (as do Desai, 2002a and b; Holliday et al., 2002; Porter and van der Linde, 1995a and b; Porter, 1990: 648). Neither regulations nor the LME institutional framework in which they have been developed in the US have been as decisive in changing industry behavior, nor created an environment in which more efficient vehicles are regarded more favorably.

NOTES

1. In terms of industrial policy, see also Hall (1999) and Leveque (1996).
2. The problem is one of conceptual stretching, as well as different levels of analysis. See Collier and Mahon (1993) and Sartori (1970).
3. She argues that while there have been pressures from 'Europeanization' as well as globalization, there are actually three Varieties of Capitalism present in Europe. She uses the distinctive attributes present in the cases of Germany, France and the United Kingdom to illustrate her point.
4. For example, Scruggs (2003: 222–223) notes that state–business relations are characterized by a corporatist/cooperative approach to managing the environment. Ministries tend to tell firms to communicate with them via their peak bodies, and standards tend to be set that industry has agreed on. In respect of environmental issues specifically, there is a strong role for industry and industry associations in making and then implementing environmental policies. However, French policy making has tended to be more centralized in the hands of small powerful groups of bureaucrats. The distance between the state and industry that results means that while regulations developed may be strict and well-specified, they are often not well-enforced. This is not to say that industry is not consulted, nor that there are not close relationships between the industry ministry and firms, but rather that the policy-making and implementation processes have tended to be somewhat more arm's length.
5. See Chapter 1, especially Table 1.4, which demonstrates that the German car industry has a 46 per cent share of the EU market, of which the European industry has a 63 per cent market share. Not only does this mean that nearly half of all cars registered in the EU are German cars, German brands outsell other European brands by a ratio in excess of 2:1.
6. One of the most entertaining is Toner et al. (1999).
7. Litigation is seen as a feature of US society generally in OECD (1996). See, in particular, Chapter 1.
8. Indeed, according to OECD (2202d: 23) the US has the lowest fuel prices of all OECD members.

9. For example, since June 1991 all emissions standards have been harmonized through the Consolidated Emissions Directive which is binding on all EU member states.
10. Since 1983, car firms have paid more than US$590 million in penalties (NHTSA, no date).
11. Light trucks as passenger vehicles have been growing in dominance since the late 1970s when they only accounted for around 10 per cent of total sales. They accounted for 53.1 per cent of new car sales by 2004 (NHTSA, 2005: 20).
12. The OECD (2004: 51) says SUVs now weigh around 2000kg.
13. In these figures, for distance travelled passenger vehicles are defined as cars seating not more than nine persons (including the driver), including rental cars, taxis, jeeps, estate cars/station wagons and similar light, dual-purpose vehicles. For consumption of road fuels, the data presented are for all autonomous road vehicles with four or more wheels, excluding caravans and trailers, military vehicles, special vehicles (for emergency services, construction machinery, etc.) and agricultural tractors.
14. Alternative fuels include ethanol, methanol, liquid propane gas (LPG), compressed natural gas (CNG) and biofuels.
15. This is indeed the finding of the National Research Council (2002).
16. This is based on a table of fuel economy versus CO_2 emission figures given in ECMT (2003: 6).
17. The industry in the EU and Japan clearly sees regulations as a necessary way of meeting Kyoto Protocol emission targets. See, for example, ACEA (2002); and JAMA (no date a), *A Better Environment for Future Generations*, http://www.jama.or.jp/eco/eco_car/en/en/, accessed 13 January 2004.
18. These are the views of the World Wide Fund for Nature which sees many industries as having captured the environmental agenda and weakened the regulatory function of the EC and EU member states (Volpi and Singer, 2000; see also Leveque, 1996).

5. Society as governance? Social attitudes and consumer demand

> When corporations, households, communities, and farmers take [environmental] measures it is not because governments are breathing down their necks. They are pursuing environmentally sound practices because they are aware of the severity of environmental problems and want to contribute to alleviating such dangers. They are being 'stung', as it were, by an ecological sensibility. This sting is a type of governance. It represents a mechanism of authority that is able to shape human behavior.
>
> (Wapner, 1996: 64–65)

INTRODUCTION

A central finding of Chapter 4 was the relative ineffectiveness, or at least uncertainty, of market mechanisms as a determinant of consumer behavior. While the argument is often made that prices must be altered to reflect the true costs imposed on the environment arising from economic activity, the data presented demonstrated that market mechanisms do not have the effects postulated: they are neither associated with reduced fuel consumption, nor distance travelled, and therefore cannot be said to (indirectly) affect firms' strategies. But what if state intervention is less important than a society-led shift in market forces? If, as Held (2006) has stressed, environmental problems such as climate change are one of the most pressing collective action issues of our time, requiring diffused authority to address them successfully, including a role for non-state actors, what can we expect of society? And how does social environmental concern get transmitted to those who can do something about it, particularly the most important non-state actors that can have an impact on finding solutions: firms, especially multinational corporations. If social concern is transmitted, is its transmission effective, so that we may say society exerts a form of governance over firms beyond the regulatory requirements of the state? These are the questions posed in this chapter.

First, arguments made about the role of society are briefly outlined, and put in the institutional context of the Varieties of Capitalism approach. Second, empirical evidence is presented for whether social attitudes are associated with consumer demand. A comparison is undertaken of social attitudes in Germany, the US and Japan revealed through three waves of the World Values Survey (WVS) from 1990–2001. Respondents' stated concern for the environment, willingness to take direct action in markets and willingness to take non-market action in respect of their environmental concern are considered. The results of analysing responses to questions asked in the WVS are then compared with trends in new passenger car purchases. Finally, the results of the analysis of social attitudes revealed through the WVS, and consumers' market preferences as evidenced by the attributes of cars they purchase, are interpreted through an institutional lens that goes to the motivations of firms explained by the VOC approach.

Two key conclusions are reached. First, social concern for the environment is not a universal force for change. Only in the case of Germany may it be said that strong environmental concern is clearly associated with consumers' purchasing decisions and firms' product offerings. Second, the effect of environmental concern is not necessarily related to its magnitude. Instead, it is contingent on national variations in capitalist relations of production that determine whether or not social concern is effectively transmitted to firms. While greater concern for the environment intuitively suggests a stronger impetus for change in the US than Japan, if national institutional variations in capitalist relations of production are factored in, the reverse is the case. A materialist analysis is most pertinent for the US, and this means that unless there is a clear market case for responding to environmental concern, the outcome is likely to be weaker than is the case for Japanese firms which take a more stakeholder-focused approach.

Therefore, a more nuanced framework is suggested for analysing the impact of social environmental concern. There is a need to move beyond simple comparisons of the magnitude of such concern between states, and generalizations about its impact. There is also a need to move beyond a generalized materialist versus post-materialist analysis. An institutional analysis, based on the VOC approach, is shown to be more appropriate because it helps to explain how firms of different nationalities perceive their interests in respect of environmental issues. While there may be ongoing analysis of the nature and strength of social attitudes, their likelihood of effecting real environmental change is also a matter of nationally conducive paths for transmitting these to firms. Rather than presuming a universal/global impact from increased environmental concern, variations in the impact of social attitudes should be the focus. The key point is this: national institutional variations in capitalist relations of production have implications for whether, and how, firms address the environmental impact of their operations as a result of social concern.

SOCIAL ATTITUDES AND THE VARIETIES OF CAPITALISM APPROACH

The optimists tell us that we are in the midst of a 'shift in the "balance of legitimacy" in environmental issues' led by civil society since the late 1980s/early 1990s. This shift means that 'environmental concern now enjoys a broad base of support' that represents a change in 'values, attitudes and practices' (Wapner, 1996: 62). Commentators on corporations and environmental sustainability such as Korten (1999), Hawken et al. (1999), and Karliner (1997) say this concern is producing an emerging shift towards more environmentally sustainable practices in global capitalism. They say capitalist relations of production are shifting from a concern for maximizing profits, to more holistic concerns for maximizing sustainability in the use of the world's resources.[1] Industry groups such as the World Business Council for Sustainable Development perceive increased environmental concern as demanding more environmentally responsible behavior, as well as offering commercial opportunities for long-term economic sustainability (see, for example, Holliday et al., 2002). This is part of the reason why others such as Florini (2003a and b) say private authority is increasingly taking responsibility for the environmental effects of profit-motivated action (see also Prakash, 2000). Indeed, authors such as Porter and van der Linde (1995a and b) have long identified environmentally responsible behavior as a strategy for efficient and profitable business.[2]

Such viewpoints reflect a belief that there is a growing shift towards post-materialism in industrialized societies. Post-materialism is the term coined to describe an increased awareness for issues of collective social concern, rather than individual concern for material wellbeing. Authors such as Inglehart (1997) and Desai (2002a) say this means politics in industrialized states is increasingly defined not by the traditional political divide between left versus right, but by a divide between materialist concern for the economy, standards of living and wealth creation, versus concern for post-material values such as gender relations, racial harmony, human rights and the environment. The shift in social attitudes is said to have played a central role in 'mainstreaming' environmental concern to the extent that deep institutional changes are being produced. Wapner (1996: 64–65 with emphasis added) characterizes it thus:

> When corporations, households, communities, and farmers take these [environmental] measures it is not because governments are breathing down their necks. They are pursuing environmentally sound practices because they are aware of the severity of environmental problems and want to contribute to alleviating such dangers. They are being 'stung', as it were, by an ecological sensibility.

This sting is a type of governance. It represents a mechanism of authority that is able to shape human behavior.

In a nutshell, as O'Riordan and Jordan (1996: 67) note in respect of the question of climate change specifically, social attitudes need 'neither structure nor regulation, but they are most certainly institutional arrangements' that affect behavior.[3] Thus, commentators on the role of civil society such as Wapner (1996: 62) perceive a 'shift in the "balance of legitimacy" in environmental issues' that started in the late 1980s and early 1990s which means that 'environmental concern now enjoys a broad base of support' that represents a change in 'values, attitudes and practices'.

What is to be made of the impact of social concern for the environment? There are a variety of approaches to answering this question, although two clear dominant strands of thought are evident (see Harrison, 2000). On the one hand, those who adopt an 'efficiency narrative' focus on the role of market signals and material returns (the liberal economic approach). On the other hand, those who adopt an 'ethics narrative' take a holistic and potentially more radical approach, imagining a world in which the rules governing humans, non-humans and the natural environment are transformed. The optimists tend to lean towards this explanation. Between these extremes are a variety of approaches in the field of environmental politics, including those that focus on the role of civil society. However, the argument in this book rests on the view (expressed at the outset in Chapter 1) that firms are the central actors responsible for environmental damage: environmental damage occurs in the production process and the act of consuming the outputs of it. If society is to exert governance in respect of the environment – by implication in addition to, or beyond, government – then social attitudes must exert a force for change on firms. Society's ecological sensibility must 'sting' firms into action. Therefore, capitalist relations of production, and whether/how these enable the transmission of society's concerns to firms, must be the focus.

In this light, the VOC approach suggests a skeptical attitude to the view that increased environmental concern can be a universal form of governance. Because firms are not placeless entities, but are 'produced through an intricate process of embedding in which the cognitive, cultural, social, political and economic characteristics of the national home base play a dominant part' (Dicken, 1998: 196), the VOC approach observes that different capitalist states have different institutional structures that inform their capitalist relations of production. Therefore, the focus must be on national variations in capitalist relations of production for how they potentially impact on the *transmission* of social attitudes to firms.

US firms, based in the archetypal LME, are most focused on the material drivers of market forces and regulatory requirements. Unless they face material pressures via market forces or government regulations, they are less likely to respond to environmental concern. However, other modes of coordinating economic activity are at least as important for CME-based German and Japanese firms. They have a stronger predisposition for a partnership approach with the state on regulations, and take more of a stakeholder, rather than shareholder, approach to business. Being more aware of their social standing/place in society, they are more willing to factor social attitudes into strategic considerations aimed at meeting their material goals. With these factors in mind, we turn to an analysis of social attitudes on the environment in Germany, the US and Japan.

SOCIAL ATTITUDES ON THE ENVIRONMENT

For a comparative analysis of social attitudes in Germany, the US and Japan, responses by those surveyed through the WVS are considered. The WVS has been conducted since 1981, and is coordinated by the Institute for Social Research of the University of Michigan. It now encompasses surveys of national samples of the populations of 80 countries carried out by an international network of social scientists. At least 1000 people are surveyed in each country in each wave of the survey, with the intention of understanding the basic values and beliefs of people in each society and how these are changing over time (World Values Survey, no date).

Questions asked in three waves of the WVS from 1990 to 2001 relating to environmental concern were aggregated and put in three categories to facilitate analysis:[4]

1. Concern for the environment: The priority respondents accord environmental versus economic imperatives, and whether they believe we should master or coexist with nature.
2. Willingness to take direct action in markets: Actions that potentially have a direct material impact on firms. These relate to respondents' willingness to act in markets by choosing, or paying more for, products that are better for the environment.
3. Willingness to take non-market action: Actions with less material impact on firms, but which nevertheless may encourage a change in their behavior. These include civil action through environmental movements; non-market financial sacrifices; and non-market other action that is environmentally-friendly. The market implications of such action are less obvious than those in the previous category, yet indicate respondents' willingness to change the 'rules of the game'

(Whitley, 1999: 5) and may lead to changes in firms' behavior if responding to such action is perceived as a more appropriate way to conduct business.[5]

It should be noted that, as with many global surveys, different questions were asked in different waves, and not all countries were included in the WVS in each wave. Therefore, data gaps exist and inconsistencies arise. The details of these are explained in Appendix A, along with adjustments to take account that were made where feasible.

Concern for the Environment

Two questions asked in Waves 3 and 4 of the WVS target respondents' concern for the environment. They are:

1. Whether priority should be given to protecting the environment or economic growth and creating jobs.
2. Whether human beings should master or coexist with nature.

Table 5.1 presents a summary of the responses to these questions. Responses indicate that concern for the environment is substantial in all territories. The majority of US and Japanese respondents gave priority to protecting the environment over economic growth and creating jobs (60 and 57 per cent respectively). A sizeable minority of German respondents (45 per cent) gave priority to protecting the environment. In addition, an overwhelming preference was expressed in all three territories for coexisting with nature rather than mastering it, particularly for Japan and Germany where almost all respondents said they believed in coexisting with nature (96 and 98 per cent respectively). Although fewer respondents in the US believed in coexisting with nature, the preference for so doing was still very high at 86 per cent of respondents.

Table 5.1   Summary of concern for the environment

Respondents' nationality	Priority to protecting the environment (%)	Humans should coexist with nature (%)
Germany	45	96
US	60	86
Japan	57	98

Source: World Values Survey.

The responses show that the two questions were viewed, and answered, quite differently. It appears that respondents would like *both* environmental protection and economic growth. When forced to choose, their responses flow close to half each way, meaning that the environment and economic growth are viewed as being of at least equal importance. Responses to mastering or coexisting with nature reflect more complex perceptions of humanity's relationship with the environment. This question may pick up cultural traits favoring harmony and balance (for example, Japanese notions of '*wa*'/harmony, and German preferences for negotiated consensus) versus individualistic achievement (e.g. US and other Anglo-Saxon cultures' belief in the virtues of competition). There is an extensive literature that discusses such cultural traits and it is reflected in the VOC approach (see, for example, Wilks, 1990; Hampden-Turner and Trompenaars, 1993). Overall, concern for the environment in all three territories is high: highest in the US and Japan on the question of the environment versus the economy, and highest in Germany and Japan on the question of coexisting with nature rather than mastering it.

Willingness to Take Direct Action in Markets

Willingness to act on concern for the environment in a way that directly impacts on firms' material returns is indicated by responses to two questions asked in Wave 3. Respondents were asked:

1.   Whether they would strongly agree, agree, disagree or strongly disagree to buying things at 20 per cent higher than usual prices if it would help protect the environment.
2.   Whether in the previous 12 months they had chosen household products that are better for the environment.

Table 5.2 presents a summary of the responses to these questions. On willingness to pay higher prices, there is a clear divide between US and Japanese respondents versus German respondents. Only around 35 per cent of US and Japanese respondents agreed with paying higher prices, whereas German respondents were approximately twice as likely in their support for this (60 per cent). Although not presented in Table 5.2, the WVS data also shows that German respondents who agreed with paying higher prices were twice as likely to *strongly* agree with so doing by comparison to US and Japanese respondents.[6] German and US respondents were most likely to choose household products that are better for the environment (88 and 73 per cent respectively), but even though Japanese

Table 5.2   Summary of willingness to take direct action in markets

Respondents' nationality	Agree to buying things at 20% higher than usual prices (%)	Have chosen household products that are better for the environment (%)
Germany	60	88
US	36	73
Japan	34	60

Source: World Values Survey.

respondents were less likely to have done so a clear majority of them had as well (60 per cent).

Willingness to take direction action in markets is therefore strongest in Germany, by paying both higher prices and choosing household products if this helps the environment. US respondents were willing to exercise a preference for more environmentally-friendly household products, but were less willing to pay higher prices. Japanese respondents were least willing to pay higher prices or choose household products that are better for the environment. Therefore, direct market signals as a result of social attitudes are likely to be strongest in Germany, followed by the US and then Japan.

Willingness to Take Non-market Action

Respondents were asked questions on non-market action that they would be prepared to take/have taken that reflects their concern for the environment. The questions are put in three sub-categories here: civil action through environmental movements; non-market financial sacrifices; and non-market other action. The results are summarized in Table 5.3.

On civil action respondents were asked:

1. How much confidence they have in the green/ecology/environmental movement (asked in Waves 3 and 4).
2. Whether they are members of an environmental organization (asked in all waves).
3. Whether they are active members of the organization (in Waves 2 and 3) or did unpaid work for it (in Wave 4).
4. Whether in the last 12 months they had contributed to an environmental organization (asked in Wave 3).
5. Whether in the last 12 months they had attended a meeting or signed

Table 5.3 Summary of willingness to take non-market action

Respondents' nationality	Civil action					Non-market financial sacrifices			Non-market other action	
	Great deal of confidence or quite confident in the green/ecology/environmental protection movement	Membership of environmental organization	Have contributed to an environmental organization	Active member/unpaid work for an environmental organization	Have attended a meeting or signed a letter or petition	Agree to an increase in taxes	Agree to giving part of income	Agree that the government should reduce environmental pollution but it should not cost me any money	Have decided to reuse or recycle	Have tried to reduce water consumption
	(%)	(%)	(%)	(%)	(%)	(%)	(%)	(%)	(%)	(%)
Germany	68	5	15	2	30	50	30	70	85	71
US	57	16	26	7	18	60	69	57	86	56
Japan	60	3	8	1	13	60	70	56	69	47

Source: World Values Survey.

a letter or petition aimed at protecting the environment (asked in Wave 3).

Around 60–70 per cent of all respondents expressed confidence in the green/ecology/environmental movement. However, far more US respondents were actually members of environmental organizations (16 per cent) compared with Germany and Japan (5 and 3 per cent respectively). Indeed, actual membership of environmental organizations in Germany and Japan is so low as to seem virtually irrelevant. It is also worth noting, though not presented in Table 5.3, that of those who had confidence in the environmental movement, a higher proportion of US respondents had a *great deal* of confidence compared to Germany or Japan.[7] US respondents were also most likely to contribute to environmental organizations (26 per cent versus 15 per cent for German and 8 per cent for Japanese respondents) and be active members/do unpaid work for them (7 per cent versus just 1 and 2 per cent for German and Japanese respondents). However, German respondents were around twice as likely to attend a meeting or sign a letter or petition aimed at protecting the environment, compared to US or Japanese respondents (30 per cent versus 18 and 13 per cent for US and Japanese respondents respectively). This suggests that Germans are potentially as willing to take civil action as their US counterparts, just in a less formal manner. They are very supportive of the environmental movement, and will take action in respect of its goals, but they are simply less likely to *belong* to environmental organizations. Overall, the conclusion is that civil action on environmental concern is most likely in the US and Germany, and much less likely in Japan. In Germany there may be less willingness to do so via environmental organizations than in the US, but nevertheless civil action may occur on a less formalized basis via attending meetings and signing petitions.

On non-market financial sacrifices respondents were asked:

1. Whether they would strongly agree, agree, disagree or strongly disagree to an increase in taxes if the extra money were used to prevent environmental damage (asked in all waves).
2. Whether they would strongly agree, agree, disagree or strongly disagree to giving part of their income if they were certain the money would be used to prevent environmental pollution (asked in Wave 4).
3. Whether they would strongly agree, agree, disagree or strongly disagree that the government should reduce environmental pollution but it should not cost them any money (asked in Wave 4).

Responses to these questions demonstrate a clear divide between US and Japanese versus German respondents. Around 60 per cent of US and

Japanese respondents supported an increase in taxes, and commensurate with this around 70 per cent were in favor of giving part of their income to prevent environmental pollution. German respondents were clearly less supportive of tax increases (50 per cent) and giving part of their income (30 per cent). On the government reducing environmental pollution at no cost, the divide is reversed. Seventy per cent of German respondents believed this should be the case, whereas only 56–57 per cent of Japanese and US respondents thought the government should take action at no cost to them. Once again, more detailed data on the strength of feeling on this not presented in Table 5.3 is informative: of German respondents who agreed that the government should act at no cost to them, a much larger proportion *strongly* agreed this should be the case than their US and Japanese counterparts.[8] Therefore, responses to these questions show that US and Japanese respondents are clearly more willing to make non-market financial sacrifices than Germans.

On non-market other action respondents were asked in Wave 3:

1. Whether in the last 12 months they had decided for environmental reasons to reuse or recycle something rather than throw it away.
2. Whether in the last 12 months they had tried to reduce water consumption for environmental reasons.

Answers to these questions demonstrate that German respondents were, on balance, most willing to reuse or recycle and reduce water consumption. Although US and German respondents were equally willing to reuse or recycle (85–86 per cent), Germans were much more likely to have saved water (71 versus 56 per cent). Japanese respondents were less likely to either reuse or recycle (69 per cent), or save water (47 per cent). Therefore, German respondents are most willing to take non-market other action, followed by US and then Japanese respondents.

Comparing Social Attitudes in Germany, the US and Japan

The only point of clear commonality between Germany, the US and Japan is strong concern for the environment. Willingness to take environmental action is mostly stronger in Germany and the US, than Japan. This is particularly so for Germany with respect to direct market action. For the US and Japan, there is greater willingness to make non-market financial sacrifices, but overall Japanese respondents' willingness to act in environmentally-friendly ways is the weakest of the three. As such, while concern expressed for the environment suggests it is at least as important as the economy, and nature is not a force to be mastered but coexisted with, this does not imply that social attitudes are a form of governance in each state to the same degree. However, before being able to answer whether or not these differences in social attitudes are associated with differences in consumer behavior, actual trends in consumer demand for new cars must be considered. This is done in the following section.

CONSUMER DEMAND

A new car is often the second most expensive durable good purchased by households, after a house itself, while in Chapter 1, the observation was made that driving a car is the single most environmentally damaging thing most of us do. Putting these two observations together, the aim here is to determine whether trends in the attributes of this most important of household purchases, in both material and environmental terms, 'squares' with social concern for the environment. Analysing the environmental attributes of new cars purchased serves as a crucial case for determining whether it can be said that consumers' revealed preferences are consistent with social attitudes, and therefore whether environmental concern is likely to provide impetus for firms to provide more environmentally-friendly products.

The fuel economy of new cars purchased in each territory is considered first, followed by an analysis of attributes of new cars purchased that impact on this: the proportion of light trucks in total sales; engine size; car class; the proportion of diesel powered vehicles in total sales; and the take-up of alternative powered vehicles. The reason for the choice of these attributes is as follows:

1. Light trucks are bigger, heavier, less fuel efficient and more environmentally damaging than 'normal' passenger cars. If consumers display a preference for such vehicles, environmental concerns are unambiguously of less concern to them.
2. A preference for vehicles with larger engines over time cannot possibly indicate a willingness to act on environmental concern. Even if all engines are becoming more efficient over time, it is still the case that bigger engines must use more fuel and are indicative of a desire for more power, acceleration and performance over lower fuel usage, lower CO_2 emissions and less impact on the environment.
3. Definitions of car class vary between the three territories so directly comparable data are not available. Nevertheless, regardless of definitional differences, smaller cars should have less environmental impact than bigger cars, so a preference for them indicates greater concern

for environmental impacts. Car class definitions in each territory are explained in Appendix B.

4. Diesel powered vehicles must always produce fewer CO_2 emissions and be more fuel efficient due to the higher density of diesel as opposed to petrol. As noted in Chapter 3, diesel provides 20 to 40 per cent better fuel economy and produces 10 to 30 per cent fewer CO_2 emissions. Consumers who know this and show a preference for diesel are therefore also showing a preference for reducing environmental damage, at least in terms of fuel efficiency and CO_2 emissions (Bradsher, 2002: 246 and 451; Harrington and McConnell, 2003: 52; OECD, 2002b: 17; Austin et al., 2003: 20).[9]

5. The take up of alternatively powered vehicles that have lower environmental impacts should indicate whether consumers are keen early-adopters of new environmentally-friendly technologies.

It should be noted that two other attributes were considered but rejected for analysis: vehicle weight and power. Although it is true that heavier, more powerful cars produce more detrimental environmental effects, both these indicators were rejected due to a lack of specificity in what they might indicate. This is because an increase in the average weight of vehicles purchased does not indicate anything, on its own, about consumer environmental preferences. Instead, it may reflect a 'trend towards installing more equipment for safety, comfort and utility' (OECD, 2004: 15). It does not indicate whether increased weight is due, say, to the purchase of larger cars and sports utility vehicles, or a rise in the proportion of mid-sized cars that might be greater than the fall in large cars. Similarly, incremental advances in engine technologies mean that regardless of the size of an engine, all engines have become more powerful. Therefore, smaller engines are now able to power heavier vehicles, and vehicles in smaller classes are now more powerful than they were without having larger engines. In fact, it is possible that a more powerful engine of the same size in a small car gets better fuel economy because it does not have to work as hard to deliver the same performance. Increases in engine power on their own cannot indicate preferences for performance over the environment, so much as advances which have simply made all engines more powerful.

Fuel Economy

Figure 5.1 presents the average fuel economy of new cars sold in each territory. Clearly, much less fuel efficient cars are sold in the US than in Germany and Japan. More important than this though, are changes over time. German and Japanese cars exhibit dramatic fuel economy improvements

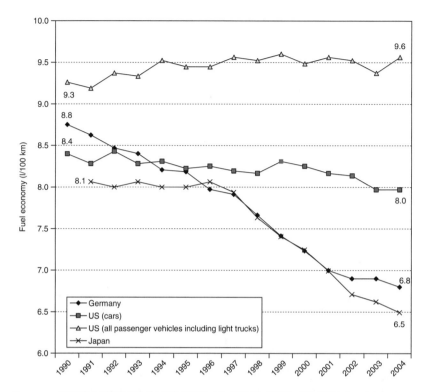

Sources: NHTSA (2005: 20); JAMA (2003: 24); JAMA (2007b: 26); VDA (no date). German data for 2001-2004 is estimated from VDA (2005).

Figure 5.1   Average fuel economy of new cars

(from around 8 to under 7 l/100km), whereas the fuel economy of US cars is virtually unchanged (around 8 l/100km). If light trucks are included in US figures, the fuel economy of all passenger vehicles in the US actually worsened from 9.3 to 9.6 l/100km. Therefore, if these data are an indication of consumer demand, market signals for firms to produce and sell more fuel efficient cars only exist in Germany and Japan.

Light Trucks

Light trucks purchased as passenger cars, such as SUVs and four wheel drives (4WDs) are bigger, heavier, less fuel efficient and more environmentally damaging than normal passenger cars. Figure 5.2 presents the share of light trucks in total passenger car registrations, and shows that only in

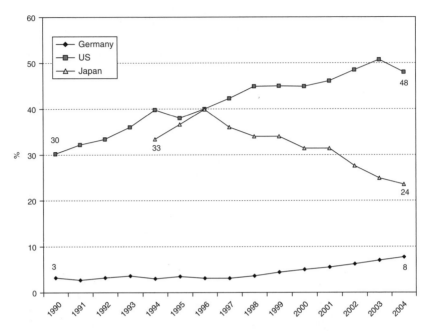

Sources: ACEA (no date d); Hellman and Heavenrich (2004a: 7-9 and 14-16); JAMA (2004a: 9); JAMA (2007b: 8-9). Data presented for Japan and Germany is for 4WDs. For Japan, there is a 'recreational vehicles' class, but this is not used as it includes station wagons, van-type SUVs, off-road 4WDs and minivans (i.e. not all of these are light trucks). Data for the US is for light trucks, which include SUVs, pickup trucks and minivans used as passenger vehicles.

*Figure 5.2   Percentage share of light trucks in total passenger car
            registrations*

the US did the percentage of light trucks in total passenger car registrations increase markedly with little sign of abating, to the point where half new passenger vehicle sales in the US were light trucks by 2002–04. Purchasing light trucks as passenger vehicles occurs in Germany and Japan as well. However, although the growth in the share of light trucks in passenger car registrations has been greatest in Germany, especially after 1997, the change exaggerates the significance. This is because for Germany the share remains very small. In Germany, where their popularity has increased more than in most EU markets, they increased their market share from just 3 to 8 per cent. For Japan, the share of light trucks peaked in 1996 at nearly 40 per cent, but declined to 24 per cent by 2004. Thus, only in the US did growth in the sale of light trucks occur to such an extent that they now account for around half new passenger vehicle sales.

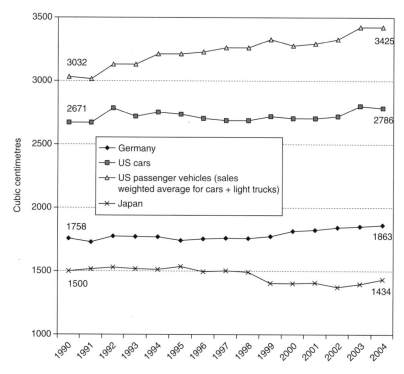

Sources: ACEA (no date b); Hellman and Heavenrich (2004a: 14-16); JAMA (2007a: 12).

Figure 5.3   Average engine size of new cars

Engine Size

Engine size is a key measure of environmental concern. Smaller engines tend to use less fuel, and technological advances mean that an engine the same size can now deliver more power in a car that is the same size, or be placed in a car that is larger/heavier with similar performance compared to that delivered by a larger engine previously. Figure 5.3 shows average engine size of new cars purchased. US consumers have always bought cars with bigger engines. For cars alone (i.e. excluding light trucks), in 2004 US car engines were around 50 per cent larger than German cars and twice the size of Japanese cars. More important, the trend is for increases in engine size in the US, for all passenger vehicles by 13 per cent and for cars alone by 4 per cent. German car engines have also increased in size by 6 per cent. Only in Japan's case have engines become smaller, by 4 per cent.

Car Class

Data on car class are available for each market, but class definitions vary between them. For comparative purposes, this means that new car purchases by class cannot be presented on a single graph.[10] Even so, what is of interest for comparative purposes is whether, over time, consumers are buying smaller, lighter, more compact cars, indicating that they are making more environmentally conscious purchasing decisions. Given the magnitude of the market share of light trucks as passenger vehicles in the US and Japan, their classes are also considered here.

Figure 5.4 presents German passenger car sales by class. It shows that the share of small cars has increased, while the share of lower-medium cars has decreased and the share of medium cars has remained steady. The share of other classes is relatively constant, with the exception of vans which increased their market share from 6 to 10 per cent, and are largely responsible for the rise in share of the 'others' class. The increase in the share of SUVs/4WDs is, as noted already, relatively marginal.[11]

Figure 5.5 presents US passenger car sales by class. It shows that for passenger cars, the small car class has suffered sustained falls in market

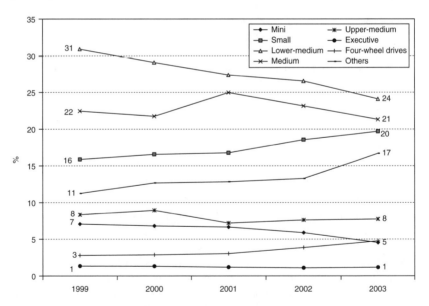

Source: VDA, provided on request 6 January 2005. 'Others' includes cabriolets, vans, utilities and other vehicles. Aggregated data by class is unavailable prior to 1999.

Figure 5.4   German passenger car sales by class

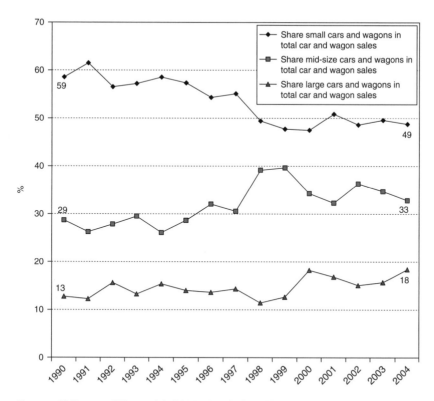

Source: Hellman and Heavenrich (2004a: 9 and 16); Hellman and Heavenrich (2004b).

Figure 5.5 US passenger car sales by class

share from around 60 to under 50 per cent, while gains have been made in the mid-size and large classes. The largest gains have been made in the large car class, the share of which has grown from 13 to 18 per cent. Figure 5.6 presents a breakdown of US light trucks sales by class, and demonstrates similar trends to those for cars. In addition to the observation that light trucks now make up just over 50 per cent of all new passenger vehicle sales, there has been a substantial rise in the share of large light trucks in total US light truck sales, from 30 to 49 per cent. In fact, by 2004 almost as many large light trucks were sold as small and medium light trucks combined. Not only has there been a shift to the purchase of light trucks, but US consumers are increasingly buying both bigger light trucks and bigger cars.

Figure 5.7 presents Japanese passenger car sales by class. It shows that the small car class has been squeezed with more sales flowing to larger

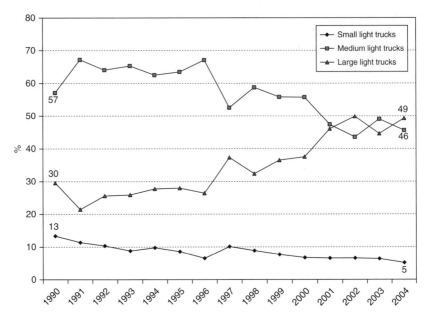

Source: Hellman and Heavenrich (2004b).

Figure 5.6   US light truck sales by class

standard and smaller mini cars. A greater polarization of the market is the result, with sales of both larger standard cars and mini cars doubling over the period. Nevertheless, it is also true to say that over the entire period around 80 per cent of car sales in Japan have been either small or mini cars, with a shift to mini cars within these two categories. Figure 5.8, which presents a breakdown of Japanese 4WD sales by class, shows that larger 4WDs have declined as a proportion of total 4WD sales from a peak of 69 per cent in 1996 to 55 per cent by 2004, while the share of mini 4WDs increased from 33 to 45 per cent. Thus, in addition to 4WDs declining as a market segment in Japan, consumers are buying smaller and therefore less environmentally 4WDs.

A lot of data have been presented in this section. The trends may be summarized as follows. For Germany, cars are getting smaller with the share of sales in the small class growing at the expense of the larger lower-medium and medium classes. While 4WDs have increased their share of sales, they remain niche vehicles. For Japan, the overall trend is also for smaller cars. Mini cars have increased their share of sales. So have larger standard cars. However, overall the market remains dominated by mini

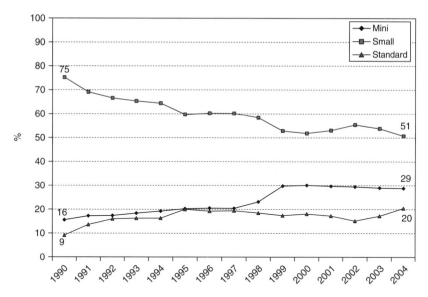

Source: JAMA (2004b: 12).

Figure 5.7 Japanese passenger car sales by class

and small cars. 4WDs, while popular in Japan, exhibit sales trends very different from their US equivalents, with sales increasingly in the mini 4WD class. The US is moving in the opposite direction to Germany and Japan with cars and light trucks both getting bigger. Mid-size and large cars have increased their share of sales at the expense of small cars, and burgeoning sales of light trucks as passenger cars have been led by sales of large vehicles.

Diesels

Diesel cars are insignificant anywhere but the EU. In the US and Japan, diesel cars account for *less than 1 per cent* of all new car registrations (Hellman and Heavenrich, 2004a: 14–16; JAMA, 2002: 12). A large part of the explanation is that the industry in Germany, and the EU more broadly, has promoted small diesel cars as a clean and technologically advanced solution to the environmental effects of car use. Thus, perceptions of diesel are different there. This is supported by the literature of the European and German peak industry bodies, as well as firms' environmental reports (e.g. ACEA, 2004a; VDA, 2004).[12]

Figure 5.9 presents diesel sales as a percentage of total car sales in the

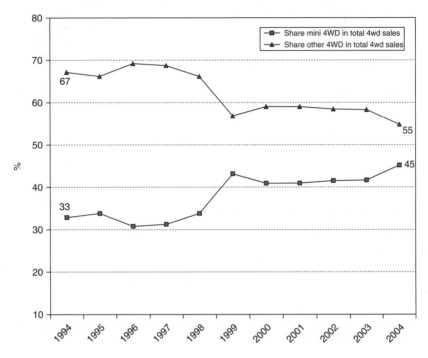

Source: JAMA (2004a: 9); JAMA (2007b: 9).

Figure 5.8 Japanese 4WD sales by class

EU and Germany. It shows that diesel's share of EU car sales increased from 14 to 49 per cent, and similarly for German car sales from 10 to 44 per cent. These trends put the 5 per cent increase in engine size for German cars shown in Figure 5.3 in perspective: consumers have purchased smaller vehicles with marginally larger diesel engines and reduced their cars' environmental impacts.

Alternatively Powered Vehicles

It seems that almost everywhere one looks there are stories about alternatively powered vehicles, especially petrol-electric hybrid vehicles and the long-term potential for fuel cell technologies which will allow cars to run on hydrogen.[13] Japanese firms are the world leaders in the commercial production of such cars, particularly Toyota and Honda which commercially released petrol-electric hybrids in the late 1990s. Demand for the second generation petrol-electric hybrid Toyota Prius is growing so much that

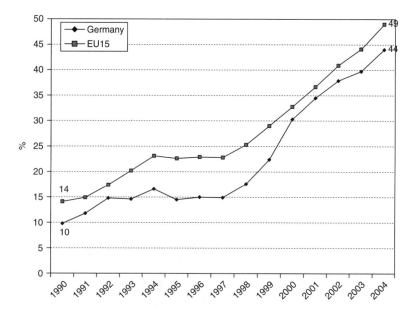

Source: ACEA (no date c; 2004b).

Figure 5.9 Diesel sales as a percentage of total car sales in the EU and Germany

Toyota had to increase production to 130 000 cars for 2004 in order to meet international demand, with an eight-month waiting list for the model in the US (McDonald, 2004; *The Economist*, 2004).

Table 5.4 presents sales data on alternatively powered vehicles from 1995 to 2004. Although at first glance sales of such vehicles appear significant, the share of alternatively powered vehicles in total passenger vehicles provides a more realistic perspective. The OECD (2002c: 11) estimates the total stock of passenger cars at around 174 million in the EU, 207 million in the US and 51 million in Japan. Combining these figures with those for alternatively powered vehicles in use in 2004, the proportion of alternatively powered vehicles in the total stock of passenger cars is greatest in Japan (0.5 per cent), followed by the US (0.3 per cent) and lastly the EU (0.1 per cent).[14] Similarly for Germany, 0.1 per cent of new car registrations are for alternatively powered vehicles (Commission of the European Communities, 2005: 17). These percentages hardly represent a consumer-led stampede to alternatively powered vehicles of the same proportion as, say, diesel in the EU and Germany, or light trucks in the US.

Even so, the trends are of interest. Sales are clearly increasing in all

Table 5.4 Sales of alternatively powered vehicles

	1995	1996	1997	1998	1999	2000	2001	2002	2003	2004
EU sales of passenger vehicles	481	1265	5271	20559	13013	17823	18080	18641	40484	22309
US vehicles in use	246855	265006	280205	295037	322355	406615	445329	505787	595479*	653764
Japan vehicles in use	11018	12208	17481	38769	56429	74770	106409	130329	180383	250293

Note: * Data were missing on petrol/diesel-electric hybrid vehicles, therefore an estimate was made based on the mid-point between the number of vehicles in 2002 and 2004.

Sources: JAMA (2004a: 52; 2007b: 28); EIA (2005); Commission of the European Communities (2005: 10; 2006b).

territories except the EU where a clear trend is harder to define – for example, there have been peaks in 1998 and 2003, but otherwise been around 20000 vehicles at most. The lack of penetration of alternatively powered vehicles in the EU is underscored by the European Commission noting that the influence on fleet average CO_2 emissions of alternatively powered vehicles remains negligible, so that until 2002 member states were not even required to include them in reports on CO_2 emission reductions (Commission of the European Communities, 2002: 11).

A word of caution is warranted on the US data. Many vehicles counted in the data are light trucks that are able to run on alternative fuels such as ethanol. However, as noted in Chapter 4, they probably never do. The data here are based on estimates by the US Energy Information Administration of the number of dual-fuel capable vehicles in the US that actually do run on alternative fuels, but even so this is just an estimate. And if one looks at the figures for alternatively powered vehicles in the US in private hands (as opposed to public authorities) that are not heavy trucks or buses, the figures are reduced to less than half the figure shown in Table 5.4.[15]

Overall, the reality is that there remains far more hype and hope surrounding the potential for alternatively powered vehicles than actual market penetration. Most importantly, the data do not suggest consumer demand is the instrumental factor in encouraging the provision of such vehicles. The trend to alternatively powered vehicles is strongest in Japan, but even there preferences remain very much with more conventionally-powered vehicles. Until the trends become clearer all that can be said is that the emerging *potential* for sales growth of alternatively powered vehicles appears most promising in Japan, and to a lesser extent the US. In all cases, consumer demand is hardly in the driver's seat.

SOCIAL ATTITUDES AND CONSUMER DEMAND: INSTITUTIONAL EXPLANATIONS FOR A PUZZLE

The evidence suggests anything but a clear-cut relationship. Social concern for the environment is not clearly related to consumer demand, and the relationship between the two is contingent on the territory considered. Any changes in the environmental performance of car firms' products cannot be clearly said to be universally explained by changing social attitudes mediated through markets. However, answers are possible to the question of whether social attitudes are associated with consumer behavior on a state-by-state basis.

For Germany, the answer is a qualified yes. Concern for the environment in Germany is supported by a strong willingness to pay higher prices and choose household products that are better for the environment. There is also a willingness to take non-market action, apart from making financial sacrifices. Consumer behavior demonstrates a growing preference for more environmentally-friendly vehicles through the dramatic uptake of diesel cars and a preference for smaller cars, albeit with larger (diesel) engines. The result is that fuel economy is improving. Germany does generally have all the signs pointing in the 'right' direction, in that social concern for the environment and willingness to act in environmentally-friendly ways is reflected in consumer demand for more environmentally-friendly vehicles.

For the US, the answer is no. There is strong concern for the environment, as in Germany. There is a strong willingness to purchase environmentally-friendly household products, plus reasonably strong non-market signals exist for environmental change based on social attitudes, especially via civil action. However, the reality is that US consumers are purchasing ever more environmentally damaging vehicles. Perhaps the clearest illustration of this is that their uptake of light trucks as passenger cars is similar to the uptake of diesels in Germany.

For Japan, a clear answer is not possible. Concern for the environment, while similar to Germany and the US, is somewhat counterpoised by the weakest willingness to take environmentally-friendly action of the three territories. The only exception is in willingness to make non-market financial sacrifices. Yet Japanese consumers exhibit a strong preference for smaller, more environmentally-friendly vehicles, and the industry is a pioneer in the development and commercial sale of petrol-electric hybrids.

What is to be made of these results? For example, why does strong social concern and a reasonably strong willingness to act in the US have no discernable impact on actual car sales? Why are good environmental outcomes through car sales in Japan not clearly traceable back to social attitudes and a willingness to act on them? Exploration of the institutional implications of the results is required, and explanations are suggested by applying the insights of the VOC approach to the findings in respect of the transmission of environmental concern to firms.

Firms in LMEs such as the US prefer market modes of coordination. Institutional support exists for responding to market forces that dictate shorter-term profits, and therefore consumer demand is their main driver. By contrast, firms in CMEs are characterized by more non-market cooperative relationships, so that it is not primarily the market and its price signals that determines firms' behavior, but relationships based on cooperative networks between them, the state and society. Therefore, institutional support for responses to social attitudes should be most acute in CMEs, in this case Germany and Japan.

Given LME-based firms' preference for market modes of coordination, based on responses to the WVS, the signals that are likely to be transmitted to US car firms are insufficient to change their behavior. This is because although US respondents are willing to choose household products that are better for the environment, they are not very willing to pay more for them. They would like to choose products that are more environmentally-friendly, but only if such products are the same price or cheaper than equivalent products. This suggests the transmission of weak material incentives to US firms. If there is little likelihood of increased profits in the short term by switching to more environmentally-friendly production or products, then the probability of increased returns to shareholders is questionable. It is therefore far 'safer' to stick with more environmentally damaging processes and products. The outcome is a feedback loop of incentives and outcomes that militate against firms producing more environmentally-friendly products. On the one hand, consumers are concerned about the environment and their concern is associated with their willingness to act on it. However, they do not demonstrate strong enough demand in markets on the basis of this concern. On the other hand, their concern suggests they might be willing to do so if only firms would offer products that reflected their concern. Unfortunately, this is unlikely because firms are unwilling to offer vehicles for sale that will attract purchasers on the basis of their environmental concerns as the market signals for so doing are not strong enough.

Being more reactive to material market pressures, and without a more apparent direct relationship between social attitudes and material market outcomes, US car firms are unlikely to drive environmental change. As long as they can sell big, gas guzzling light trucks, social attitudes are unlikely to flow through to changes in the products offered by them. They will be 'happy' for consumers to feel guilty while they sell them more light trucks.[16] Even if respondents indicate that they have decided to reuse or recycle, or reduce water consumption, the only clear market signal this sends to US firms is that there are material (i.e. profit) opportunities in products embodying these attributes. Even then, a product that uses less water or is made from recycled products will probably not be preferred by respondents unless it is the same price or cheaper than an equivalent product.

Related to a tendency to reject collective coordination in favor of market competition, is the adversarial relationship between the state and business in US LME capitalism. Social groups attempt to affect the outcomes of this relationship, so that many 'voices' take part in the regulatory process. As such, it is not surprising that civil action and a robust network of social groups feature so much more than is the case for Germany and Japan.

The fact that many more US respondents are members of environmental organizations, contribute to them and are active in them is therefore not necessarily so much an indication of the increased importance of the environment, as a feature of the institutional foundations of US capitalism. This is how change occurs in the US: through competition for ideas, through many voices seeking to influence business and government, and advocacy via organized social groups. What responses to the WVS demonstrate more than anything else, is that the environment is an issue that is attracting attention in the US, and therefore such groups are a factor in raising environmental concern. It does not indicate that this concern will necessarily be *transmitted* and bring about change. This requires firms' material returns to be affected. Therefore, unless such groups can either alter market forces (via consumer demand), or successfully lobby for government regulations, they are likely to be ineffective.

Based on responses to taking direct market action, US non-market civil action appears to have had limited success in encouraging an impact on market forces. So what of the government? There is more hope on this front because US respondents are willing to make non-market financial sacrifices, including via increased taxes. They expect government action to cost them money. The question is, given a laissez-faire ideology that supports the separation of the state and markets, is their willingness enough? This is a hard question to answer. The fact that US respondents are willing to make non-market financial sacrifices is not, in and of itself, necessarily a force for change. The missing ingredient is a *business case* for change, which is not very likely given that respondents' willingness to make financial sacrifices is more non-market.

Therefore, one thing seems clear. If the development and offering of more environmentally-friendly products by US firms will only occur if these are cheaper, US firms will have to be subsidized by government for these products to be offered, or their existing products will have to be taxed. Respondents support this happening, but there is still the need to overcome the pervasive antagonism between the state and business which reflects a belief in minimal government intervention in markets. Seen in this light, the absence of a business case flowing from social concern indicates an up-hill battle for US regulators.[17]

Where the VOC approach suggests that the US responses produce weaker signals for firms than might be expected, the opposite is the case for CME-based Japanese firms. They are less coordinated by market competition, and more concerned with their social standing and responsibility to stakeholders. They are less driven by providing short-term returns to shareholders, and more by longer-term strategies. As such, despite a similar willingness to purchase products at a higher price to US respondents, and slightly less willingness to choose household products that are better for the environment, the impact of this on Japanese firms may be stronger. The reason is that social attitudes *matter* more, even if they are not as clearly related to short-term material gains. Even if the relationship between social attitudes and actual market outcomes is more tenuous, the fact of the existence of environmental concerns may have more impact due to the greater importance accorded social attitudes. Being *seen* to be environmentally-friendly is more important for Japanese firms. They may even offer more environmentally-friendly products on the basis of the existence of social concern, and *lead* the market despite respondents' lesser willingness to take direct market action. In such a context, even a more moderate tendency to reuse or recycle, or save water, may be regarded as a signal to Japanese firms to change the market (as opposed to responding to it).[18]

Turning to civil action, where membership of social groups is a part of the US institutional landscape, it simply is not in Japan. Therefore, the fact that very few respondents are members of such groups, let alone whether they are active or inactive members, is not necessarily significant. What is significant is that Japanese respondents' confidence in the environmental movement is similar to that of US respondents, and they are only slightly less likely to have attended a meeting or signed a petition. What matters is that Japanese respondents' support for the environmental cause is comparable to that of US respondents, rather than whether or not they have joined environmental social groups.

Japanese respondents are willing to make similar financial sacrifices to US respondents, including paying more taxes, so that their government may take action. However, unlike the US, the CME features of Japanese capitalism do not include an ideology of separation between the state and markets. Government and business have a partnership rather than adversarial relationship. Throw this into the equation, and while once again it is a hard to answer the question of whether social attitudes are enough to encourage government action, it is clear that the need for a strong business case in material terms is not as acute as in the US. Social concern may be enough to stimulate (perhaps informal) agreements between business and government, even in the absence of strong market imperatives, once again in order to lead the market. Support for non-market financial sacrifices and other action is therefore more likely to transmit an impetus for government pressure on industry to improve environmental outcomes.

Finally, turning to Germany, concern for the environment is supported by a strong willingness to both pay higher prices and choose household products that are better for the environment. Respondents are also willing to take action such as reducing water consumption and recycling. They are similarly willing to take non-market action. There is strong support for environmental movements, and a willingness to take action via attending meetings, signing letters or petitions that is stronger than US respondents' membership of actual environmental organizations. Therefore, one can say social concern for the environment and willingness to act on this concern exists on almost all levels. In fact, whether it is a matter of material, market drivers or concern for social attitudes due to more of a stakeholder approach on the part of business, is almost a redundant question. In terms of both market and non-market action there are strong incentives for firms to offer more environmentally-friendly products, with improved environmental outcomes likely regardless of whether Germany is a CME or LME. The need for an institutional analysis drops out of the equation.

The one exception for Germany is in less willingness to make non-market financial sacrifices. Does this matter? If one considers the historical political context in which German respondents said they would prefer government to take action at no financial cost to them, the answer is probably no. The phenomenon of the Green Party as a coalition partner in German government during the 1990s means that environmental issues entered mainstream politics there to an extent not seen in the US and Japan. Therefore, it is entirely possible that German respondents saw no need to pay more taxes or make similar financial sacrifices to effect change. Their government incorporated an environmental party, so it is not so much a matter of making financial sacrifices to bring about change at a political level, as believing that the government bears responsibility for reducing environmental pollution regardless of this. Responsibility for addressing environmental concern moved from society to the state, as much as business.

Overall, a more nuanced perspective is suggested by the VOC approach that results in a different interpretation of the data. The impetus for change from environmental concern remains strongest for Germany, which is then followed by Japan rather than the US. In the case of Germany, social concern and willingness to act on it is so strong across the board that the need for an institutional analysis is questionable. Even so, because of the CME-basis of capitalist relations of production in Germany and Japan, firms from these states are less likely to await clear market signals before reacting. They are more likely to be proactive in driving environmental change on the basis of social attitudes in advance of such market signals, or externally imposed regulations that alter market conditions. For US firms, despite respondents' willingness to act on their environmental concern, unless this results in market forces that exert material influences on business, the impetus for change is weaker.

EXPLAINING THE NATURE OF THE CHANGE IN MARKETS

Many commentators note that the CME features of Germany and Japan are expressed in different ways. An important difference that has relevance here is the idea that state involvement in the Japanese economy has 'technonationalist' aims – that is, technological leadership is the goal. As noted in Chapter 2, while Japanese corporations aim for technological leadership, German firms are more likely to incorporate technological advances more incrementally and conservatively to improve the quality of existing products. US firms exhibit an LME-propensity for radical technological change, but only in response to market forces, and then more in emerging industries rather than established ones.

The shift to diesel cars in Germany (and the EU) represents a shift to a technology that is more environmentally-friendly, in a technologically incremental manner. Petrol and diesel are existing well-defined technologies, and what German firms have done is to switch their focus to diesel and improve the efficiency and performance of engines so that they exceed the environmental performance of existing petrol engines (see Volkswagen, 2003; DaimlerChrysler, 2004).[19] In contrast, the technonationalist nature of Japanese CME institutional arrangements means there is an emerging shift on a more radical technological front to, in particular, petrol-electric hybrid vehicles. Although such new technologies are very much at a nascent stage, Japanese companies are the pioneers in commercially releasing them on the market. The Japanese Energy Conservation Centre sees the development of such technologically advanced alternatively powered vehicles, combined with Japan's Top Runner Method of setting fuel economy standards, as a way for firms to 'strengthen their international competitiveness, because manufacturers who possess advanced energy-saving technologies can develop new business opportunities that respond to consumer needs by applying their basic technology [because] consumers' preference for equipment with higher energy efficiency is expected to increase' (Energy Conservation Centre, no date).

A word of caution is warranted though, in the sense that perhaps the point should not be too overstated. There is no doubt that most of the improvement in the fuel economy/CO_2 emissions of new Japanese cars is related to other factors (e.g. buying smaller cars). Even so, it is possible that technonationalist features of Japan's CME mean that petrol-electric hybrid technologies are an emerging strategy for revitalizing a mature industry and seeking new markets. This, combined with the possibility that social attitudes on the environment are taken more 'seriously' by firms than in an LME like the US, provides greater incentives for commercializing investment in such radical new technologies. Following from this line of argument is the suggestion that Japanese firms are leading the market. Rather than following it, as one would expect in the case of LME firms, Japanese firms are investing in the development of the latest technologically-advanced products that they believe consumers *should* buy.

The point has already been made that in the US a shift to more environmentally-friendly products is unlikely without clear market signals. US car firms continue to produce and sell ever bigger light trucks as passenger vehicles. It is hardly surprising then, that when US firms think of technological advances they think in terms of equipping their largest and most fuel-thirsty SUVs with the capacity to run on alternative fuels like ethanol, or purchase the technology from Japanese firms to equip them with petrol-electric hybrid drivetrains (see Ford Motor Company, 2004; General Motors Corporation, 2004).[20] Neither represents the technological shift evident in German and Japanese firms' product line-ups.

So, there is the unavoidable fact of the path dependence of established competitive advantages. This is related to the VOC approach in the sense that the institutional basis of for capitalist relations of production in states to some extent determines how such advantages are developed (e.g. via the market versus state guidance, via incremental technologies versus radical technological change), but more generally the point is that the competitive advantages developed are themselves 'sticky' as much as the institutional basis for their development. If technonationalist attributes of Japan's CME lead it to produce ever more advanced fuel efficient vehicles; if voluntaristic aspects of German and Japanese industry approaches to setting standards which reflect a CME partnership approach to state-business relations is the case; and if US firms prefer LME arm's-length relations with regulators and a focus on giving consumers what they demand, these produce different competitive advantages that endure over time. In other words, institutional path dependence produces material capabilities that are also resistant to change. Production data for 1998 to 2004 indicates that 30 to 50 per cent of the output of the two major US producers, Ford and General Motors, is accounted for by 'light commercial vehicles' by comparison to 3 to 6 per cent for Volkswagen and 6 to 21 per cent for Toyota, the largest German and Japanese firms. These production profiles have implications for firms' profit sources. Ford and General Motors rely on light trucks for over 70 per cent of their profits and they therefore face a much more significant redesign of their product portfolios than German and Japanese firms in order to be more environmentally-friendly (OICA, no date; Austin et al., 2003: 32 and 63–64).

The implications are that the path dependent effects of entrenched competitive advantages, in terms of production and profits from producing larger vehicles, outweigh the signals provided by social attitudes. This could certainly be the case in the US, but it may equally be true that a competitive advantage in the production of smaller, more fuel efficient vehicles on the part of German, Japanese (and European) manufacturers has the opposite effect. Thus, consumers are not so much sovereign/'in charge' of products offered for sale as firms. They must accept the products firms produce regardless of their attitudes or demand preferences. What drives firms – i.e. their organizing principles – is therefore pertinent, and is the focus of the following chapters.

CONCLUSION

For anyone accustomed to applying the liberal economic model to the motivations of economic actors, US firms' rationale for action seem most 'rational' (or even 'believable'). They are more instrumentally driven by materialist concerns, particularly what the market dictates. Their preference for market modes of coordination means they prefer arm's-length government involvement in markets. Social attitudes are more likely to be addressed for how they impact on, or relate to, material interests. Although social concern is important to US firms, it is seen more in terms of how it affects material outcomes, and the interests of shareholders predominate (i.e. those with an interest in, and who are directly affected by, firms' material interests). The LME model, based as it is on competitive market modes of economic coordination (including a concern for concepts such as shareholder value and profits in the shorter term) supports such a perspective.

For German and Japanese CME-based firms, non-market modes of coordinating economic activity rival the short-term material imperatives of market forces. They are more inclined to consider social attitudes in addition to short-term material returns, and therefore are able to focus more on environmental concern as a strategic motivator. Material interests flow from (or are more dependent on) responsibility to stakeholders encompassing society more broadly, rather than the short-term material interests of shareholders. Therefore, as in the case of the Japanese industry, social concern for the environment may be addressed even if there is less of a willingness on the part of consumers for this to be reflected in material outcomes.

Two conclusions are possible. First, concern for the environment in Germany, the US and Japan is not a universal cause of change. Only in the case of Germany may it be said that strong environmental concern is likely to be reflected in consumers' purchasing decisions and firms' product offerings. Second, the successful transmission of environmental concern to firms is not simply related to its magnitude, nor willingness on the part of consumers to translate it into material outcomes. Instead, it is contingent on national variations in capitalist relations of production. Given US firms' LME institutional setting, a lack of strong market signals favoring environmental action potentially overrides significant social concern. A materialist analysis remains appropriate even in the face of substantial environmental concern. However, German and Japanese CME-based firms have clearer incentives for environmental action. Even if Japanese respondents' willingness to act on their concern is weaker than that of US respondents, the resulting impetus for environmental improvements transmitted to car firms is likely to be stronger because social concern *matters* more.

The evidence counters the idea that social attitudes, let alone post-materialist values (concerning the environment and the car industry at least), are a universal source of behavioral change. Indeed, it disproves any sweeping hypothesis that society, or at least social attitudes, is/are a form of governance from the point of view of firms. Although such a clear causal path is intuitively appealing and logically reasonable, the evidence does not support it as a universal phenomenon. However, explanations for the findings are suggested utilizing the insights of the VOC approach, on the basis that the different institutional settings faced by firms in their home states have implications for their corporate strategies. For social attitudes to perform a governance role in respect of firms' environmental initiatives requires assumptions regarding the institutional basis for capitalist relations of production. They *can* if they affect firms' material interests in LMEs. They *may* if they affect firms' normative perceptions of appropriate behavior in CMEs.

Ultimately, what we have is a case of 'chickens and eggs'. Associations have been examined more than causal links. It is hard to clearly determine whether German car firms are reacting to social concerns and leading the market, or reacting to consumer preferences expressed in the market. For institutional reasons, they and Japanese firms are more likely than US firms to lead the market (on the basis of social concern) than react to its signals. This is true for German firms even if they are likely to be acting less for post-materialist reasons than firms in the other territories. But regardless of their home state, in an industry where production is concentrated in a handful of enormous corporations and less than two or three of these dominate their home territories, to some extent consumer choice will always be defined by these firms. Their established competitive advantages produce a path dependence in their product offerings that may override shifts in social attitudes, at least in the short term. Thus, if consumers are buying more environmentally-friendly vehicles in Japan and Germany maybe this is because this is where their production expertise lies. Similarly in the US, despite an expressed willingness to act on environmental concerns, it may be that the industry offers less environmentally-friendly vehicles than German or Japanese firms because their production structures mean that these products are instrumental to their ongoing profitability.

One final observation is that the institutional factors considered in this chapter are largely exogenous ones. What is required is an examination of firms' endogenous institutional factors (i.e. their internal cultures), as it is the interplay of both exogenous and endogenous factors that completes what remains a more complex picture than that presented here (and indeed a more complex one than that presented by more optimistic commentators). This is the focus of Chapters 6 and 7 which examine firms' rationales for their environmental initiatives as expressed in their environmental reports and in interviews with key personnel.

NOTES

1. Some cases in point include the World Trade Organization recognizing that 'environment, gender and labour concerns are on the agenda in ways that would have been deemed illegitimate in the 1970s', and establishing its Committee on Trade and Environment in 1995 at its inception (O'Brien et al., 2000: 231). At the same time, throughout the 1990s a series of international agreements with business also emerged. One of these is the Global Compact, announced in 1999 to bring companies together with UN agencies, labor and civil society to support nine principles in the areas of human rights, labour and the environment (UN, no date b). Another is the Global Reporting Initiative, started in 1997 by the Coalition of Environmentally Responsible Economies and now an official collaborating center of the UNEP that works in cooperation with the UN's Global Compact (GRI, 2002).
2. Porter actually foreshadowed the perspectives outlined in these articles in Porter (1990). In this now classic work, he noted that any environmental damage caused by firms is, as much as anything else, a sign of waste and therefore economic inefficiency.
3. This perspective would seem to agree with, and flow from, the definition given for institutions in Chapter 1 as 'a set of rules, formal or informal, that actors generally follow, whether for normative, cognitive, or material reasons' (Hall and Soskice, 2001: 9).
4. The waves in question are: Wave 2, 1990–1993; Wave 3, 1995–1997; and Wave 4, 1999–2001.
5. The questions in category 3 go to March and Olsen's logic of appropriateness (March and Olsen, 1989 and 1998). They are also very much at the heart of comparative institutional approaches, and the normative basis for institutions in the VOC approach.
6. The percentages for respondents who strongly agreed with paying higher prices was: Germany 9 per cent, US 5 per cent and Japan 4 per cent.
7. In Wave 3, 10 per cent of US respondents had a great deal of confidence in the environmental movement by comparison to 8 per cent in Germany and 6 per cent in Japan. In Wave 4, the question was not asked of German respondents, but the gap between US and Japanese respondents was even greater: while again only 6 per cent of Japanese

respondents had a great deal of confidence in the environmental movement, 16 per cent of US respondents did.

8. Thirty-three per cent of all German respondents strongly agreed that the government should reduce environmental pollution but it should not cost them anything, by comparison to 25 per cent in the US and 13 per cent in Japan.

9. It is also true that other emissions from diesels, such as particulate matter, tend to be much higher than from equivalent petrol engines. However, tougher regulations for such emissions in all three territories in recent years, along with technical advances by manufacturers, mean that such environmental concerns are increasingly being addressed (e.g. see ECMT, 2001).

10. As noted earlier, the exact car class definitions are provided in Appendix B.

11. There is a slight discrepancy in the data by comparison to Figure 5.2. The reason for this appears to be that the data are from different sources, and therefore reflects different criteria for allocating sales to particular classes. Even so, comfort may be taken from the observation that in either case the point that 4WDs represent a very small niche market still stands.

12. The annual report of the German peak industry body is liberally sprinkled with references to the environmental benefits of diesel, especially vis-à-vis climate change. German firms' environmental reports also highlight diesel technologies as central to their environmental strategies, but this is not the case for US and Japanese firms.

13. A search on *Factiva* on 29 July 2005 for the specific term 'petrol-electric hybrid' alone produced 336 hits for the preceding 12 months. Petrol-electric hybrids are driven by a combination of two power sources, one a traditional internal combustion engine and the other an electric motor. The Toyota Prius and Honda Insight are examples of such cars. Cars that run on hydrogen, when available, will produce nothing but water vapor as exhaust gases. Depending on the source of the hydrogen they thus have the potential to have minimal environmental impact by comparison to cars today. Other alternatively powered vehicles include those that can run on other fuels such as ethanol, liquid propane gas (LPG) and compressed natural gas (CNG).

14. The EU calculation is an overly-optimistic one calculated on the basis that all vehicles sold remain in use.

15. This is based, for example, on 197 284 light duty vehicles in use in 2001 and 221 542 in 2002, exclusive of petrol-electric hybrids of which only 19 872 and 34 689 were offered respectively in 2001 and 2002 (EIA, 2005).

16. The Alliance of Automobile Manufacturers (AAM), the US industry's peak body, supports such a conclusion when it says that US firms could be more proactive in developing more environmentally-friendly vehicles but consumers simply will not buy them (AAM, no date a; see also Newton-Small, 2003).

17. This is in fact DeSombre's (2000) point when she says that in the US alliances of 'Baptists' (social groups) and 'Bootleggers' (business) are required before regulatory action is taken on environmental issues.

18. These points are supported by authors such as Katzenstein (1996: 25–26) who notes that 'visibility characterizes Japan's social order' and that this reinforces the importance of public and published opinion which can give rise to 'social sanctions'. This may help to explain why, as a result of the Kyoto Protocol, firms like Toyota invested in the production of hybrid petrol-electric cars which they fully expected would be loss making, whereas US firms waited for the market for such vehicles to mature.

19. DaimlerChrysler (2004: 32–35) stresses its history of expertise in diesel dating back to 1936, and its developments of the technology as a process dating from its first pioneering efforts.

20. This is clear from the strategies that firms such as General Motors and Ford outline in these environmental reports, as discussed in Chapter 3.

6. Firms' rationales: environmental reporting

[N]orms prompt justification for action and leave an extensive trail of communication among actors that we can study.

(Finnemore and Sikkink, 1998: 892)

In Chapters 4 and 5, state regulations and market forces were considered as the key material factors impacting on the car industry. In Chapter 4, it was shown that institutional factors determine the environmental performance of the industry in the European Union, United States and Japan more than regulations themselves. Market mechanisms do not necessarily encourage consumers to use their cars less, nor purchase less fuel. It cannot be said that they are clearly a mechanism for encouraging firms to change their product strategies. And neither the timing, nor stringency, of standards is as important as the institutional context of state–business relations which inform their development. In Chapter 5, it was shown that although strong social concern for the environment exists in Germany, the US and Japan, willingness to act on this is by no means universal, and social attitudes are not necessarily reflected in consumer demand. For Germany, there is strong concern for the environment, willingness to act on this concern, and demonstration of this via actual consumer demand. In the US, there is a reasonably strong willingness to act on environmental concern, but not in markets. This is associated with little demonstration of this willingness in practice via consumer preferences. For Japan, the opposite situation to the US is the case. Concern for the environment and willingness to act on this concern are the weakest of the three, yet ever more environmentally-friendly vehicles is the market outcome.

These results go against the grain of the mainstream liberal economic perspective which holds that rational firms with instrumental material goals aim to maximize profits in markets, while being bound by state regulations. Instead, institutional factors provide more compelling explanations for the empirical evidence. Specifically, the extent to which a car firm's home state variety of capitalism is characterized more by a liberal or coordinated market economy (LME versus CME) better explains variations in the outcomes. Only in the case of US firms is the materialist liberal economic view sufficient to explain their behavior. This is to be expected because institutional LME features of the US mirror the value system of the liberal economic model (a point also made in Dore, 1997: 31). For example, US firms appear to be adopting a reactive, and barely sufficient, approach to fuel economy standards, and are responding more to consumer demand than social attitudes. The environmental action they take/ do not take is primarily the result of market forces and state regulation. By contrast, CME-based German and Japanese firms focus less overtly on such material factors. German firms, as part of the European car industry, take a more cooperative approach to setting regulations and appear to be acting on the basis of social attitudes as much as actual consumer demand. In addressing their carbon dioxide emission commitments they are promoting diesel vehicles, commensurate with a CME preference for incremental technological advances in established industries. Japanese firms are taking a more radical technology-driven approach befitting their technonationalist version of a CME. Proactively acting in concert with, and possibly ahead of, the state, and certainly ahead of consumer demand, they appear to be more internally driven in their environmental initiatives, and more concerned with social attitudes than actual consumer demand.

Such insights as these, supported by the empirical evidence presented so far, are examined in more detail in the following two chapters via an evaluation of the major German, US and Japanese firms' rationales for their environmental initiatives. Two major questions are posed. First, what do car firms themselves say motivates them to take environmental initiatives? This includes an assessment of whether they highlight reacting to material factors versus proactively taking steps for more normative reasons.[1] Second, what are the implications for how action on environmental concerns occurs within the industry in each territory? Answering these questions involves exploring whether firms' nationality matters, and whether firms of different nationalities are key drivers of change and why.

There is a problem in seeking to identify rationales. Implicitly, one is examining attitudes and beliefs, but these cannot be directly observed. They must be inferred on the basis of other indicators (see, for example, King et al., 1994). While recognizing this, the objective is to attempt to get inside the 'heads' of firms to 'observe' such attitudes and beliefs via first-hand perspectives derived from what they say in their environmental reports, and views offered by key personnel in interviews which are analysed in Chapter 7. The nature of the perspectives expressed, whether in writing or verbally, are informative because, as Finnemore and Sikkink note, 'norms prompt justification for action and leave an extensive trail of communication among actors that we can study' (Finnemore and Sikkink, 1998: 892), particularly in the light of hard evidence and data. The two go together: without first-hand opinions that represent a normative justification for action, hard evidence and data can only produce conclusions based on a priori assumptions. Similarly, opinions and justifications for action cannot be taken merely on face value, but must be viewed in light of the empirical evidence.

While this book takes a historical snapshot of the period 1990 to 2004, this chapter considers a moment in time by examining firms' 2004 environmental reports. All quotations in the following analysis are from these.[2] They are analysed by applying codes for references to material versus normative factors, then for codes in subcategories below these – e.g. material factors include subcategories such as market forces and state regulation; normative factors include social attitudes and internal company strategies. The methodology applied is explained before a quantitative summary of coding on material versus normative factors is presented. This is followed by a largely qualitative discussion of coding in the subcategories. In addition, coding for the overarching concern of 'sustainability' as a concept referred to in firms' environmental reports is considered, before conclusions are reached on the different rationales for action offered and the strategies these suggest.

What is found is that material factors, especially market forces, are stressed by US firms. Normative factors are stressed more by German and Japanese firms, especially social attitudes for German firms and internal company strategies for Japanese firms. Therefore, it becomes clear that the institutional basis of capitalist relations of production in their home states illuminates how firms perceive and communicate their environmental initiatives. The findings support the insights of the VOC approach, in that institutional explanations are important for understanding the rationales firms *themselves* believe most important to highlight when presenting their environmental product development initiatives.

WHY DOES WHAT FIRMS SAY IN THEIR REPORTS MATTER?

Firms' environmental reports are not an objective representation of firms' attitudes. After all, objectivity is unattainable precisely because attitudes are always subjective phenomena. In fact, these reports are produced teams of people qualified in, and tasked with, presenting information in the best possible light.[3] There are therefore two important reasons for examining them. First, they show what firms themselves perceive as constituting the best possible light in which their environmental initiatives may be cast. What do they see as most convincing and brand-enhancing for their readerships? What do they think will inspire confidence? What do they think will convince readers that they are a firm committed to environmental concerns and acting on them? These reports present firms' understanding of how their environmental strategies should be 'best' presented, so from them their attitudes may be inferred.

Second, because considerable effort goes into publishing a written report, it presents what each company believes to be its *key* messages. While all the firms examined have websites that contain a plethora of environmental information, these are updated regularly and evolve over time. However, a written report endures and presents, in one comprehensive document, the activities a firm believes are most important to communicate at a moment/period in time.[4] Such a historical snapshot allows for a more robust comparative analysis on a like-to-like basis.

The sections of the environmental reports analysed, the codes applied to statements in these sections and the manner in which these were analysed are described before presenting the findings of the analysis.

Sections of Firms' Environmental Reports Analysed

Three sections of each firm's environmental report were analysed. First, executive statements presenting the view of the Chief Executive Officer (CEO) and other board members that introduce the report were examined. These 'set the scene' of the report by introducing it and presenting the view of its contents by the firm's highest office holder/s. Second, environmental 'vision' statements were examined. These are the section/s presenting the firm's vision with respect to environmental performance, laying out the rationale for its embrace of environmental sustainability. Taken together, the executive and vision statements articulate *why* the firm is taking environmental action, as opposed to simply reporting on actions taken. Third, the firm's environmental policy guidelines were examined. These guidelines operationalize the company's vision by setting out concise rules for all employees for action on environmental issues. Although these three sections account for a small proportion of each report, focusing on them permits a comparative analysis between what are otherwise often stylistically dissimilar reports. They are also where one would most expect to find *rationales* for environmental action rather than simply descriptions of action taken.

Codes Applied

Codes were applied to the executive statements, environmental vision statements and policy guidelines. First, codes were applied to statements pertaining to the two material factors of market forces and state regulation. Market forces relate to statements that identify forces that affect the firm's financial performance as a result of the products it sells. These include responding to consumer demand and pressure from competitors; safeguarding financial returns in the sense of maintaining sales, market share and ensuring shareholder value, as well as managing risks that affect these; and proactive action to ensure market leadership and the realization of business opportunities. State regulation relates to references to national and international voluntary agreements, as well as national and international legislation, plus input to the policy process in the development of regulations.

Second, codes were applied to statements regarding the normative factors of social concerns and internal company strategies. Codes in both these categories relate to motivators beyond material factors alone. Social concerns relate to statements highlighting non-market forces to do with social perceptions of the environment. These include statements regarding general social concern for the environment; the way in which brand image and trust in the company is affected as a result of them; and a stated belief that the firm bears responsibility to society and stakeholders in respect of its environmental performance. Internal company strategies relate to statements that demonstrate endogenous factors leading firms to take the environment seriously, such as corporate policy; the path dependence of previous commitments to the environment; and the 'vision' of senior management.

The rules for coding statements were that:

1. All coding was based on *rationales* for action, not on action itself. All coded statements answer the question of *why* action is being taken, rather than the simple fact that it is.
2. Passages could be coded more than once. For example, a statement that it is necessary to respond to social concerns, and that in so doing market share will be increased, would be coded for both market forces and social concerns.
3. Paragraphs were the maximum unit for coding. No coding was applied across paragraphs for the reason that each represents a new idea, or a new idea on the same subject.
4. Sometimes the same code was applied more than once within a paragraph if separated by a sentence/sentences that represented another idea. However, contiguous sentences expressing a rationale for action based on the same idea were not coded separately.
5. Because products and product development is the focus of analysis, as explained in Chapter 3, the environmental impacts of passenger cars in use was the focus for coding.

The following analysis of the codes applied is both quantitative and qualitative. The relative percentages of codes for material versus norma-tive rationales are examined first. A qualitative analysis is then applied to investigate the underlying reasons for variations in the distribution of material and normative rationales for action. Therefore, the analysis aims to highlight the actual proportional differences in codes between firms (i.e. relative emphasis), as well as the qualitative nature of the statements codes represent (i.e. how motivations are ascribed). Further details on the defini-tions of codes and their application is provided in Appendix C.

MATERIAL VERSUS NORMATIVE FACTORS

The VOC approach predicts that material factors should be of greater importance for LME-based US firms (for example, competition in markets) than CME-based German and Japanese firms. The latter should focus more on normative rationales for action (e.g. relational coordination). This prediction is borne out by the rationales presented by firms them-selves in their environmental reports. Table 6.1 summarizes the results of coding for material and normative factors, and their sub-categories, on a national average basis. Figures 6.1 to 6.4 show the relative coding propor-tions on a firm-by-firm basis for each of the subcategories within material and normative factors.

There is almost a 50:50 split on average in material versus normative factors for US firms. Both are offered as rationales for action. However, for the German and Japanese firms there is a clear bias towards normative factors: on average 59 per cent of German and 68 per cent of Japanese firms' codes.[5] This supports the VOC prediction that US firms should be more motivated by exogenous material factors than German and Japanese firms.

Examining the subcategories of material and normative factors reveals that the material component in the US firms' rationales that loomed largest was market forces. They coded for this more than twice as much as the German and Japanese firms (40 per cent on average by comparison to 18 and 16 per cent for the German and Japanese firms respectively). Ford outstrips all other firms by having 45 per cent of its codes on market forces, around three times the proportion for most of the German and Japanese firms. The German firms coded more for state regulation on average than the US and Japanese firms, although there is a large spread of coding percentages between firms of the same nationality.

The reason for normative factors' importance for the Japanese firms is their focus on internal company strategies. On average, 36 per cent of codes

Table 6.1 Summary totals of material versus normative factors

	Market forces	State regulation	Total material	Social attitudes	Internal company strategies	Total normative	All codes	All codes
	(%)	(%)	(%)	(%)	(%)	(%)	(%)	(No.)
German average	18	23	41	37	22	59	100	227
Japanese average	16	16	32	32	36	68	100	177
US average	40	10	51	28	21	49	100	124

Source: Company environmental reports.

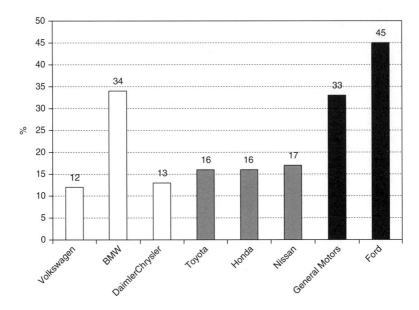

Source: Company environmental reports.

Figure 6.1   Proportion of all codes on market forces by firm

applied to the Japanese firms' reports relate to these, versus just over 20 per cent of codes on average for the German and US firms. The reason for normative factors' importance to the German firms is that they are more inclined than Japanese or US firms to code for social attitudes. On average, they have 37 per cent of their codes on these, while the US and Japanese firms have around 30 per cent. The exception to the rule is Toyota which codes more than any other firm for social attitudes (42 per cent). However, like the other Japanese companies, Toyota still skews more towards internal company strategies than the US and German firms. Therefore, it remains true to say that rather than having an internal rationale for action like Japanese firms, the German firms are more likely to cite social attitudes.

BMW deserves special mention. While other individual firms may be somewhat at odds with their national counterparts on subcategories within material versus normative factors, BMW skews towards material factors to the extent that it has a coding profile more like a US – for example, it codes for market forces similarly to General Motors. BMW also has the lowest coding of any firm on internal company strategies (12 per cent). However, while BMW is somewhat at odds with the other German firms in these regards, on social attitudes its coding is comparable

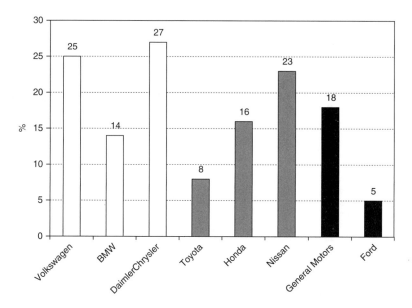

Source: Company environmental reports.

Figure 6.2 Proportion of all codes on state regulation by firm

to them (40 per cent by comparison to 37 per cent for Volkswagen and DaimlerChrysler). Therefore, while sharing a German focus on social attitudes, BMW also shares the US firms' concern for market forces.

Overall, it is clear that the US firms are most concerned with material factors, especially market forces. This seems to relate to an LME preference for market coordination of economic activity. If one excludes BMW from the German average, the difference is even greater with Volkswagen and DaimlerChrysler having only 12–13 per cent of their codes on market forces. Therefore, excepting BMW, the CME-based German and Japanese firms cite normative factors more than their US counterparts. Japanese firms code strongest for internal company strategies, while German firms code strongest for social attitudes, reflecting the different stakeholder focus in each of their home states.[6]

MATERIAL FACTORS IN DETAIL

The material factors of market forces and state regulation are considered in detail in this section. The way in which codes within these subcategories

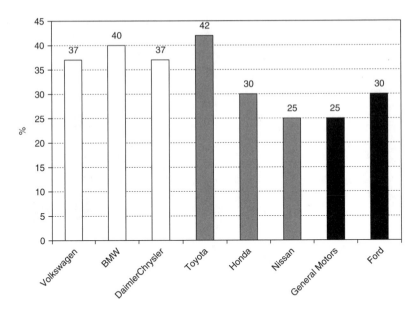

Source: Company environmental reports.

Figure 6.3 Proportion of all codes on social attitudes by firm

inform firms' rationales for environmental action is investigated to more clearly contextualize the observations made above. For example, market forces are more important for US firms than German and Japanese firms, but just *how* are they important? Are they more important from the point of view of responding to competitive pressures such as consumer demand, or taking proactive action to increase market share?

Within the subcategory of market forces, codes were applied for competition in the form of consumer demand or competitive pressure from other firms; safeguarding financial returns in the form of profits and sales, promoting shareholder value or minimizing risks; and proactive action aimed at increasing market share/leadership or exploiting business opportunities. Within the subcategory of state regulation, codes were applied for national and international voluntary agreements; national and international legislation; and input to the policy process. Given that subcategories of subcategories are considered,[7] the coding frequencies are often quite low. Therefore, in the following analysis, qualitative differences in the actual statements made are often brought to the fore. Subsequent to discussing these, the key observations are related to the VOC approach.

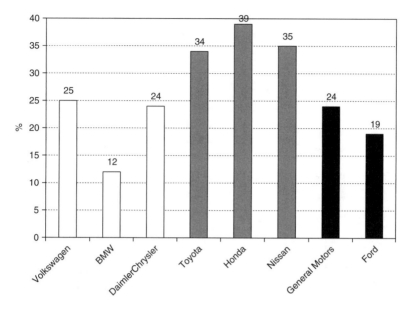

Source: Company environmental reports.

Figure 6.4 Proportion of all codes on internal company strategies by firm

Market Forces

Only the US firms and BMW have a large proportion of their codes in the subcategory of market forces (33–45 per cent of all codes by comparison to 12–17 per cent for the Japanese and other German firms – see Figure 6.1). With this in mind, Table 6.2 shows the composition of firms' codes on market forces. The three codes within the subcategory of market forces are considered in turn: consumer demand and competitive pressure from other firms; safeguarding financial returns; and proactive action.

Competition: consumer demand and competitive pressure from other firms
Competition in the form of consumer demand or competitive pressures from other firms accounts for over 40 per cent of the US firms' market forces codes. In addition, around a third of their market forces codes come from a drive to respond to consumer demand specifically. Clearly, competition in markets is a key driver for US firms, as one would expect of their LME heritage. The statements they make are also qualitatively strong. For example, on consumer demand Ford says:

Table 6.2 *Material factors – market forces*

	Competition			Safeguarding financial returns				Proactive action			Total	Total
	Consumer demand	Competitive pressure from other firms	Total (No multiple coding)	Profits and sales	Share-holder value	Risk management	Total (No multiple coding)	Market share/ leadership	Business opportunity	Total (No multiple coding)		
	(%)	(%)	(%)	(%)	(%)	(%)	(%)	(%)	(%)	(%)	(%)	(No.)
Germany Volkswagen	54	8	62	8	8	0	15	15	8	23	100	13
BMW	5	0	5	19	33	24	75	14	5	20	100	20
DaimlerChrysler	0	13	13	13	0	0	13	50	25	75	100	8
Japan Toyota	10	10	20	20	0	10	30	50	0	50	100	10
Honda	33	0	29	17	0	0	14	50	0	57	100	7
Nissan	58	0	58	8	0	17	25	0	17	17	100	12
US General Motors	35	6	41	6	6	0	12	47	0	47	100	17
Ford	31	9	42	14	9	3	24	17	17	33	100	33
Total	28	6	35	13	10	7	29	26	10	36	100	120

Source: Company environmental reports.

It's not that our customers want these environmental benefits at any expense. Quite the opposite. They're saying they want it all at little additional cost. They don't want tradeoffs between environmental performance and the power, comfort and safety they've grown to expect. Our products must reflect this 'no compromises' attitude.

Indeed, the 'no compromises' approach to consumer demand is reflected in the primacy accorded it in Ford's executive statement where the company's Chairman declares that 'the fastest way to bring about the [environmental] transition we are seeking is through the market and competition'.

General Motors' statements about competition, particularly responding to consumer demand, are similarly strong. The firm outlines its commitment to giving customers 'gotta have' products and states from the outset that 'a report on our behavior must start with delivery on our promise to design, build and offer great cars and trucks that meet the full range of consumer needs and preferences in the markets where we compete'. Like Ford, consumer demand, in the context of responding to market forces generally, is the firm's primary strategic driver. Its bottom line is that it must 'offer vehicles that people want to buy' because 'if no one buys the product, the new technology has no real impact'.

Although BMW exhibits the US firms' focus on market forces, this is not expressed in terms of competition in markets. It, like two of the Japanese firms (Honda and Nissan), does not code for responding to competitive pressure from other firms *at all*, and has only 5 per cent of its material factors codes on consumer demand. Therefore, despite sharing the US firms' concern for market forces, BMW does not share their concern for responding to competitive pressures. While it might be a stretch to say this indicates a CME preference for cooperation/coordination between firms, it certainly does not indicate an LME-like preference for market competition.

Not only do the other German firms code less in proportional terms for market forces, the statements they make are qualitatively different to the US firms. Volkswagen says that 'companies are obliged to act in line with economic considerations' and that 'their primary function is to create value and satisfy the needs of their customers', and echoes General Motors in saying that 'eco cars which fail to find buyers are of no use to us or the environment'. But Volkswagen additionally notes that 'the negative associations . . . which in the past have linked environmental protection with self-sacrifice or scaremongering have already put off far too many customers'. Unlike the US firms, this is a statement embracing environmental factors as a way of potentially *encouraging* customers. Of the other German firms, which have a very small proportion of their market forces codes on either consumer demand or competitive pressure from other firms, statements are made along the lines that they must manage to 'satisfy' (BMW) their customers and develop products and technologies that 'take account of and drive the market trends of the future' (DaimlerChrysler) in order to be competitive. Not only are these quite restrained statements, but the latter indicates DaimlerChrysler sees its role as a mixture of responding to and leading the market, rather than primarily reacting to the demands of consumers. Like Volkswagen, consumer demand is seen as more of a 'two-way street', in the sense that it may be influenced as well as responded to.

The Japanese firms' statements on competition in markets are quite weak. Honda simply says that it wishes 'to meet the expectations of customers' and 'provide customers with products that totally satisfy them'. Toyota talks of providing 'products and services that fulfill the needs of customers worldwide' by being mindful of market forces but striking a balance between them and environmental imperatives. Similarly, Nissan declares that 'customers want environmentally friendly cars, but they expect a sound value proposition, so we have to find solutions'. Therefore, environmental product development initiatives are not as contingent on consumer demand, as for US firms. Instead, consumer demand is more a consideration given a *prior* commitment to the development of environmentally-friendly products. Concomitant with Japanese CME firms' internal drivers for strategic decisions, the decision to undertake environmental initiatives comes first, or is at least balanced with, consumer demand.

Safeguarding financial returns: profits and sales, shareholder value and risk management

There is one clear observation on firms' coding for safeguarding financial returns. It is the strength with which BMW codes for it, with 75 per cent of its market forces codes in this subcategory. Therefore, although BMW stresses market forces to a similar degree to US firms, the reason is not so much a preoccupation with reacting to competitive pressures as safeguarding its financial returns. The reason would seem to be that it knows it has a good product and a significant share of the prestige car market, and it wants to make sure it keeps it. It makes statements along the lines that 'by consistently serving the premium segments of the car market, the BMW Group creates the right conditions for profitable, long term growth'. As a prestige car maker, BMW is playing a different 'game'. It is not so much competing in markets as maintaining its position as a niche producer of prestige cars.

In addition to coding less for market forces in general, Japanese firms and DaimlerChrysler do not mention shareholder value *at all*. This reflects the less stockmarket-focused nature of financial markets in CMEs.

Beyond quantitative coding variations, firms' statements about safeguarding financial returns are qualitatively rather similar. The clearest differences are that Toyota, when mentioning sales, refers specifically to sales of its petrol-electric hybrid Prius rather than sales in general – i.e. the spotlight is clearly on its environmental initiatives. However, when US firms mention profits and sales, they refer to 'razor thin profit margins' (General Motors) and action in the face of 'difficult economic conditions' (Ford). This can be contrasted with the German firms which note their 'excellent sales, revenues and profits' (BMW) and the need to remain profitable generally over the long term. The difference in emphasis for US and German firms no doubt reflects differences in their underlying profitability.

Proactive action: gaining market share and exploiting business opportunities

As a proportion of their codes on market forces, DaimlerChrysler, Toyota, Honda and General Motors code more than the other firms for proactive action, particularly in respect of acting to increase market share/ leadership. But given the small number of codes involved for firms other than BMW and the US firms, it would be dangerous to draw conclusions on the basis of coding proportions alone (for example, DaimlerChrysler has 75 per cent of its market forces codes on proactive action, but this only relates to eight statements). However, examining the qualitative differences reveals that the German and US firms are more explicitly materialist in their references versus the more 'poetic' visions of the Japanese firms.

The US firms make statements about seizing opportunities to ensure they remain competitive, often couched in terms of market leadership. For General Motors, it is a matter of 'product leadership', being an 'industry leader' and indeed 'being the world leader in transportation products and related services'. Ford similarly sees environmental action in terms of a 'leadership choice' based on 'sound business drivers' on which the company 'must deliver'. Environmental sustainability is thus described in materialist terms as 'a tremendous business opportunity'.

The German firms make similar statements. DaimlerChrysler says its 'aim is to safeguard future mobility and secure a competitive edge by developing innovations and future-oriented technologies that benefit the environment, safety, and comfort'. Thus, being proactive on environmental matters is a matter of being competitive in markets and creating opportunities from a position of leadership. BMW talks about ensuring it remains 'the most successful premium manufacturer . . . with a comprehensive product range in all the relevant segments of the automobile market' and taking action to 'expand on new markets'. Volkswagen also sees its environmental commitments as opening up 'additional scope for the company to break new ground on its own initiative and at its own responsibility' because 'together, commercial success, far-sighted environmental protection and social competence enhance the global competitiveness of the Volkswagen Group'.

The language of the Japanese firms, in contrast to their German and US counterparts, is less materialist. They have strategic visions that can only be described as matters of the *heart*. Honda wants to act to increase its market share, and talks about its efforts to be a market leader, but sees the end result of this as acting 'to share our dreams and joys with more customers'. When Honda talks of being a leader it mentions its successes in fuel economy and the like, but also says 'we continuously strive to be a leader in bringing forth new values and creating joy'. Although Toyota reports on its product leadership aspirations in materialist terms, it then goes further to note the need to 'strive to become a leader and driving force in global regeneration by implementing the most advanced environmental technologies'. As part of its policy guidelines, Toyota states that it desires to 'be at the vanguard of the times through endless creativity, inquisitiveness and pursuit of improvement'. Nissan makes a similarly strong statement:

> As we face global environmental issues, we will act with a sense of volition. We will turn every issue we face into a motivating force for improvement as we aspire for a society with a symbiosis of people, vehicles, and nature.

Such statements suggest more normative rationales to do with how Japanese firms conceive their *raisons d'être*. They also suggest that, in Japanese CME fashion, they are more internally driven for their strategic decisions.

Market forces and the Varieties of Capitalism approach
The analysis of the coding on market forces produces the following three observations in respect of the VOC approach.

First, the US firms not only stress market forces more than the other firms, but only they stress responding to consumer demand as a leading consideration in environmental product development initiatives. For the others, consumer demand and competition more broadly are more underlying concerns to be balanced against environmental initiatives, rather than primary motivators that drive or constrain them. This is consistent with the importance of market forces in the US LME variety of capitalism, as opposed to one factor among many, and more an underlying than primary concern, in CMEs.

Second, safeguarding financial returns is a major strategic driver for BMW, though not by virtue of its home state's variety of capitalism as much as it being a prestige car producer. This explains why BMW appears more like a US firm in its coding for market forces overall. In addition, there were no references to shareholder value for Japanese firms and DaimlerChrysler. This reflects the lower priority accorded stockmarkets in CMEs. Qualitatively, the main observations are that Toyota stresses sales of its petrol-electric hybrid Prius, whereas the other firms are not so environmentally-focused in their statements about profits and sales, and that US firms stress their financial pressures.

Third, when it comes to taking proactive action in markets, US firms see market leadership and business opportunities in LME materialist terms. The German firms' statements are similar. However, Japanese firms express their leadership aspirations and identification of business opportunities in language that implies something more than market success via winning a competitive battle. In CME-style, broader strategic goals are the aim, and in the Japanese CME tradition these are based more on an internal vision, rather than external motivations.

State Regulation

On average, the German firms are more likely to cite state regulation as a rationale for environmental action than the US and Japanese firms, but the variation between firms of the same nationality is considerable (see Figure 6.2). Therefore, no strong quantitative statements have been made so far on coding for state regulation overall. Table 6.3 shows the composition of firms' codes on state regulation. The three codes within the subcategory of state regulation are considered in turn: national and international voluntary agreements; national and international legislation; and input to the policy process (in terms of attending international meetings and input to national policy/regulations).

National and international voluntary agreements
The US and German firms are far more likely to cite voluntary agreements as a rationale for environmental action than the Japanese firms (41–63 per cent versus 0–14 per cent of state regulation codes). It is also notable that the Japanese firms make *no statements at all* on national voluntary agreements.

Beyond these quantitative differences, there is a qualitative similarity about the statements made by all firms. When mentioned, voluntary agreements are noted as existing along with firms' support for/adherence with them. Firms cite international agreements/guidelines such as Agenda 21, the Global Compact, Coalition of Environmentally Responsible Economies (CERES) guidelines, the Global Reporting Initiative (GRI),

Table 6.3 Material factors – state regulation

		National and international voluntary agreements (%)	National and international legislation (%)	Input to the policy process (%)	Total (%)	Total (No.)
Germany	Volkswagen	44	15	41	100	27
	BMW	63	25	13	100	8
	DaimlerChrysler	41	29	29	100	17
Japan	Toyota	0	100	0	100	5
	Honda	14	57	29	100	7
	Nissan	13	63	25	100	16
US	General Motors	56	22	22	100	9
	Ford	50	25	25	100	3
Total		37	35	28	100	92

Source: Company environmental reports.

the Organisation for Economic Co-operation and Development's *Guidelines for Multinational Enterprises* and the International Chamber of Commerce (ICC) *Charta of Sustainable Development*. German firms also cite national voluntary agreements, particularly the initiatives of the Forum for Sustainable Development of German Business, known as 'Econsense', founded in 2001 by 19 major German corporations. Ford mentions that voluntary carbon trading schemes are emerging that mean it will need to develop appropriate strategies. Therefore, the major observation is the lack of Japanese firms' coding on voluntary agreements, particularly national voluntary agreements.

National and international legislation
The overriding observation on national and international legislation is the degree to which the Japanese firms code for this by comparison to the German and US firms – i.e. the converse of voluntary agreements. At least 57 per cent of the Japanese firms' codes for state regulation are accounted for by codes on legislation specifically (100 per cent in the case of Toyota), versus 15–29 per cent of the US and German firms' codes. Therefore, although US and German firms are more likely to cite voluntary agreements, and German firms are most likely to cite national voluntary agreements, Japanese firms are most likely to cite adherence to national and international legislation.

When the Japanese firms mention adherence to such legislation, they refer to national legislation more often than international legislation. By contrast, US firms make no mention of complying with national legislation at all, and Volkswagen is the only German firm that does. This is not to say that performance against specific national regulations is not contained elsewhere in all firms' environmental reports, but it is only Japanese firms who mention them specifically in executive, vision and policy statements, citing examples of how they meet or exceed national regulatory requirements. The following statement by Nissan is typical of how the Japanese firms do this:

> Approximately 90% of new Nissan vehicles sold in Japan and, increasingly, in other parts of the world, are certified as ultra-low emission vehicles (ULEV), and we are pushing our lead further with super ultra-low emission vehicles (SU-LEV). Our Bluebird Sylphy was the first car ever to be certified as a SU-LEV.

They focus on how they meet or exceed specific Japanese regulatory targets.

Input to the policy process
Excepting Toyota and BMW, all firms are quite likely to note the policy process and sometimes allude to their role in it. Volkswagen does so the

most, with 41 per cent of its state regulation codes on input to the policy process. There are no striking national patterns in their coding proportions. However, there is a clear qualitative split between US and Japanese firms versus the German firms. The former talk in terms of being aware of and attending meetings, providing input to discussions, etc., whereas the latter adopt a more proactive stance.

Ford notes that 'pension fund managers and administrators globally, including a number of US state and local treasurers convened by CERES, have joined together to discuss the financial risks they may face because of investments in companies whose products and services have an adverse effect on climate change'. Ford says it participates in such discussions. General Motors does as well, declaring that it 'will continue to work with all governmental entities for the development of technically sound and financially responsible environmental laws and regulations'. The key observation is that the purpose of being 'at the table' for both the US firms is not so much to promote the cause of environmentalism, as it is to ensure financial outcomes are safeguarded, the technical challenges more manageable, and that their voice is heard. Japanese firms are simply willing participants in the policy process – for example Nissan notes that it is a 'participant in the WBCSD Sustainable Mobility Project'.

However, German firms describe how they intend to *shape* the policy process, rather than just participating in it. BMW declares that 'by jointly planning and cooperating with all areas of politics, society and government administration, the BMW Group is able to offer perspectives for the future where mobility and responsibility for the environment no longer represent a contradiction in terms'. DaimlerChrysler says it 'contributes its expertise to non-corporate scientific, technical and governmental activities designed to improve the environment'. To stress the proactive role it plays in making this contribution it further declares that 'companies need to play a proactive part [and] to this end, DaimlerChrysler is committed to a process of dialogue with politicians, trade associations and social interest groups'. Volkswagen makes a number of similarly proactive statements, such as 'Volkswagen works hand-in-hand with society and policymakers to shape a development process that will bring sustainable social and ecological benefits'. German firms are not just participants in policy dialogue. They want to help drive the process for improved environmental outcomes.

State regulation and the Varieties of Capitalism approach

The analysis of coding on state regulation produces the following three observations in respect of the VOC approach.

First, in addition to coding slightly more for state regulation by comparison to US and Japanese firms, the German firms have a preference for a more voluntaristic approach to regulation. The German firms stress providing input to government on regulations and driving the policy development process. These observations fit with the CME-style of regulation setting and implementation in Germany and Europe: a voluntaristic approach based on extensive state–firm discussion and consensus building, in the context of a belief that private firms have public responsibilities to fulfill.

Second, the LME-based US firms would rather avoid regulation. Although they share a preference with German firms for voluntary agreements, they also indicate that when involved in discussions on policy development the aim is not so much to proactively shape environmental outcomes, as to ensure their views are represented and their material interests not overly infringed.

Third, the Japanese firms stress compliance with, or exceeding, legislative requirements more than their US and German counterparts. They also refer more to national legislation, suggesting they are more focused on their home country regulatory settings than the US or German firms. Not only does this support the notion that national institutions matter, it specifically supports the CME-nature of Japanese state–firm relations: Japanese firms are focused on regulations they have agreed (often informally) with regulators, particularly at the national level, and then set about achieving and exceeding compliance with such regulations.

NORMATIVE FACTORS IN DETAIL

Turning to the normative factors of social attitudes and internal company strategies, the way in which codes within these subcategories inform firms' rationales for environmental action is investigated in a similar way to those for the subcategories of material factors. While quantitatively social attitudes are more important for the German firms, and internal company strategies for the Japanese firms, in their environmental reports firms refer to these normative factors in qualitatively different ways. Within the subcategory of social attitudes, they mention general social concern and raised awareness of environmental issues; the importance of environmental considerations from the perspective of the firm's image; a responsibility to society (generally); and a responsibility to stakeholders (those directly affected by the firm's activities). Within the subcategory of internal company strategies, firms cite environmental action on the basis of corporate policy; the importance of the firm's history and therefore path dependence in its actions; and leaders' vision. As with material factors, both quantitative and qualitative differences in coding are analysed, subsequent to which the key observations are related to the VOC approach.

Social Attitudes

German firms, and Toyota, stress social attitudes more than the US and other Japanese firms (see Figure 6.3). With this in mind, Table 6.4 shows the composition of firms' codes on social attitudes. The four codes within the subcategory of social attitudes are considered in turn: responding to general social concern/raised awareness of environmental issues; firm image (as perceived by society in terms of trust, or in terms of brand loyalty stemming from its actions and products); a belief in responsibility to society; and a belief in responsibility to stakeholders.

General social concern/raised awareness of environmental issues

There is one key quantitative observation on responding to general social concern/raised awareness of environmental issues. It is that while Honda and Nissan have fewer codes than the other firms for social attitudes, only they have more than 20 per cent of their codes for social attitudes on responding to general social concern/raised awareness of environmental issues. They are also the only firms to make qualitatively strong statements in this regard. Honda talks of environmental problems being 'recognized as common problems for everyone in the 1990s', so they developed their environmental guidelines 'amid the increasing momentum toward environmental conservation and the acceleration of environmental measures all over the world'. Nissan similarly cites 'strong interest in the world today about how to balance economic development with environmental protection'. Indeed, Nissan sees 'society demanding a shift from conventional environmental management to consolidated environmental management, to include our consolidated subsidiaries'. Even though Toyota does not have as many codes for general social concern, it believes that only firms that respond to environmental problems 'will be acceptable to society'. This suggests social concerns require a response if the firm is to endure.

Therefore, for the Japanese firms, particularly Honda and Nissan, social concerns are significant motivators for environmental action. This is a key finding because it illuminates the conundrum of Chapter 5 that Japanese firms' market profiles are at odds with Japanese social concern for the environment by comparison to Germany and the US. It supports the hypothesis suggested in Chapter 5 that the existence of such concern, as much as its degree, is taken more seriously by Japanese corporations.

Volkswagen makes similarly strong statements to the Japanese firms, such as the following:

Table 6.4 Normative factors – social attitudes

		General social concern/raised awareness (%)	Firm image (%)	Responsibility to society (%)	Responsibility to stakeholders (%)	Total (%)	Total (No.)
Germany	Volkswagen	13	13	41	33	100	39
	BMW	0	52	17	30	100	23
	DaimlerChrysler	4	13	52	30	100	23
Japan	Toyota	4	35	38	23	100	26
	Honda	23	46	15	15	100	13
	Nissan	28	6	33	33	100	18
US	General Motors	8	23	31	38	100	13
	Ford	14	41	9	36	100	22
Total		11	27	32	31	100	177

Source: Company environmental reports.

> Social interest groups including consumer and environmental associations, and
> thus the political sphere, set the bar high for companies, be it at national or
> international level [*sic*]. As a result, large international companies with promi-
> nent global brands are today caught more firmly in the spotlight of public atten-
> tion than ever before. It is a challenge which, like other major international
> players, we at Volkswagen have taken up from the outset not least by making
> a voluntary commitment to enter into target agreements and reduce the fuel
> consumption of our cars.

Like the Japanese firms, Volkswagen sees the 'challenge' posed by social
groups as one that must be met. However, this is not the case for the other
German firms. BMW does not mention general social concern at all, and
DaimlerChrysler merely notes that 'corporate governance issues have
rightly attracted considerable attention and are now the subject of wide-
ranging public debate'. Environmental concerns for these firms are subsumed within the wider question of corporate governance generally, and
then only referred to in the context that a lot of debate is going on.

The US firms refer to general social concern in similarly oblique terms.
General Motors merely notes the increased 'visibility as the public, government, and nongovernmental organizations have looked to corporations and the private sector to play a leading role in addressing the impact
of globalization on living standards, economic development and environmental improvement'. Ford notes that 'times are changing', 'questions
about fuel economy' are being asked, and that fuel economy is recognized
by people as a 'quality issue'. Ford says that 'customers are demanding
accountability' on climate change. However, these statements of recognition of changing social attitudes do not quite amount to the 'call to arms'
implied by Nissan, Honda and Volkswagen.

Firm image
Firm image relates to statements about how firms wish to be perceived for
their environmental credentials. Toyota, Honda, BMW and the US firms
code most for acting to boost firm image. However, as one would expect
of a concept such as 'image', the qualitative rather than proportional differences in the coded passages reveal clearer national trends.

US firms take the attitude that building trust and brand image is part
of doing business. Ford's chairman says 'transparency and open dialogue
can be uncomfortable at times, but I believe these are prerequisites for
building the trust required to move forward'. Along with statements about
the importance of behaving with integrity, Ford says that the reason for
so doing is building trust and respect with 'investors, customers, dealers,
employees, unions, business partners and society'. Underlying such statements are material goals: 'focusing on customer satisfaction and loyalty

and keeping our promises' and 'seeking enhanced stakeholder loyalty as a route to competitive advantage and long term growth'. General Motors' statements are similar. Although it talks of doing business the 'right way' and being 'measured' by its conduct, the reason for behaving responsibly towards the environment (and in general) is to 'earn our customers' enthusiasm through continuous improvement driven by the integrity, teamwork and innovation of GM people'. Clearly, a desire for ongoing material success is a significant part of why firm image is important to the US firms.

On the other hand, Japanese firms (excepting Nissan) want to be seen as societal leaders, commanding respect and standing in the community for their actions. Rather like their statements on being market leaders, one finds highly emotive and 'organic' statements in their reports. Honda is 'striving to become a company that people will want to exist' and that 'all people can look up to'. It wants to 'share its joys' with its customers and people generally. In its policy statement, Honda declares it 'will consider the influence that [its] corporate activities have on the regional environment and society, and endeavor to improve the social standing of the company'. Toyota similarly desires social standing and respect 'by all peoples around the world' by acting in 'good faith':

> Good faith means acting with sincerity and without betraying the confidence and expectations of others, keeping one's promises, and fulfilling one's duties, and this is embodied in the following way in the guiding principles at Toyota Motor Corporation: 'undertake open and fair corporate activities to be a good corporate citizen around the world'.

Therefore, image is not just a matter of selling more cars at higher prices,[8] but also of sincerity, confidence, keeping promises and fulfilling duties. Being 'kind and generous', and with a desire to 'strive to create a warm, homelike atmosphere', Toyota virtually wants to move in and be part of the family!

Where Japanese firms are emotive, German firms make the most holistic statements in relation to image. For example, DaimlerChrysler says: 'we believe that only a policy of openly providing information on environmental protection measures and reporting on achievements and problems in the implementation of these measures will motivate employees and create credibility in the general public'. Thus, 'credibility in the general public' encompasses, yet also goes beyond material success, although the firm links the two in saying 'in order to safeguard the future of the company and increase its acceptance in society at large, we have committed ourselves to the principle of sustainable development'. Impressing people with its products is also seen as a matter of convincing them with the firm's 'philosophy'. Volkswagen too sees 'reputation among clients and the general public' as tied up with the broad goal of 'access to – and the long term safeguarding of – resources at all levels'. The overarching aim is that 'the name Volkswagen is inseparably linked with (sustainability) principles'. At a policy level, as one would expect of Germany's CME state–business relations, there is also recognition that 'cooperation with policy-makers and the authorities is based on a fundamentally proactive approach founded on mutual trust'.

BMW, which codes proportionally most for firm image, exemplifies the German holistic perspective. It makes many statements, but perhaps the best illustration of this perspective is found in the following:

> The BMW Group's commitment to social, economic and ecological responsibility as an international company is in keeping with its performance as a corporate citizen. Thus, reputation management serves to develop the company as a responsible partner in the global community. A company that is firmly anchored in society as a reliable partner creates acceptance for its products. This acceptance is particularly important for a premium supplier, such as the BMW Group.

For BMW, firm image is about selling cars and material success, but also about a broader aim of being 'a good corporate citizen' and 'a partner in the global community'.

Overall, what is clear is that image is most about material success in markets for the LME-based US firms, versus a more socially-embedded, or holistic vision, of responsibility in the case of the CME-based Japanese and German firms. For Honda and Toyota in particular, firm image is not just a matter of material benefits, but their standing in society in terms of trust and respect.

Responsibility to society

On average, the Japanese and German firms have more codes for responsibility to society than the US firms. However, the low percentage of codes for Honda and BMW, and the particularly noticeable coding divergence between General Motors and Ford, make it difficult to reach clear conclusions about national differences. The qualitative nature of firms' statements is more illuminating. While all firms refer to their responsibility to society, some of the German and Japanese firms see themselves as *part* of society and enmeshed in it, whereas the US firms see themselves as outside society with responsibility *to* it.

Despite coding significantly less than its German counterparts, BMW nevertheless sees itself as 'anchored in society as a reliable partner', the result being that it 'creates acceptance for its products'. This anchoring in society is mirrored in DaimlerChrysler's statements. It sees itself as 'bound up in an intricate web of relationships' that mean 'over and above our commercial status as an automaker, we are very much a part of the society in which we operate'. Volkswagen stops short of saying it is part of society, but comes close when it says it is a 'partner to society', and 'hand-in-hand with society'.

Of the Japanese firms, Nissan does not quite make the link. Like Volkswagen it is close to being part of society, but still primarily sees itself as 'contributing' and 'collaborating'. Honda makes the link, in saying it is 'a responsible member *of* society' (emphasis added), but it is Toyota that waxes most lyrical declaring that 'as a member of society [it will] actively participate in social actions'. In its policy statements, Toyota says its employees should 'be contributive to the development and welfare of the country by working together, regardless of position, in faithfully fulfilling [their] duties', and 'pursue growth in harmony with the global community through innovative management'.

There should be no doubt that US firms' statements on their responsibility to society are strong. Ford identifies the need for 'a public commitment to strengthen our connection with society' and wishes to bring about a transition to a more environmentally sustainable society in this context. It seeks to 'contribute to the communities around the world in which we work'. General Motors also seeks to be a 'constructive influence' and wants to 'meet the needs of both our customers and society as a whole'. There is nothing weak about these sentiments, but they clearly make the firms 'us' and society 'them'. German and Japanese firms make as strong, if not stronger links, and in some cases there is no gap to bridge between the two.

Responsibility to stakeholders

The main difference in the codes for statements of responsibility to society versus responsibility to stakeholders, is that the former refers more to social responsibility generally (for example, local communities, national and global society, etc.) while the latter refers to those directly impacted by the firm's business (e.g. customers, suppliers, employees and government). US firms clearly have a higher proportion of their social attitudes codes for responsibility to stakeholders. General Motors and Ford have 38 and 36 per cent of their codes on responsibility to stakeholders, whereas German firms have around 30 per cent, and Japanese firms code in a range from 15–33 per cent. Given that Ford and General Motors are LME-based firms, it is perhaps not surprising that they make more statements of responsibility to those directly affected by their business, rather than society more generally. This is commensurate with the point made in the previous section that their statements separate them somewhat more from 'society' than is the case for the German and Japanese firms. Yet, concern for stakeholder relations in addition to short-term market outcomes should also hold weight for CME-based firms.

Qualitative differences shed light on this puzzle. The key difference between the German and Japanese firms on the one hand, and US firms on the other, is the degree to which material versus normative motivations are stressed. The US firms see responsibility more in instrumental materialist terms. For example, Ford talks of 'seeking enhanced stakeholder loyalty as a route to competitive advantage and long term growth', and 'actively pursuing the benefits derived from a diverse workforce, as well as those from the diversity of perspectives provided by our stakeholders'. Similarly, General Motors notes that it has 'long recognized the importance of government policies, international relations, environmental performance and labor and community responsibilities to [its] business'. Responsibility to stakeholders is not always stressed for environmental reasons as much as it is beneficial to firms' material interests. Therefore, although responsibility to stakeholders is highlighted by US firms (a motivation not predicted by the VOC approach), this is for material reasons (a motivation that is predicted by the VOC approach).

By contrast, the German and Japanese firms view responsibility to stakeholders as valuable *in and of itself*. Although DaimlerChrysler notes that it considers 'commitment to the interests of our employees and of society at large not an obligation but an investment in the future of DaimlerChrysler', and Toyota mentions 'work with business partners in research and creation to achieve stable, long term growth and mutual benefits', the Japanese and German firms tend to go beyond the purely material benefits. The following statement by Toyota illustrates the point:

> Toyota hopes that the 21st century will be truly prosperous for society, and aims to grow as a company together with its stakeholders, including customers, shareholders, business partners, and employees, through making things and making automobiles, while seeking harmony with people, society, the global environment and the world economy.

Responsibility to stakeholders is coupled with concern for a prosperous society and the interests of all people generally. In fact, Volkswagen and BMW reverse causality by saying that acting responsibly is actually in the material interests of their stakeholders, rather than the firm. The other Japanese firms make no mention of material interests in the context of responsibility to stakeholders *at all*.

Social attitudes and the Varieties of Capitalism approach

The analysis of coding for social attitudes produces the following clear observations in respect of the VOC approach that relate to the different emphasis accorded material factors in LMEs versus CMEs.

Honda, Nissan and Volkswagen (and Toyota to some extent qualitatively) are most likely to see changing social concerns as a cause for action, or a demand that must be met for their firm's survival. Apart from the post-material values implications analysed in Chapter 5 (that is, that social attitudes are taken most seriously in Japan) this suggests that these firms are more proactive than reactive to social attitudes. They anticipate rather than respond to these to enhance their image, and act in a manner that they see as responsible to society and/or their stakeholders. It also indicates that CME-based firms can substantially alter their environmental performance on the basis of social concerns, not just on the basis of material market forces. Japanese (with the exception of Nissan) and German firms also see their image regarding the environment *specifically* as highly important. While the former have proportionally more codes than the latter, both make strong statements on image in this regard. And while there is considerable variance in proportional terms on responsibility to society, in qualitative terms, Japanese and German firms make stronger statements than their US counterparts. Only on responsibility to stakeholders do US firms quantitatively lead Japanese and German firms in coding proportions. However, again, in qualitative terms they remain more materially focused.

The implications are clear and go to the CME/LME divide between the firms. Not only do the German firms and Toyota code most for social attitudes overall, the German and Japanese firms are more disposed to place themselves *within* society and take account of their social responsibilities, image and social concerns in a more holistic fashion than the US firms. When the US firms report their rationales in respect of social concerns they are clearly thinking more about their material returns factors. Their focus is more on the impact their business has on those most closely related to it, rather than on society generally.

Internal Company Strategies

The Japanese firms stress internal company strategies most (that is, 34–39 per cent of all their codes by comparison to 12–25 per cent for the German and US firms – see Figure 6.4). With this in mind, Table 6.5 shows the composition of firms' codes for internal company strategies. The three codes within the subcategories of internal company strategies; corporate policy; history/path dependence; and leader's vision are considered in turn.

Table 6.5 Normative factors – internal company strategies

		Corporate policy	History/path dependence	Leader's vision	Total	Total
		(%)	(%)	(%)	(%)	(No.)
Germany	Volkswagen	78	22	0	100	27
	BMW	86	14	0	100	7
	DaimlerChrysler	93	7	0	100	15
Japan	Toyota	81	14	5	100	21
	Honda	65	35	0	100	17
	Nissan	64	32	4	100	25
US	General Motors	75	25	0	100	12
	Ford	50	7	43	100	14
Total		73	21	6	100	138

Source: Company environmental reports.

176

Corporate policy

German firms and Japanese firms code more for corporate policy than their US counterparts (64–93 per cent versus 50–75 per cent). This suggests they are more endogenously motivated on environmental matters as they cite firm-wide guidelines or corporate beliefs and strategies in place. It further suggests they have a stronger *commitment* to environmental considerations because they have internalized them as part of how they do business. This is especially the case for the Japanese firms which proportionally code most for internal company strategies overall.

Such suggestions are borne out by the qualitative nature of the statements made. Of the US firms, Ford's strongest statement of corporate policy is as follows:

> Our ultimate goal is to build great products, a strong business and a better world. As with the vehicles we create, this goal is evolving over time from initial concept to final product. We know that true leadership will require strong vision and values, as well as perseverance and patience. It also will require dedicated leaders and active partners.

This is a highly aspirational statement (that is, a 'goal' of 'great products, a strong business and a better world'). General Motors' strongest statement is similar:

> Integrity is one of our core values; we live it every day, with each decision we make and each action we take. Integrity transcends borders, language and culture; it's all about creating an environment that supports, and demands, proper business conduct. Doing the right thing is not always convenient, but it's essential to sustaining our culture of integrity and our leadership position in corporate responsibility. It means honest and accurate reporting of our performance, both internally and externally. It means competing – and succeeding – by the rules, whether they are laws, regulations, or simply GM policy. It means making our actions match our words.

General Motors wants to 'do the right thing' with 'integrity' and be 'honest', and declares its commitment to corporate responsibility. However, neither of the US firms gives a sense of exactly *why* they have such policies. This is left implicit, or such policies are presented as a 'good thing' in and of themselves.

DaimlerChrysler makes similar statements to the US firms, but the other German firms elaborate further. BMW and Volkswagen see elevating the corporate priority of environmental concerns as good for business. For example, BMW says:

> Corporate governance is an all-embracing issue that affects all areas of the company. Taking responsibility for our actions, transparency and trust in

others have long been the principles of our corporate culture. This corporate culture is essential for the success of the BMW Group both today and in the future.

BMW further says that its 'product and market offensive' incorporates environmental responsibility in order to 'safeguard the future of the BMW Group on a sustainable basis'. Volkswagen makes similar statements, but also cites cultural reasons for adopting corporate environmental policies. It says: 'Volkswagen is a company with German roots, European values and global responsibility. The rights, personal development, social security and economic participation of its employees are core elements of corporate policy'. Thus, for Volkswagen there is something 'German' and 'European' about its corporate policy.

Where Volkswagen and BMW start, Japanese firms take off, waxing lyrical once again. Honda has its environmental policies because it 'wishes to preserve the environment for future generations', and to 'pass on the beautiful natural environment' to them. This is all part of the firm's desire 'to pass on our joys to the next generation'. Such a view of the firm's role in ensuring inter-generational equity is said to flow through to its employees who adhere to company policies because they are 'both a member of the company and of society'. Nissan also has a corporate vision that is about more than the firm's material position. As Honda wants to pass on 'joy', Nissan has a 'corporate vision of enriching people's lives', and therefore is on a 'social mission'. The reason is elaborated as follows:

> It is our view that the basis of environmental protection lies in the human capacity to show kindness and concern. Along with striving to understand the environment better, all of us at Nissan bring a shared concern for people, society, nature and the Earth to bear on our activities.

Nissan's aim is to bring about 'symbiosis of people, vehicles and nature'. Like Honda, Nissan's environmental policies are based on notions of inter-generational equity, as it says: 'we will not accept short term gains if it means compromising our future needs or the ability of future generations to meet their own needs'. Toyota makes similar statements, and cites the precepts of its founding father, Sakichi Toyoda, who enjoined Toyota as a company to 'be at the vanguard of the times through endless creativity, inquisitiveness and pursuit of improvement', and to be 'practical and avoid frivolity'. As a result, everyone at Toyota is required to 'dedicate [them]selves to providing clean and safe products and to enhancing the quality of life everywhere through all our activities'.

Qualitatively, it appears that statements on corporate policy fall into three categories: we do it because it's a good thing to do (that is, no explicit reason); we do it because it's good for us (that is, instrumental material motivations); and we do it because of a higher vision (that is, a strong statement of belief that goes above and beyond material concerns). US firms' statements are very much in the first category, German firms to some extent belong in the second category. The third category goes to statements of belief based on higher principles than financial returns that Volkswagen hints at in its cultural references, but Japanese firms make explicit. Their statements demonstrate visions of inter-generational equity, and a concern for the wellbeing of society and the natural environment that go well beyond material motivations.

History/path dependence
The Japanese firms code most on citing their histories, and thus the path dependence of previous action/concern/decisions in taking their current environmental initiatives – 17–35 per cent of Japanese internal strategy codes relate to this, versus 7–25 per cent for the US and German firms. This suggests that in coding strongly for internal company strategies, Japanese firms do so from the perspective of an enduring firm culture. It also suggests that they have a 'head start' on their US and German counterparts by being more historically 'locked in' to embracing environmental initiatives.

A qualitative analysis reveals further that only the Japanese firms, and Volkswagen, identify a history of environmental product development initiatives *specifically*. Volkswagen says its environmental policies date back to the 1970s when its Environmental Department was established, and cites its experience in environmental technologies. Of the Japanese firms, Toyota traces its environmental concern to the Toyoda Precepts handed down by its founder, Sakichi Toyoda, and the codifying of its environmental principles in 1992. Nissan presents a summary of its environmental efforts and achievements dating back to the 1960s, noting that its current environmental initiatives flow from 'the accumulation of technology over the years'. Similarly, Honda discusses its environmental initiatives since the 1960s to highlight that it 'has long been engaged in environmental conservation'.

None of the other German and US firms specifically refer to a history of *environmental* commitments in the same manner. For example, DaimlerChrysler says it has a '115 year tradition of technological leadership and innovation', echoed by General Motors which notes its history of innovation as well, while BMW and General Motors say they have a long history of strong principles in terms of taking responsibility for their actions more generally – for example, General Motors talks of a legacy of 'doing business the right way'. Ford somewhat obtusely refers to 'building on our heritage'. Therefore, although path dependence is important for all firms, quantitatively it is most important for the Japanese firms, and only they and Volkswagen refer to path dependence in environmental product development initiatives specifically.

Leader's vision

There is only one observation to make on this rationale for action, and that is its importance to Ford. Although Nissan and Toyota's executives make statements in support of their firms' environmental initiatives, the support of Ford Chairman and CEO Bill Ford is *personal*. For example, he declares: 'when I became Chairman of Ford Motor Company five years ago, I pledged that we would distinguish ourselves as a great company through our efforts to make the world a better place' and 'one thing that has not changed is my belief that improved sustainability performance is not just a requirement, but a tremendous business opportunity'. He relates his beliefs to his place in the lineage of the firm's founding family:

> My family connects me to the automotive business in a unique way. I feel a special responsibility and pride in the contributions Ford makes to the quality of life of our employees, customers, business partners and neighbors worldwide. I am dedicated to ensuring that we are the best automotive company in the world, by any measure.

Statements such as these reveal that environmental initiatives are not so much a case of corporate policy, or even path dependence in the sense of previous strategies, as personal beliefs and vision held a man ancestrally related to the firm's founding father.

In fact, a noticeable feature of Ford's environmental report is the importance of its leaders' visions generally. There is no distinct 'vision' section, but rather Bill Ford says at the outset that he has 'asked a group of our senior leaders to develop a sensible approach to the issues of climate change, energy security and fuel economy'. Their thoughts and views, sprinkled throughout the report as it provides evidence of the company's environmental performance, thus largely constitute the firm's vision. They are therefore what was coded as the vision statement of the company in this analysis.

Internal company strategies and the Varieties of Capitalism approach

There are three clear observations on internal company strategies that relate to the VOC approach.

First, the internally-driven nature of firm strategies under Japanese CME capitalism is evident. Quantitatively and qualitatively this is where their strategic drive for environmental initiatives lies. And having taken action to focus on the environment as a strategic priority early, there is a path dependence about their ongoing environmental initiatives.

Second, the internal drivers are not just quantitatively weaker for the German and US firms, they are qualitatively less clear. Of the German firms, only Volkswagen approaches the Japanese firms in the importance accorded internal company strategies. For the others, the more outwardly-driven stakeholder model of German CME capitalist relations would seem to explain their divergence from the Japanese firms. Even so, their statements indicate that they are more internally driven than their US counterparts, which is to be expected as LME-based firms focus more on the exogenous factors of market forces and state regulations. This may explain why when US firms highlight the corporate policy aspects of their environmental commitments, though the language they use is strong, their rationales are not.

This brings us to the third observation, which is the importance of the leader's vision in US-based LME firms. The greater unilateral power of top management in LMEs suggests that if environmental commitments are a management priority, they are more likely to be a firm's priority too. Hence the importance of the views of a firm's leaders in whether environmental strategies are embraced. In the case of Ford, top management commitment is evident. In the case of General Motors it is not.

SUSTAINABILITY

Although not specifically related to the VOC approach, the frequency with which the concept of sustainability appears in the reports prompted coding for it as a separate category. Table 6.6 summarizes the results of coding for the degree to which environmental sustainability is stressed, and the degree to which it is seen as intertwined with firms' economic fortunes. It shows that firms are three to four times more likely to cite environmental sustainability as a rationale for action, than explicitly linking it with economic sustainability. When they do, Japanese firms are the most likely to make the connection, although Ford and BMW come close.

Clearly though, the concept of environmental sustainability occurs most in German firms' reports: Volkswagen mentions it 66 times, BMW 45 times and DaimlerChrysler 21 times. The frequency of codes also explains why the proportion of codes linking environmental sustainability and economic sustainability appears slightly lower for the German firms as opposed to the Japanese firms. Given that the German firms code so much more for the concept of environmental sustainability, although they draw the link between it and economic sustainability, the sheer magnitude of coding on the former makes the percentage of coding on the latter smaller. There is no doubt that, based on the sheer *number* of times the concept of sustainability is mentioned, the German firms (especially Volkswagen)

Table 6.6   Summary totals of concern for sustainability

		Environmental sustainability	Environmental and economic sustainability linked	All codes	All codes
		(%)	(%)	(%)	(No.)
Germany	Volkswagen	88	12	100	66
	BMW	67	33	100	45
	DaimlerChrysler	81	19	100	21
	German average	80	20	100	132
Japan	Toyota	60	40	100	5
	Honda	57	43	100	7
	Nissan	67	33	100	18
	Japanese average	63	37	100	30
US	General Motors	100	0	100	3
	Ford	69	31	100	16
	US average	74	26	100	19
Total		76	24	100	181

Source: Company environmental reports.

have comprehensively adopted the concept of sustainability as something to be cited and taken seriously in their environmental reporting.

There are also qualitative differences that relate to the *way* in which the two concepts are linked. At one end of the spectrum are firms that see their future economic and environmental sustainability as inextricably intertwined. They make statements that elevate environmental concerns and sustainability not just to sit alongside, but to be part of, economic sustainability. These firms include the Japanese firms of Toyota and Honda, the German firms of Volkswagen and DaimlerChrysler, and Ford. For example, Toyota says:

> If the automobile is to remain a beneficial tool in the twenty first century, environmental responses are essential. Without environmental responses, the automobile industry has no future, and Toyota is convinced that only automakers that succeed in this area will be acceptable to society.

Honda similarly says that only through 'preservation of the global environment . . . will [it] be able to count on a successful future not only for [the] company, but for the entire world'. Volkswagen makes statements such as: 'we can only achieve lasting economic success if our business activities are guided not only by social considerations but by ecological aspects as well'. DaimlerChrysler expresses similar sentiments. Ford recognizes that the task of 'integrating' economic, social and environmental responsibilities is difficult, and that these can sometimes appear to be 'at odds', but even so sustainable development must be elevated 'to sit alongside other business imperatives'. It looks like more a question of balance for Ford, were it not for the firm's Chairman and CEO saying that environmental concerns are 'a key element in building [the] company for the next 100 years' and that it is only through addressing environmental questions that automobiles can 'secure their role in providing mobility to a growing and changing world'.

Nissan and BMW conceive the link between economic and environmental sustainability more in terms of balance where both are, to some degree, competing aims. Nissan makes several statements to this end, such as the following:

> There is strong interest in the world today about how to balance economic development with environmental protection. Economic growth does not necessarily threaten the environment. To the contrary, investments in technology can greatly benefit our understanding of the world we live in and how to preserve it. Collaboration among corporations, civic organizations, governments, and society in general will help move the world towards an effective balance between a healthy environment and healthy growth.

This statement clearly reflects a concern for balance between competing, or at least alternative, interests. It is reflected in others made by the company, along the lines that 'continued innovation is crucial to achieve a balance between economic development and the protection of the natural environment'. However, there is also a sense in Nissan's reports that economic growth hinges on environmental sustainability. For example, Nissan states that 'protecting the environment is the single most important aspect of sustainability', with environmental initiatives 'needed to allow economic development to continue'. Perhaps the nuances are subtle, but while Nissan suggests the need to strike a balance, Toyota, says that not just economic development, but the very future of the automobile itself, *depends* on environmental action.

The distinction is clearest in the case of BMW. Although a belief is expressed that 'the company's economic success and the efficient use of resources in the entire value added chain depend upon one another', this is coupled with the idea that 'economic efficiency and sustainability can be compatible with one another'. It is not that they are/must be, but that it is possible that they *can* be, and then in rather a material sense of using resources efficiently. The firm's vision statements make the distinction plainer, such as: 'for the BMW Group, long term economic success provides the basis for its activities. It is only on this basis that the company can assume responsibility permanently and sustainably'. Similarly: 'for the BMW Group, economic success is both the prime objective and stable basis for assuming responsibility for . . . the environment'. Therefore, environmental sustainability is *contingent* on economic success. In BMW's environmental policy, the focus then is on how to 'reconcile the interests of people and nature, technology and progress with the right of future generations to an intact environment'.

All of this is not a matter of 'black and white', but more 'shades of grey'. BMW, like Nissan, recognizes the need to reconcile competing interests, whereas Toyota, Honda, DaimlerChrysler, Volkswagen and Ford see their economic future as depending on both. But one thing is clear: General Motors does not draw the link at all. The closest it comes is acknowledging that its operations have environmental impacts, and recognizing this it works to 'continuously reduce the environmental impacts of our business in line with a commitment to contribute to sustainable development'. The idea that environmental and economic sustainability are linked, or that one is dependent on the other, is an association never explicitly made. It is also the case that General Motors codes least on environmental sustainability, with a mere three statements.

In summary, with the notable exception of General Motors, all firms explicitly associate their economic fortunes with environmental sustainability. As a proportion of their codes for environmental sustainability, Japanese firms are most likely to do so and to see the two as inextricably intertwined. German firms are less likely to code for the linkage than Japanese firms. BMW's statements, like Nissan's, are somewhat weaker as they refer more to balancing competing aims than ones that are mutually reinforcing. However, the German firms are most likely to mention the concept of environmental sustainability in the first place.

Not only does General Motors not make an explicit link between environmental and economic sustainability, it also refers to the concept of environmental sustainability the least. The suspicion this raises is that without the strength of commitment to environmental strategies of its Chairman and CEO, Ford too, LME-style, might also downplay the importance of environmental concerns as a strategic business issue in favor of more material priorities.

CONCLUSION

At least three caveats are worth bearing in mind in respect of the analysis in this chapter. First, a caricature has been drawn. National similarities and points of difference have been emphasized rather than variations within them. However, this is necessary in any comparative analysis. One wishes to tease out the similarities and differences within and between groups/categories, whether in terms of absolutes or degree, and the resulting implications (see Sartori, 1970; Collier and Mahon, 1993; Adcock and Collier, 2001; Collier and Adcock, 1999). Second, the analysis has focused on distinct sections of the firms' reports. All the rationales for action within these sections may be found to varying degrees elsewhere in them. However, the intention was to compare similar report sections, and particularly those sections where rationales for environmental action would be most likely to be found. Third, the dichotomous division of material versus normative factors is to some extent a simplification for the sake of empirical analysis. The idea was to tease out whether firms ascribe their motivations more to material (logic of consequentialism) versus normative (logic of appropriateness) factors. It is worth acknowledging again here, as in Chapter 1, that in either case firms' interests are 'material' in the sense that they matter to them, are perceived by them as being important in how they convey their motivations, and no doubt are perceived as affecting their performance.

Bearing these caveats in mind, clear differences in the rationales presented by firms have been revealed. The US firms couch their environmental initiatives more in material terms of market forces. In taking action that is environmentally positive, the rationales they present are of market imperatives: what consumers demand, what the competition imposes and what safeguards their financial returns. This reflects a preference for market modes of economic coordination in LMEs. In adhering to regulations, voluntary rather than imposed regulation is preferred, and the purpose of being involved in the policy process is to ensure their material interests are not overly compromised. This reflects a preference for arm's-length government involvement in markets in LMEs. Although social concerns are important, these are seen more in terms of how they affect business interests, and the interests of stakeholders predominate (defined here as those with an interest in, and who are directly affected by, the firm's material interests). Again, the LME model, based as it is on shareholder value and a resulting preoccupation with profits in the shorter term, supports such a perspective. In LME fashion, internal drivers for change are not as important as external (mainly market) imperatives unless, as in the case of Ford, individual leaders' perspectives result in them coming to the fore. This is because of management's more unilateral control over firm strategies in LMEs. Commensurate with this, sustainability as a concept is recognized, but not necessarily mutually supportive of economic interests, unless such top management commitment is present.

The German and Japanese firms' rationales look almost irrational, perhaps even non-genuine, when viewed through an LME lens. One is tempted to declare that Honda is pulling our collective legs when it says it is motivated not by profits but 'joy'! However, such statements make more sense if viewed through a CME lens.

The German firms are more focused on normative than material factors, particularly social concerns. This is commensurate with the German CME model which sees firms as bearing public responsibility for their actions and looking to social attitudes in upholding such responsibilities. Their image and standing matters to them from an economic perspective, but also in terms of their role in society. Market forces are more an underlying concern than one given primacy for action. Even if BMW is as concerned as US firms about safeguarding its financial interests, it remains otherwise less focused on market forces in terms of consumer demand and competitive pressures than on social attitudes. While German firms share a US preference for voluntary agreements, they couple this with a desire to be proactive in the policy process in achieving consensus-based agreements that serve environmental as well as material/business agendas. Close and cooperative, consensus-based state–business relations, predicted by the VOC approach, are therefore central to their perspective on state regulation. They are therefore likely to develop internal corporate policies to further their environmental goals in the light of social concerns and their close relations with the state, and the result is a commitment to environmental sustainability not just as a concept, but for its links to their future economic interests.

The Japanese firms share similar drivers for action with their German counterparts, including in respect of social attitudes. But while German firms exhibit traits of the German 'machine', in which a more integrated approach to the environment involving more than material factors pertains, the Japanese firms do so in a more 'organic' way that reflects the enterprise community aspects of Japanese CME capitalist relations of production. They have a tendency to be 'poetic' and wax lyrical. They are particularly driven by their internal cultures, as predicted by the importance ascribed to communitarian company group, consensus-based strategy development and implementation within CME-based Japanese firms. They are therefore driven by internal corporate policies and a strong sense of history/firm culture that gives them impetus for environmental action. They are also focused on social concerns, but in terms of leading society, being respected and doing their social *duty*. They are most likely to see environmental and economic sustainability as linked, especially from the point of view of social acceptability. They are not so much focused on voluntary regulations as German and US firms, but on achieving and exceeding the legislative requirements they have agreed with national regulators. As their CME variety of capitalism would suggest, a longer-term view based on future benefits and market leadership, rather than shareholder value, is the result. Their aim is not just to get products on the market, but to lead the market in new and uncharted directions with more radical products. They want to lead not just in material competitive terms, but in meeting broader (in this case environmental) goals.

Despite the national differences a final point should be stressed. It is that these German, US and Japanese firms may all be on a journey that leads to the same destination: more environmentally responsible behavior. It is just that they are taking a different path, largely based on the VOC of their home states. Where the US firms are focused on material factors, such as consumer demand and market forces generally, and even see normative concerns in more instrumental terms, the German and Japanese firms are more focused on social attitudes and internal company strategies so that a more normative approach to their business interests is shifting them to more environmentally friendly behavior. Ultimately, they all may arrive at the same destination, but the US firms will have got there with an eye on their financial bottom lines, whereas the German and Japanese firms will have taken a course of action that they believe to be normatively 'right' and which at the end of the day has delivered material benefits. It is not so much a matter of 'greenwashing' versus real commitment, but considering different paths to that commitment, and the different drivers that facilitate it in different institutional contexts.

These conclusions have been derived, or perhaps suggested, via an analysis of firms' executive statements, vision statements and environmental policy guidelines in their environmental reports. They support the findings so far in Chapters 4 and 5, vis-à-vis state regulations and market forces, and add the perspectives of individual firms' internal strategies. However, to build on the insights these environmental reports shed on individual firms' rationales for action, the views expressed by key personnel willing to be interviewed within them are the subject of analysis in Chapter 7.

NOTES

1. Although, as noted in Chapter 1, a more nuanced conception of the divide between material and normative factors is not an either/or one. More accurately, it is one in which it is recognized that economic actors such as firms have material interests, and the question then is whether the material 'facts' of these should be the focus for analysis, versus normative aspects of how these interests are perceived (see, for example, Hay 2006a and b).
2. These were their most recent reports as at March 2005 when the analysis was conducted. They are: Volkswagen AG (2003), *Environmental Report 2003/2004: Partners*

in Sustainability, Wolfsburg: Volkswagen AG; BMW Group (2003a), *Sustainable Value Report 2003/2004: Innovation. Efficiency. Responsibility*, Munich: Bayerischen Motoren Werke; DaimlerChrysler (2004), *360 Degrees: Environmental Report 2004: Alliances for the Environment*, Stuttgart: DaimlerChrysler Communications, including accompanying CD ROM; Toyota Motor Corporation (2004), *Environmental and Social Report 2004*, Tokyo: Toyota Motor Corporation; Honda Motor Company (2004), *Honda Environmental Annual Report 2004*, Tokyo: Honda Motor Company; Nissan Motor Company (2004a), *Environmental Report 2004*, Tokyo: Nissan Motor Company; General Motors Corporation (2004), *2004 Corporate Responsibility Report*, Detroit: General Motors Corporation; Ford Motor Company (2004), *2003/4 Corporate Citizenship Report: Our Principles, Progress and Performance: Connecting with Society*, Dearborn: Ford Motor Company. Two additional reports were coded for Honda and Nissan: Honda Motor Company (2002), *Honda Ecology*, Tokyo: Honda Motor Company; and Nissan Motor Company (2004b), *Sustainability Report 2004*, Tokyo: Nissan Motor Company. The reason for this is that while both produce specifically 'Environmental Reports', these are augmented with additional reports that put their initiatives in a broader perspective. In the case of Honda, its 'Ecology' report, produced every three years, presents an overview of the company's policy, vision and future directions in relation to the environment, as opposed to its 'Environmental Report' that covers performance in the past year. Nissan produced its 'Sustainability Report' for the first time in 2004 in addition to its 'Environmental Report'. In addition, Volkswagen's environmental policy guidelines were also coded because they are referred to and summarized in the 2003/4 report, but printed in full on the firm's website and in the firm's 2001–02 report. It was therefore thought prudent to include them. They are available at: Volkswagen AG (2001) *Environmental Report 2001/2002: Mobility and Sustainability*, Wolfsburg: Volkswagen AG. Similarly, BMW's environmental policy guidelines were included from BMW Group (2003b), *Environmental Protection: BMW Group Environmental Guidelines*, http://www.bmwgroup.com/e/0_0_www_bmwgroup_com/5_verantwortung/5_4_pub-likationen/5_4_4_downloads/pdf/BMWGroup_Umweltleitlinen_E.pdf, accessed 13 January 2005. These are only available from the website, although the website address where they may be found is provided in the firm's written report.

3. DaimlerChrysler (2004: 85) notes that 'the contributor line-up for the 2004 Daimler-Chrysler Environmental Report is once again a blend of experienced writers and award-winning newcomers – an alliance of journalists, photographers, and graphic designers who share a passion for high-quality copy, striking images, and topics that open a window on the future'. General Motors expresses the hope that its report 'provides you with a valuable insight into General Motors, our performance, culture and values' (General Motors Corporation, 2004: 1.1).

4. Ford acknowledges that what appears in its written report is what is most important. For example, Ford says the following in its report for 2003/04: 'we have expanded our coverage of the environment and safety issues in the print report because of their importance to us and to our stakeholders' (Ford Motor Company, 2004: 11).

5. These averages are calculated as a weighted average of the codes for individual firms. For example, if one firm has 100 codes in total and 40 of these are for market forces, and another has 150 codes in total also with 40 on market forces, the average is calculated as $(40+40)/(100+150)\times100=32$ per cent.

6. That is to say, the enterprise community is more the focus for Japanese firms, versus society as a whole for German firms.

7. That is to say, market forces and state regulation are subcategories of material factors, and the categories considered here fall below them.

8. As a matter of policy the firm does say that it wants to 'promote the appeal of cars throughout the world and strengthen the Toyota brand image.'

7.　Firms' commitment: interviews

There's not green flowing through our veins, we're a car company after all!
(Ford interviewee)

Recycling, not taking plastic bags from the supermarket and taking your own canvas bags etc., these are all little things but they're slowly building a level of consciousness about the environment that makes us rush to introduce a vehicle like Prius into the market.
(Toyota interviewee)

Firms' rationales for their environmental commitments reflect the institutional context of their home states where they are economically, politically, socially, culturally and historically embedded, as well as physically headquartered. This key point, at the center of this book and implied by the Varieties of Capitalism approach, was borne out by the analysis of the major German, US and Japanese firms' environmental reports in Chapter 6. What was shown was that national institutional variations in capitalist relations of production produce different perceptions of what is important in addressing the environmental impact of firms' operations. The analysis also highlighted some key differences at the subnational level. For example, German firms are particularly mindful of consensual cooperation with regulators while taking account of social concerns, whereas Japanese firms place more emphasis on leading society and being internally driven by company policies.

To build on these findings, this chapter seeks to marry firms' stated rationales for environmental commitments with the results of interviews conducted with key personnel from Volkswagen, BMW, Ford and Toyota. Mirroring the analysis in Chapters 4 to 6, interviewees' perceptions of state regulations, the role of market forces, including consumer demand versus social attitudes, and internal company strategies are considered in turn. Therefore, as well as inviting interviewees to comment generally on their firms' environmental product developments, the interviews had a significantly semi-guided component.[1]

For state regulations, interviewees' responses fell broadly into two categories: the role they saw government playing, and the nature of state–business relations in the light of this. The key differences noted are that German and European Union regulations were identified as leading environmental strategies there, and even worldwide, to an extent not high-lighted for Japan and the US. This was associated with a different causal relationship between business and government that interviewees identi-fied. The state was seen as developing environmental strategies in partner-ship with firms in the case of the German companies. Toyota personnel said that their firm is leading government. Ford interviewees said that their company acts in a more reactive manner to state regulations. This supports the model proposed in Chapter 4 in Figure 4.9.

For market forces, the role ascribed to consumer demand versus social attitudes was highlighted. The key point made by interviewees was that, as suggested by the analysis in Chapter 5, social attitudes on the environment have not flowed though to consumer demand as clearly as some com-mentators might hope. The role played by social attitudes in influencing company strategies varied between interviewees. Social attitudes appear to be discounted in favor of consumer demand in the case of Ford, but the German and Japanese interviewees stressed the role of social attitudes more in shaping their firms' environmental strategies.

For internal company strategies, interviewees made comments that suggested the main drivers for environmental attributes in the cars they produce, the way in which this is associated with their firms' desires to be 'leaders', the role played by senior management, and the role of path dependence. Analysing their comments demonstrates that, as suggested by the analysis in Chapter 6, Japanese firms such as Toyota are most internally-driven, while US firms are least internally-driven on environ-mental strategies. Indeed, when it came to 'leadership', the Japanese and German firms' interviewees were prepared to identify their firms' environmental strategies as a key aspect of their leadership strategies generally, particularly in the case of Toyota, while for Ford interviewees environmental leadership was more contingent on material factors. The exception for Ford was the key role ascribed to senior management, in that the firm's Chairman and CEO, Bill Ford, was identified as a key driver of Ford's environmental strategies. This goes to the more unilat-eral control exerted by management in liberal market economy (LME)-based firms. Finally, the point is made that with all the various drivers for environmental strategies, interviewees identified what amounted to path dependence as a key factor, as indeed it is for the VOC approach more generally.

Therefore, the aspects of their firms' rationales for environmental commit-ments highlighted by interviewees are related to the points made in previous chapters, and build on them. They support the insights of the VOC approach. The chapter concludes with observations made by interviewees on the impli-cations of their opinions for future strategic directions, and the international implications of national variations in capitalist relations of production. Two clear conclusions are reached. First, interviewees' responses indicate that the rationales offered by firms in their environmental reports reflect attitudes that filter down to lower management levels worldwide. Therefore, the institutional context of firms' home states permeate their operations internationally. Second, and most important, the relative importance ascribed by interviewees to market forces versus social attitudes, state regulations and internal company strategies confirms the conclusions reached in the preceding chapters based on the empirical evidence at a national level, and firms' rationales expressed in their environmental reports.

CONDUCTING THE INTERVIEWS

All firms whose environmental reports were analysed in Chapter 6 were invited to participate in interviews. Volkswagen, BMW, Ford and Toyota accepted the invitation.[2] In total, interviews were conducted with three personnel from Toyota, five from Ford, and one each from Volkswagen and BMW. In being granted interviews with personnel from these firms, access was given to first-hand perspectives from leading firms within the German, US and Japanese car industries. Volkswagen and Toyota dominate their home markets. Volkswagen also dominates the European market. Ford co-dominates its home market with General Motors. BMW dominates the prestige car segment of the market in Germany and internationally (Deutsche Bank, 2004).

All interviews were with senior Australian personnel, except for Volkswagen. There are three reasons for this. First, all the firms have Australian branch offices. Second, their presence in Australia is not purely of an import and distribution nature. Ford and Toyota have the full array of operations from research and product development, to manufacturing, distribution and sales. Therefore, strategic product development decisions for these firms go beyond simply 'shifting product'. In addition, it is fair to say that the Australian market is a microcosm of the international market because all the major firms are represented in it (Productivity Commission, 2002). Third, interviewing Australian nationals working for these firms tested whether Australian, as opposed to German, US or Japanese, perspectives prevail. This revealed the relative importance of host versus home market conditions, and therefore the strength of the VOC thesis. Volkswagen is the exception to the rule because an interview was conducted with a senior office holder from the firm's German head office. This is because Volkswagen Group Australia recommended this course of action.

As well as inviting interviewees to speak generally on their firms' environmental product developments and motivations behind them, the interviews had a significant semi-guided component through which interviewees were directed to comment on state regulations, market forces (in terms of consumer demand versus social attitudes), and internal company strategies. Time was allowed at the end of interviews for interviewees to express any views they may have felt pertinent that were left out in the course of the interview. The questions asked, and the rationale for asking them, is explained in greater detail in Appendix D.

In the following analysis, direct quotations and views expressed are presented anonymously. This is despite all interviewees bar two being happy for quotations to be attributed to them. Even so, I am mindful of the surprise (and despair) expressed by the late, charismatic, former General Motors executive, John de Lorean, that during his time with the company airing *any* view in the public domain was usually viewed negatively. However pure the motivations of an employee commenting on their company's strategies, there are always others within it who may draw their own conclusions based on personal prejudices and seek to attack that individual (Wright, 1979).

One final point is worth noting. When commenting on the environmental product development initiatives of their firms, all interviewees focused primarily on fuel economy and carbon dioxide emissions. This mirrors to a large extent the focus on these aspects in environmental reports. It also supports the focus on fuel economy, CO_2 emissions and the issue of climate change in this book.

STATE–BUSINESS RELATIONS

All interviewees believed governments need to provide an agenda-setting role, informing and educating their citizens on environmental matters and acting in the interests of society. In practical terms, they all agreed with government support for research and development and for business generally. This includes tax breaks to encourage consumers to purchase more environmentally-friendly vehicles, as well as subsidies to firms. Beyond these points of agreement, there were clear differences of opinion on the role of government regulations, the nature of state–business relations and, as a result of these relations, differences in the causal relationship between regulations and business strategies. These differences appear clearly related to the VOC of firms' home states. Ford interviewees, working for an LME-based firm, primarily saw the government's role as setting regulations to which the firm must adhere.

Interviewees from the German and Japanese firms, based in CMEs, saw state–business relations in more partnership terms, desiring a closer relationship with regulators and, in the case of Toyota, greater state support. As noted in Chapter 4, the differing role ascribed to the state, and the resulting differences in state–business relations, have causal implications in the sense that US firms respond to regulations, whereas German and Japanese firms are instrumental in co-developing regulations and, in the case of Japanese firms, taking the lead in their development. Both the role of government and the resulting differing state–business relations are discussed below.

Although all firms agreed that governments play a key role, some regulations were viewed negatively by Ford interviewees. LME-style, these were market interventions that penalize environmentally-damaging behavior, such as taxes, which were seen as 'blunt instruments' because their effects cannot be clearly predicted.[3] Instead, a preference was expressed for research and development grants to 'accelerate the commercialization and introduction of new technologies' – that is, market *enhancing* initiatives. However, CME-style, support for broader-based state intervention was expressed by the Volkswagen and Toyota interviewees. The Volkswagen interviewee expressed strong support for technologically-neutral regulations based on environmental impact, including standards and excises. Toyota interviewees wanted governments to 'come on board' more and cooperate with their firm in all ways. Therefore, a greater range of state interventions were accepted, even welcomed.

Raised awareness of environmental issues and the influence of the Kyoto Protocol were widely cited as reasons why governments are taking a tougher stance on issues like climate change. Yet when pressed, interviewees could not identify any dramatic changes in regulations that had impacted on their product development strategies. Instead, existing regulations were said to have been incrementally strengthened.[4] Therefore, environmental product development initiatives were not seen as driven by tougher state regulations. This included the petrol-electric hybrid Toyota Prius and Ford Escape. The latter was said by one Ford interviewee to be attributable to state regulations only in the broadest 'directional' sense. Only the Volkswagen interviewee saw his firm's product development initiatives as being the result of state regulations, but then significant impetus was provided by the industry itself. He said:

> When we developed these hybrid cars and so on, and the diesel engine, that was a bit compelled by the agreement between the car industry in Europe and the governments and the European Commission in Europe, because Volkswagen is the largest mass producer here on this continent so we had to carry, I would say, most of the obligations we made there.

Therefore, Volkswagen developed advanced diesels in response to industry co-sponsored EU regulatory targets.

Concomitant with the Volkswagen interviewee's perspective, most interviewees cited the EU as a regulatory leader. The German firms' interviewees saw this as reflecting long-standing initiatives to address environmental concerns over the last 15 to 20 years in both Germany and Europe. Because of their stringency, Ford interviewees said European standards are now *de facto* global standards, as no firm wants to make a unique car just to meet European requirements. Therefore, there is an international trend to harmonize regulations with those of the EU. However, one Toyota interviewee noted that outside the EU, 'pragmatism at the end of the day rules' with progress on environmental matters by the US government particularly slow (unless one counts Californian regulations),[5] and Japan 'responding' to, and slightly lagging, the EU. Any regulatory changes impacting on the international industry were thus said to be largely the result of 'substantial change over the last ten years driven largely by Europe'.

This leads to the key point of difference between German firms and the others: the extent to which governments reflect or lead public opinion. The Volkswagen interviewee said the German government is the protagonist on environmental matters:

> Normally in most countries in the world the Greens are not in the government, so they are the public, so to speak, and they influence the government. Whereas here in Germany they are in the government and there they shape, in a way, public opinion because, of course, they are the strongest exponents for environmental action and the public is less environmentally-friendly than the government.

Therefore, the German government *leads*, rather than reflects, public opinion. The rise of the German Greens to coalition government in the 1990s, mirrored in the rise of similar parties as a political force in a handful of other European countries, was said to mean that 'the government quite often starts, or at least strengthens, the political debate or public debate'. One Toyota interviewee made similar comments on the German Greens' role. Even though the BMW interviewee noted that governments are generally 'more responsive rather than proactive', and tend to react on the basis of 'some external, dramatic, radical, unplanned for change' or a change in public sentiment that affects their re-election chances, he still identified 'a very high level of maturity and thinking about the environment' in Europe reflected in EU legislation and regulations.

Outside Germany and the EU, and agreeing with the BMW interviewee's view of governments generally, one Ford interviewee said that governments are 'reflecting what society thinks or wants'. He explained the reason why as not being related to any grand leadership vision, but because growing environmental awareness affects their re-election chances. One Toyota interviewee was particularly dismissive of government policies saying 'we see a lot of, I suppose, fairly cynical policy statements put out and a lot of window dressing' at worst, or at best 'the ideas and the willingness are there, but they're just not implemented'.

Overall, interviews saw governments playing an important role. Government intervention was expected and desired, although Ford interviewees expressed dislike for governments extensively constraining market forces, as one would expect of their LME view of the primacy of markets and market forces as organizers of economic activity. Although government regulations were not seen as having dramatically changed, there was the feeling that they have incrementally been made more stringent. This is especially the case for Germany and the EU, to the point where the EU was seen as a regulatory leader because the concept of environmental sustainability has been most deeply and strategically institutionalized. The result is that for Germany and the EU, government regulations are playing a leading role in driving environmental sustainability, whereas elsewhere they tend to reflect broader social concerns.

The interviewees' views on the role of governments suggest differences in state–business relations, and the causal relationship between the two. All interviewees' said their firms worked with government in setting and meeting environmental regulations, but their reason for doing so varied. LME perceptions of the state intervening to correct market failure were reflected in Ford interviewees seeing government imposing environmental regulations to which the firm must adhere to remain in business. CME preferences for greater coordination between the state and business were reflected in the Volkswagen interviewee perceiving state regulations as complementing firm strategies, while Toyota interviewees desired more support for their firm's environmental initiatives. The BMW interviewee was relatively silent on the firm's relationship with government, but did stress that BMW always exceeds regulations.

Ford interviewees saw state regulations in the most adversarial terms. This is not to say that the government is somehow the 'enemy'. After all, they cited Ford's voluntary commitments under programs such as the Greenhouse Challenge.[6] Even so, because state regulations temper market forces one Ford interviewee noted that they can be 'unnecessarily stringent', because 'if the customer preference is for high powered thirsty vehicles but the individual company has a particular target to meet, that means they may need to produce unprofitable product to balance that out which doesn't really do anyone any good'. Regulations are too stringent

when they work against market forces too excessively. Another interviewee noted that Ford 'would comply with the regulations in order that
(the firm is) involved in establishing those regulations'. Thus, involvement
in negotiations about regulations was seen as important in order to limit
their impact on market outcomes.

Why sign up to voluntary agreements then? Ford interviewees said the
reason was more to demonstrate that the company is a good corporate
citizen. In respect of the Greenhouse Challenge, one Ford interviewee
said 'big companies' had signed up to it because 'they'd be silly not to'.
He said:

> It's not legislation but it's a strong encouragement to demonstrate that you're
> doing some good things to the rest of the community. So, why are 500 compa-
> nies already signed up to the Greenhouse Challenge? Well, because we all think
> we're good corporate citizens and we want to be able to demonstrate that.

A key reason for voluntary commitments is thus to be seen to be setting a
good example. Indeed, the same interviewee followed up the above statement with the observation that such initiatives are a matter of 'an indirect
carrot and stick that says, well, if you don't do these things there'll be a
penalty further out, not today, but further out'. The motivation implied is
an instrumental desire to reduce the interference of government in future
product development strategies, while using corporate citizenship as a
marketing strategy.

It is important that this finding on Ford not be taken too negatively,
because although they might not always like how the state intervenes,
Ford interviewees also saw the government as having 'a critical role
to play' in 'setting a vision [of] where we need to go'. It was all part of
'the fine balance between industry going forward and progressing, and
the government setting a vision and finding that fine balance between the
economic reality of it and the fact that, yes, we have to progress'. All Ford
interviewees stressed that part of being a responsible corporation and
legitimately remaining in business involved regulatory compliance. As one
Ford interviewee put it, you have to 'hit those regulatory targets otherwise
you literally can't sell your vehicles . . . so the regulatory environment has
a huge role to play in terms of shaping outcomes'. In addition, one Ford
interviewee stressed constructive consultation with government as the key
to achieving good regulatory outcomes. Interestingly though, and in line
with the competitive/confrontational tendencies of such interactions in the
US LME variety of capitalism, the same interviewee conceded he did not
'see that in the US (where) it seems much more confrontational'.

For Ford, meeting environmental regulations is therefore important because these constrain how the firm responds to consumer demand. One interviewee said: 'what we'll look at is what does the customer want, and what are the corporate and regulatory requirements' because 'the regulatory environment will mandate that we deliver certain things'. In other words, business is about reacting to the material imperatives of consumer demand and government regulations. Indeed, 'if there weren't set targets that had to be achieved then [environmental] progress would be made, but knowing you have to hit certain targets naturally makes them more evident and helps shape outcomes and resource allocation'. The result is that for Ford regulations are seen more as a ceiling to be 'hit' than a floor the company is well above.[7]

Although the Volkswagen interviewee shared a belief that the government plays a crucial role, his perception was not so much one of the government intervening to impose regulatory targets that must be hit, as one where the industry and government move forward together in strategic harmony. As he put it, while environmental regulations in Germany and the EU are important, the industry 'actually wants to go in the same direction' as the government. He said:

> There's not so much that one leads and the other follows. It's more the space that grows because companies will of course look more to costs and competitiveness, whereas the government sees more of the health aspects and environmental aspects purely without looking so much at costs and the international competitiveness of their companies.

In other words, Volkswagen does not so much respond to state regulations as share a similar strategic agenda. The emphasis might be different, but the agenda is broadly similar, and it is less a matter of action (by government) and reaction (by industry) as a 'space' in which consensus is reached. This is very much what one would expect of the negotiated consensus attributes of Germany's CME.

While one Toyota interviewee agreed that 'regulations and the forecasted regulations introduction scenario will definitely shape what we do', all Toyota interviewees stressed that the firm is well ahead of regulations. The point was made that Toyota has a corporate policy of certifying all its vehicles in excess of regulatory requirements. Toyota interviewees actually saw state leadership on environmental issues as a thing of the past. Two Toyota interviewees described the visit of a senior environmental director from Toyota's head office and his message to staff to illustrate this point. One said:

> Somebody asked that question: how do you think government can help Toyota move forward? He basically said we don't think you can because 20 years ago a lot of the legislation and guidelines helped direct us, gave us direction, but now

we're waiting for government to catch up because they've already surpassed every form of legislation. They already meet or exceed the 2010 emission and fuel economy guidelines for virtually all their range in Japan. He basically said the benchmarks aren't high enough.

His reply, indicating the company does not take its strategic direction on environmental matters from government any more, was summed up in the following terms: 'he wasn't trying to be smug, but he basically said that 20 years ago we needed you but now we're waiting for you to give us more direction and work with us'.

The BMW interviewee made similar points to Ford in saying the firm was always 'mindful of where government policies are going to go' and recognized that 'most legislative criteria are the result of negotiation and compromise', but like Toyota he also stressed that BMW always seeks to exceed government regulations as a matter of corporate strategy. However, unlike Toyota, it was not so much a matter of leading government as being aware of regulations and designing products to meet forecast future regulations. The reason for this was explained as BMW's ethos of leadership in everything it does as a premium producer. The BMW interviewee said:

> Our focus [is] on being innovative and not just being responsive to proposed or existing legislation. We take that into account in our planning. I mean, we wouldn't say that we're only going to do this because it's required by government. We'd say no, let's go a bit further.

Regulations for BMW thus establish a 'floor', rather than a 'ceiling' to be hit. The BMW interviewee summed up this outlook saying 'we'd probably be looking well beyond [current regulations] to make sure that at our lowest base we were well past it so there is no chance of running into any legislative issues down the track, but also to make sure that we remain ahead of the pack'.

State–business relations were thus seen very differently by interviewees from each firm. Ford interviewees, in true LME fashion, saw them as a constraint on reacting to market forces, but necessary because the government's role is to drive the environmental agenda. The German and Japanese interviewees did not see government regulations as setting their environmental agendas as much, although for Volkswagen it can be said that, in CME fashion, working *with* government is a key reason why environmental initiatives have been undertaken. Toyota interviewees went a step further. While sharing BMW's strategy of always exceeding regulations, the Toyota interviewees desired more government involvement to support their firm's environmental strategies.

These results suggest clear causal differences in the relationship between state regulations and business strategies. Ford reacts to and meets current regulations. But Volkswagen travels the same road as government in a cooperative manner, while BMW aims to be aware of proposed future regulations in order to ensure its products always exceed rather than respond to regulatory requirements. Therefore, the German firms have a co-regulatory relationship with government or exceed regulations as a matter of corporate policy. For Toyota, governments were seen as lagging the company's environmental initiatives, and a desire was expressed for them to catch up. The causal relationship this suggests supports the model hypothesized in Figure 4.9. US firms react to regulations, German/ European firms have a more co-regulatory relationship with government (or, in the case of BMW, exceed regulations as a matter of corporate policy) but Japanese firms go beyond the co-regulatory model of Germany/Europe to lead regulators.

MARKET FORCES: CONSUMER DEMAND VERSUS SOCIAL ATTITUDES

All interviewees saw market forces as important because their firms are driven by economic imperatives to maintain/increase their market share and profits. However, perceptions of the strategic role played by social attitudes versus consumer demand differed markedly. Concomitant with the findings of Chapter 5, the analysis of environmental reports in Chapter 6 and the insights of the VOC approach, Ford interviewees stressed the importance of consumer demand above all other factors, while interviewees from the CME-based firms stressed normative factors relating to consumer attitudes. The result is that different forces drive firms' environmental product developments based on different perceptions of just what the market is: consumer demand as 'money on the table' in the case of LME-based Ford, versus a range of more intangible attitudinal factors for the CME-based firms.

All interviewees agreed that concern for the environment has increased. A major reason cited was media exposure of global environmental issues, especially climate change. There was general agreement that concern for the environment will continue to increase, although the Volkswagen interviewee noted that it has actually waned slightly in Germany and Europe in recent years because of 'social problems, mostly labor problems' in Europe that have diverted public attention. Even so, he said Volkswagen expects concern to rise again in future, as there remains a strong underlying awareness of environmental issues as a legacy of the emergence and growth of the German/European environmental movement over the last 20 years.

If concern for the environment is present, the key question is the one asked in Chapter 5: does it flow through to market outcomes via consumer demand? All interviewees agreed that for the most part it does not. Environmental features do not encourage consumers to purchase a vehicle, nor will they pay a premium for them. Other attributes such as comfort, reliability and performance remain higher priorities. Even though Toyota is the market leader in petrol-electric hybrids, one Toyota interviewee admitted that 'the attributes customers are looking for remain "grunt", comfort and space'. Ford interviewees noted an increase in consumers' expectations of all car attributes, including environmental performance, although 'not necessarily in its relative weighting versus the others'.[8] Therefore, consumer demand for more environmentally-friendly products specifically was seen as lacking.

While good environmental performance may not impact positively on sales, the Volkswagen interviewee noted that bad environmental performance can impact negatively. Volkswagen customers expect their cars to meet environmental standards and will not buy cars that fail to do so. Similarly, the BMW interviewee said that environmental performance is an attribute BMW customers expect as a matter of course because they conceive environmental attributes as intrinsic to a product that is the latest, the best, the most efficient and highest performing. He said:

> The focus is on efficiency rather than merely economy, because we are in the prestige or luxury part of the market where from customers' perspective they're not totally driven to BMW by the amount of petrol they'll save by driving economically in one of our cars, but they want to know whether it is efficient, and they want to know they're getting the most performance they can out of their engines.

Therefore, environmental performance is a *quality* attribute for BMW.

The only way in which all interviewees agreed consumer demand positively affects environmental outcomes is in the area of fuel economy, but then primarily from the perspective of operating cost. The Volkswagen interviewee described this as a 'financial problem' with consumers driven by a desire 'to have smaller cars, cheaper cars, and cars that do not need so much fuel'. Ford interviewees strongly echoed this argument, and one Toyota interviewee noted that while the environmental aspects of the Prius may have brought customers into showrooms, customer surveys indicated that the number one reason why they purchased the car was fuel economy. So, from a consumer demand perspective, material concerns remain very much to the fore.

On such material concerns, it was noted in Chapter 4 that many analyses attribute the greater fuel efficiency of European and Japanese cars to higher fuel prices, and the success of diesels in Europe to the price differential between diesel and petrol (e.g. see Deutsche Bank, 2004: 72). The fuel economy point made by interviewees tends to support such a view. However, the Volkswagen interviewee made three points to refute such arguments that, he said, he had mostly heard 'in the American discussion'.[9] First, he cited the higher purchase price of diesel cars. In part, this is because they tend to have larger engines than petrol cars, and in Germany there is a purchase tax based on engine size.[10] The result is that despite cheaper fuel, diesel car owners do not 'break even' with petrol car owners until they have driven approximately 100 000km. Second, he noted that the price differential between petrol and diesel has narrowed over time, providing less financial incentive for favoring diesel cars. Third, he suggested that substantial variation in the price differential across EU member states means that there is no clear correlation between this and the percentage of diesel cars purchased.

From a liberal economic perspective these are bold claims, so evidence was sought for them. His point on the higher purchase price of diesel cars is corroborated by the fact that ownership taxes as a percentage of the price of a new car in Germany are, on average 32 per cent for a diesel versus only 22 per cent for a petrol powered car (Harrington and McConnell, 2003: 22). His point about the narrowing price differential is supported by OECD data. Table 4.1 in Chapter 4 demonstrated that across EU member states the average per litre price of diesel increased from 56 to 69 per cent of the petrol price over 1980 to 2000 (OECD, 2002c: 23; ACEAc, no date). His point about price differential variations across EU member states is supported by the same OECD data which demonstrates that the percentage petrol is more expensive than diesel varies from 15 to 61 per cent, and that the price differential is not clearly correlated with the share of diesels in total car sales. For example, petrol is approximately 50 per cent more expensive than diesel in Germany, France and Denmark, yet the share of diesels in total car sales is 30, 49 and 13 per cent respectively (OECD, 2002c: 23). The alternative explanation offered by the Volkswagen interviewee was that it is more 'an image question', based on 'emotional aspects', coupled with the material security afforded by greater fuel economy because conventional fossil fuel sources are running out.

If social attitudes on the environment have not flowed through to consumer demand, except in a quality sense in the case of Germany and the EU, or in an operating cost and fuel economy sense more generally (that is, not for environmental reasons) what role do market forces play in encouraging environmental attributes? A clear division was evident between Ford and the other firms' interviewees on the extent to which consumer demand drives product development versus social attitudes. In LME fashion, Ford bases its product development on actual consumer demand expressed via revealed preferences in markets. In CME fashion, social attitudes were of more concern for the German and Japanese firms whose interviewees exhibited a broader conception of market forces beyond short-term profits. The extent to which firms respond to, versus lead, consumer demand is a related point of difference. Ford seeks to respond to consumer demand, while the other firms seek to lead it on the basis of social attitudes.

On the role of consumer demand in product development planning, one Ford interviewee said 'all of our product planning is driven by what the market needs'. Therefore, 'ultimately [Ford] want[s] to design and develop vehicles, and promote and sell them, that respond to market demand'. 'What the customer wants' was highlighted as the most powerful incentive for investment in environmental product initiatives because 'the easiest way to generate a business case for any new concepts and technologies [is] if there are strong consumer forces'.[11] But the interviewee who made this point went on to note that 'in reality, consumer forces don't always work on this subject'. Therefore, a lack of consumer demand for environmental attributes constrains environmental product development. The result is that environmental initiatives are 'largely driven by the regulatory environment'.

A related point is that social attitudes were clearly discounted in favor of consumer demand by all Ford interviewees. One said:

> Both are important but developing a car is a very expensive business and it's a very sophisticated product, and there's always limitations on the amount of funds that you have available to you no matter what you'd like to do. So, when it comes to trade offs we will always be biased towards the consumer preference in terms of how it translates to purchase. So, that is what we are all about. We're about producing cars that our customers will be excited about and want to buy.

For Ford, what matters most is what happens 'when it comes down to outlaying $20 000'.

Toyota's decision to produce its petrol-electric hybrid Prius, and to focus on hybrids as a key driver of its environmental product development initiatives, was said to be based on a belief that a car with good environmental credentials that uses less fuel will be seen as a superior product for its quality and lower operating costs. Even if not directly demanded by consumers, environmental product attributes were said to be 'good for the brand'. One Toyota interviewee said it was a matter of acting on 'latent consumer desires', which he described as follows:

I think people understood that provided that there is no compromising the operation of the vehicle and it was a benefit to society, then I think there were people looking out for that kind of creative solution. And that's what Prius has done. That's what I mean by there was a latent desire for that kind of product and we just tapped into it.

If this amounts to responding to consumer demand, it is a very nuanced understanding of the concept. It suggests attitudes trump 'money on the table'. Indeed, the same interviewee went on to say that 'listening to [consumers'] attitudes will give you the edge in terms of providing products that will suit them in five to ten years' time'.

Ultimately, in listening to consumer attitudes over demand Toyota seeks to lead the market. If one was to sum up the firm's strategic thinking on the environment expressed by its interviewees, it would be that it has a future-focused way of conceiving consumer demand. The following explanation by one interviewee captures this thinking best:

Global warming, I mean, it's in newspapers all the time. I think people are concerned about that. You watch little campaigns that are being promoted at the moment, say for example recycling. Recycling, not taking plastic bags from the supermarket and taking your own canvas bags etc., these are all little things but they're slowly building a level of consciousness about the environment that makes us rush to introduce a vehicle like Prius into the market. It doesn't take a lot of convincing people that a vehicle like this will provide a benefit to them. At the beginning in 1997 when we first introduced the vehicle that 'latentness' was quite small and the thing that we had to appeal to people with was technology: look at the amazing technology in this car, and by the way it gives you environmental benefits. With this new generation, sure there's an awareness that's grown through the previous model, but I think just general awareness of the environment has grown as well so that when you introduce this vehicle you could go out there on the front foot and say this is an environmentally friendly drivetrain called hybrid, and by the way it's got this 'whizzo' technology. You totally swap the story around that gets the hook into people because they understand the importance of the environment.

As such, Toyota develops products for the future, then promotes them in a manner palatable to present market preferences. The focus is on convincing, educating and shaping consumer preferences, rather than providing a product that accurately reflects them. It is the possibility of latent consumer desires that makes the firm 'rush' to develop products rather than the existence of actual demand.

For the German firms, there was a strong sense that consumer demand is the *least* important consideration. Instead, in typical CME fashion, the Volkswagen interviewee said a range of other factors take greater precedence. He said: 'consumer preferences are mostly a bit later than the internal strategic considerations of the company or the government and NGO positions. In that respect, I think the consumer is the slowest'. When asked specifically about the relative importance of consumer demand versus attitudes, like Toyota a clear preference was expressed for attitudes. At times, the BMW interviewee referred to the market and consumer demand in more Ford-like terms, but the firm's relationship with the market was also described as a two-way street in which the firm responds to *and* influences the market. He said: 'we want to supply the market with vehicles that they want to buy, and we want to stimulate the market to buy our vehicles, which is two sides of the same thing'. Like Volkswagen and Toyota, the BMW interviewee said the firm desired to be ahead of the market by producing products to stimulate it. Although no strong view on social attitudes versus demand was expressed, reacting to consumer demand was seen as less important than acting on a vision of what a car *should* be, especially for a prestige firm like BMW. He described the firm as a 'massager' of demand: 'we're not just sitting there saying, well, we'll build a car because we think people [want it]. We want to actually show them something and make them want it after they've seen it'. Like Toyota, BMW seeks to define the market rather than react to it.

Overall, Ford interviewees' responses indicated a predilection for *responding* to consumer demand. This is commensurate with an LME preference for market competition over cooperative coordination, and a material imperative to make short-term profits. For the CME-based firms, there was greater emphasis on the relationship between firms and markets as a two-way street, in which they often sought to *lead* markets. This point was clearly made for environmental reasons in the case of Toyota, which rushes to introduce environmentally-friendly products that it believes consumers only latently desire, and then attempts to convince them of their product's desirability. For Volkswagen and BMW it was a more general aspect of overall corporate strategy. For example, environmental aspects of BMW's products' performance are one of many ways it seeks to excel as a prestige car maker. But the point of commonality for all the CME-based firms is a focus on factors beyond what will drive consumers to put their money down *now*.

By implication, without material pressures via strong consumer demand for environmental attributes, the incentive for Ford to produce more environmentally-friendly products is the weakest of the firms here. This supports the findings of Chapter 5 where it was shown that the US market is characterized by increasingly environmentally damaging vehicles despite increased social environmental concern. By contrast, the German and, especially, Japanese firms take social environmental concern more seriously as a sign of latent/future demand. In fact, echoing the point on voluntary commitments made with governments, the main way in which social attitudes affect Ford's behavior was said by one interviewee to be how the company is perceived, rather than how it acts. It wants to be seen as a good corporate citizen. It is not surprising that this same interviewee concluded that Ford has 'a very difficult path to tread'.

INTERNAL COMPANY STRATEGIES

The observation that German and Japanese firms seek to lead the market more than follow it has implications for internal company strategies. It suggests, as noted in Chapter 2, they are potentially driven more by endogenous than exogenous forces. Hailing from CME states, they focus less on exogenous material factors and more on internally derived 'visions' of their purpose. This should be especially the case for Japanese firms whose internal stakeholders within the enterprise community are key drivers of their business strategies. However, analysing this is not straightforward, because the line between exogenous and endogenous factors is often blurred. For example, interviewees often noted that their firms' strategies are affected by state regulations and market forces. Conversely, they have strategies that aim to affect these exogenous factors. Determining what is exogenous versus endogenous is problematic.

Nevertheless, interviewees' responses demonstrated that the environmental impact of firms' products was perceived in different ways, and the drive for environmental attributes came from within them to different degrees. In particular, all interviewees mentioned the concept of 'leadership', but just what this meant differed between firms. It certainly produced different perceptions of the environmental attributes of their products. The role of senior management was stressed more by Ford and Toyota interviewees, but the insight of the VOC approach that top management has more 'unilateral control' than in CMEs appeared crucial in the case of LME-based Ford (a point also highlighted in Chapter 6). All interviewees also made statements concerning the path dependence of the products their firms produced, and the capabilities and constraints flowing from this. These are considered in turn below.

Turning first to perceptions, it was clear that the drive for environmental attributes emanates more from within Toyota, Volkswagen and BMW than Ford. Commensurate with the greater focus on internal stakeholders for Japanese CME-based firms, Toyota's interviewees noted that protecting the environment is a matter of corporate philosophy. The firm believes that 'if you don't look after the environment now, whatever business you currently have will not be protected and you won't have a business in the future'. In other words, business and environmental interests are seen as one and the same. Given this philosophy, the ultimate goal of the company was said to be 'the search of the ultimate "eco car"'. The petrol-electric hybrid Prius is obviously the clearest expression of this philosophy, but more broadly the belief was expressed that 'it's important to say we're going to strive to make the most efficient vehicle we can in each segment'. A key reason for such a philosophy was said to be *kaizen*, the Japanese term for continuous improvement. *Kaizen* and the environment were linked by one Toyota interviewee because 'where you can make a more fuel efficient car and then make it for less, what you've actually got is a better environmental outcome: you've got less waste, less emissions, all those other things'. Therefore, the *kaizen* principle coupled with Toyota's corporate environmental philosophy leads to the environmental attributes of its vehicles occupying a central strategic position.

The result of Toyota's corporate environmental philosophy is that hybrid technologies and working on environmentally-friendly vehicles are now 'prestigious' areas within the company. They were described as 'the "gun" job', 'sexy' and 'cutting edge'. All divisions of Toyota 'want to put hybrid in their next generation car'. The *esprit de corps* created means that Toyota employees 'have a real sense that what they're doing has a real impact on the environment and society as a whole'.

Similar, albeit more muted, internal company strategies drive BMW and Volkswagen's efforts. The BMW interviewee said his firm generally pays less heed to exogenous factors because 'the imperative for development comes from inside BMW rather than government or consumers'. The Volkswagen interviewee made a similar point, explaining that 'it's more the company, the people in the company's strategy and the company saying OK, first we have to avoid environmental problems, and second our expectations of the next ten to 20 years are such that we have to do it before the consumer really knows it'. Therefore, in a similar manner to Toyota, the German firms' interviewees saw environmental attributes of their firm's cars as being more internally driven than exogenously imposed. Indeed, the BMW interviewee said his firm possesses 'a very strongly environmentally aware mindset [that] permeates through all the layers of engineering, the engine manufacturers, the drivetrain manufacturers, right down to the body manufacturers, the people who design bodies and all that sort of stuff. BMW's performance, technological innovation and prestige objectives are always tempered by 'an environmentally conscious brake'.

Where does this leave Ford, given its LME preference for responding to exogenous material factors? Ford interviewees said their firm wishes to take environmental initiatives because it is the 'right thing to do', and perhaps good for business in the longer term. One Ford interviewee explained the conflicting internal and external forces faced by the company in the following terms:

> We're very concerned about corporate citizenship, recognizing we're in an industry which some may view as not necessarily in the best interest of the planet. We don't agree with that. We're really talking about benefits to society as a whole, and trying to do whatever we can to have vehicles which are fun to drive and are still sustainable. But it doesn't do anybody any good if we produce a radical product that's unaffordable because people won't buy it, we go out of business and no one wins.

Therefore, Ford struggles with conflicting exogenous material forces versus endogenous desires. In this light, the introduction of the Ford Escape petrol-electric hybrid is a phenomenon that interviewees struggled to explain. It was said to probably be due to 'an internal company desire to be a good corporate citizen and to be seen as such'. It was also described as a 'foray into the market to see how it's received'. After all, 'you have to get your feet wet somewhere and the learning from that can build to newer technologies down the track'. It appears to represent an attempt to marry the imperatives of consumer demand with a desire to be a good corporate citizen and improve brand image.

Overall, Toyota, as a Japanese firm, exhibits the Japanese CME trait of being more internally strategically driven, but the German firms are also more internally driven on environmental matters than Ford. Headquartered in the US and desiring to be a good corporate citizen, Ford struggles with its LME predilection for market forces, especially consumer demand, and securing material financial returns in the shorter term. This has implications for the concept of 'leadership', which was raised *voluntarily* by all interviewees. But just what constituted 'leadership' differed considerably. Notions of leadership were more likely to be defined in corporate philosophical terms by the Japanese and German firms, than in the case of Ford where leadership was more narrowly defined, LME style, as primarily a matter of market leadership.

Toyota and BMW interviewees stressed leadership and innovation as key considerations behind everything their firms do. As a prestige car maker less bound by pricing constraints, and therefore with more leverage to invest in new technologies, the BMW interviewee stressed his company perceives itself as 'a technological leader' that tries 'not to be bound by conventional thinking'. This was said to be BMW's 'point of difference' that distinguishes the brand. BMW's leadership perspective impacts on environmental outcomes because environmental performance is seen a key factor in the firm's overall technological leadership. BMW's pre-eminence in hydrogen technologies was given as an example of this in practice, through which it is not sacrificing performance, but seeking to lead technologically by being ahead of the market, ahead of the oil industry, and ahead of government and infrastructure. Fundamentally, the BMW interviewee said 'it's probably up to companies like BMW, and other people in this market, to expose the decision makers in society to whom we sell our cars to the reality of cleaner energy, which we have for our cars'. BMW therefore has a holistic vision of leading governments, society and markets via the environmental attributes of the cars it sells.

Toyota interviewees discussed technological leadership in a thematically similar manner. However, the environmental attributes of Toyota's cars appeared more central than for the other firms. Indeed, Toyota interviewees said their company is now casting itself as *the* environmental car firm. Like the latest technology is BMW's 'point of difference', this is what gives Toyota its distinctive brand. For example, the launch of the petrol-electric Prius was said to come from 'a strategic decision to take a leadership role' in hybrid vehicles, not required by regulation and with no expectation of immediate financial benefits. It was described as 'totally our own initiative', 'not driven very strongly by demand' and 'regardless of any government direction'. Ultimately, one Toyota interviewee predicted the introduction of environmental technologies that also improve performance by 'combining a hybrid [drive]train with a V6 engine in all-wheel-drive version where you get phenomenal fuel consumption, incredibly lowered emissions plus blistering performance'.[12] Toyota interviewees also saw their firm as performing an educative role on the environment. One noted that since launching the Prius, the firm is regularly invited to participate in environmental conferences or discussions on sustainable development. Therefore, Toyota exercises a leadership role not just in respect of markets or government, but also in shaping the environmental agenda more broadly in society.

The Volkswagen interviewee talked not so much of leadership, as cooperatively reaching consensus positions with a range of stakeholders internal and external to the firm. This is clearly the 'negotiated consensus' model of German CME capitalism. Indeed, he specifically mentioned the German system of 'co-determination' for management–employee relations in this context. Commensurate with this model, rather than one exogenous factor being more important than the other, or internal strategies taking precedence in environmental matters, the environmental *issue* in question was said to be most important:

It depends very much on the individual aspect of environmental improvement or environmental performance. So, for example, the recycling discussion has been mainly a discussion put forward by the government, whereas the CO_2

climate discussion is mainly put forward by the NGOs, and the cost of fuels, and that means the amount of fuel, the fuel efficiency, is mainly put forward by the market. So, it depends very much on the environmental aspect where we see which one is the strong force.

For Volkswagen, addressing environmental concerns is a matter of balancing internal and external stakeholder concerns, with the primary aim of effectively addressing the issue in question.

For Ford, no strong internal drivers for environmental initiatives were mentioned in a leadership sense, unless one counts leadership in markets on the basis of consumer demand. Even though doing the 'right thing', being a good corporate citizen and meeting government regulations, etc. were seen as important by all Ford interviewees, one Ford interviewee declared that 'there's not green flowing through our veins, we're a car company after all!' Yet, the role of the firm's Chairman and CEO, Bill Ford, in driving the firm's environmental agenda, and his position as a member of the founding family of the company that retains a significant stake in its fortunes, was stressed by all Ford interviewees. The interviewee who expressed it most articulately said:

> Certainly a lot of it stems from an unstated desire on the part of the company to be sustainable, in Bill Ford's words, harking back to the heritage of his great-grandfather, that we're a company that's here to improve society. We want to be profitable, but we also want to contribute to society, and we want to do it in an environmentally sustainable fashion as well.

Apart from his association with the cultural heritage of the firm, Bill Ford was said to have almost single-handedly raised environmental issues to be a key strategic priority for the company. His role in doing this was expressed by one Ford interviewee as follows:

> I would say his personal standard of 'greenness', if you want to use that term, on the company is quite significant. I don't think we would be where we are now if he hadn't pushed that. So, arguably a lot of our unique driver is Bill Ford.

In fact, Bill Ford was described by the same interviewee as the key reason why the environment is on the company's strategic agenda.

Like Ford, Toyota interviewees recognized the role played by their senior management who, as one noted, 'for many years have had this sustainability agenda and they're focusing on it because they've got a long-term vision for the company'. The continuing focus on environmental sustainability by Toyota's senior management makes it one of the firm's 'number one management issues'. The impetus for the commercial launch of the Prius was said to come from the President of Toyota himself who directed staff two years before the Kyoto Protocol 'to have a car that's mass produced, on sale, ready at that meeting'. While this could look more like opportunistic behavior than enlightened environmental concern, the point is nevertheless clear. While other firms saw the importance of the Kyoto Protocol in regulatory terms, Toyota's management saw it as an opportunity for a new product launch given the firm's branding focus.

Finally, in terms of internal strategies, all interviews discussed their firms' environmental initiatives as part of a historical process that enables and constrains their current initiatives. They used this to explain why German firms had opted for advanced diesels, Japanese firms for petrol-electric hybrids, and why Ford faces significant challenges in improving the environmental performance of its products. The points interviewees made support the observation of Chapter 6 that path dependence in environmental initiatives enable the German and Japanese firms, rather than constrain US firms such as Ford.

German firms' shift to advanced diesels was explained in terms of their existing expertise and technological capabilities. The Volkswagen interviewee cited a history of expertise in diesel technology, plus the view that hybrids are not seen as an 'elegant technical solution' because they require drivetrains with two engines rather than one. The BMW interviewee echoed the sentiments of Volkswagen, saying that 'our view on hybrid is that we can't see the value in two power sources in the vehicle'. Commensurate with the German CME role of technology, he also said they were keener to incrementally develop existing technologies rather than introduce new ones. He elaborated on this as follows:

> Car companies have invested a hundred years' worth of know-how into building and producing internal combustion engines. That's a reasonably efficient process and to abandon all that investment and go off into a completely different type of technology would be very difficult and quite a lot of goodwill, heritage and brand reputation is tied up in the engine systems. Our aim is to make our petrol engines as efficient and clean as they can be. . . . So, we think there's still more life left in the current technology, and maybe by the time hydrogen is more practical we'll be ready to 'push the button' on that as well.

On hydrogen power, the BMW interviewee also noted that it was a better 'fit' with BMW's image than hybrids because 'one of BMW's core elements is driving excitement and driving pleasure', and hydrogen is believed to confer such attributes. In short, a belief in the 'elegance' of diesels, a history of expertise in them and petrol internal combustion engines, and their ability to deliver performance attributes (in the case of BMW) were all reasons why German firms have taken the diesel route in Europe.

Toyota has a history of producing efficient, smaller cars, so to some extent its drive to develop more environmentally-friendly cars is the natural progression of an established product development path. One Toyota interviewee explained this as follows:

> Most of the cars Toyota has made over the years have been smaller cars rather than larger cars. We make Land Cruisers of course at the heavier end, but most of the cars have tended to be small four- and six-cylinder cars, so just by the virtue of having good fuel economy you actually have low emissions.

Toyota's drive for further environmental efficiencies is therefore the continuation of a path it has been following over many decades.

Given that Ford relies on sales of light trucks and luxury cars, largely sold in North American markets, this places strong economic sustainability constraints on the company in dealing with environmental concerns. One Ford interviewee therefore said:

> The challenge for us is to be able to continue to produce [large cars with larger engines] in a sustainable way that meets customer expectations, what we call the 'DNA' of the product, and at the same time recognize that we are in an organization that wants to be responsible for corporate citizenship.

Apart from the path dependence of the firm's products' 'DNA', there are the barriers that exist due to consumer demand (or lack of it) for environmentally-friendly vehicles. The launch of hybrid vehicles such as the Escape SUV was seen as a way around the conundrum, yet even though such vehicles 'show a lot of promise [they] still fundamentally have barriers to consumers which relate to the cost of the product'. Ford's material limitations mean that Bill Ford is probably doing all he can given a strong LME-driven market focus, and the inescapable fact that the short to medium-term success of his family business is dependent on Ford continuing to produce and sell larger vehicles.

THE FUTURE

The interviews concluded with a question about the major challenges facing firms over the next 10–20 years. An invitation to openly speculate, it was answered in remarkably different ways, because although all firms' interviewees saw a hydrogen-powered future for their vehicles eventually, probably in 20 years' time, the path to this and the motivations for it were quite different.

The future for Ford was seen in terms of responding to a range of challenges in much the same way as the firm has in the past. The challenges were seen neither as radical as for Toyota, nor as far-sighted in terms of the implication of environmental concerns as for Volkswagen and BMW. Growing concern for the environment was seen as something to be factored into product developments in the same way as increased consumer demand for other features such as performance and handling. As one Ford interviewee put it:

> Customers want more power and performance and handling and quietness, but there's basic issues of physics that our brilliant engineers work to tackle and overcome every day. How do you get more performance but less fuel? How do you meet ever increasing, whether it be regulatory or just socially acceptable levels of environmental impact, in terms of fuel economy and emissions? So, I think that continual striving of getting better, better, better on emissions and fuel economy are two big ones. Noise is another one: the drive by noise and setting better targets for those all the time and getting better on that. So, I just think that overall thing of technological advancement, continually getting better, using less, being quicker: the eternal struggle. Is there one particular stand out? I don't think so.

The future was therefore primarily conceptualized in terms of continuing to meet consumer demand and tougher regulatory standards. Corporate responsibility imperatives for improved environmental performance were also cited, but not given primacy. One interviewee summed up Ford's perspective as not necessarily more environmentally-friendly products but generally 'more of everything'.

For the German firms, real challenges in the form of environmental constraints and threats were identified as priorities that require a response. The Volkswagen interviewee said that the pre-eminence of the issue of climate change in Germany and Europe means that it *must* be addressed. As such, the future environmental challenges of the company were very much seen in terms of the political and social concerns of its home state, and the region where it has its major markets. Volkswagen sees the answer as moving to advanced biofuels and hydrogen in the next 20 years. The BMW interviewee's responses were similar. For BMW the future entails the eventual move to a hydrogen-based economy, while always having such advanced products that it can continue to succeed in business no matter what regulatory constraints or market forces may arise. A shift to alternative drivetrains was seen as inevitable because 'there has to be an answer to petroleum internal combustion engine cars for the long-term future'. The environment is a key problem these German firms must address. There is no alternative.

One Toyota interviewee envisaged a 'multi-fuel future' in a similar manner to the German firms, with hydrogen the ultimate outcome. But for Toyota, there was a sense that the future is here now. More accurately, rather than attempting to be ready for what the future may hold in the way of challenges, and rather than just working in partnership with government to find solutions, Toyota sees its role as *creating* the future of passenger cars. Toyota interviewees were the only ones that envisaged their firm competing in markets on the basis of environmental attributes specifically, with the endpoint being 'the ultimate eco car'.

If one was to summarize their perspectives, it would be that Ford interviewees again exhibited an LME preoccupation with material factors and remaining competitive in markets. German and Japanese firms, with longer-term perspectives, are in CME fashion looking beyond immediate material factors to shape the future of their industry in response to real environmental constraints that must be addressed. In Toyota's case, this is occurring regardless, and ahead, of regulations or the reality of these constraints when they may arise.

THE INTERNATIONAL IMPLICATIONS OF NATIONAL VARIATIONS IN CAPITALIST RELATIONS OF PRODUCTION

It is clear that not only do interviewees' responses support the insights of the VOC approach, but that the impact of national institutional variations filter down to lower management levels within companies worldwide. This is because firms are institutionally embedded in the home states where they have their headquarters, where their policy and strategic decisions are made. These decisions, expressed in respect of the environment in their environmental reports, and exhibited in their product development strategies, permeate their operations internationally.

The evidence speaks for itself, but so do the views expressed by interviewees. For example, one Ford interviewee said that despite designing and manufacturing unique cars for Australia, the firm's Australian branch always does so given the constraints and overall corporate policy settings of its head office. On environmental technologies, he said the role of Ford Australia was therefore relatively minimal as the 'technology is going to be driven globally'. In a similar vein, the Volkswagen interviewee noted that 'the culture of a company is quite often the culture of the place where their [*sic*] headquarters is'. One Toyota interviewee noted somewhat colorfully that what might seem 'airy fairy' and more peripherally related to core business from an Australian perspective is very much central to the way the firm operates from a Japanese perspective. In relation to Toyota's reports he said: 'there are a lot of words in there about our commitment to living in harmony with the environment and so forth. That's not just rhetoric. It's a Japanese company so it's a commitment that's believed in, and our product designs reflect it'. In all cases, there was something American, German or Japanese about each firms' strategies, environmental or otherwise. The fact that these points were made by Australian branch office personnel (with the exception of Volkswagen) lends further weight to the idea that national variations in capitalist relations of production have international implications. If one were to draw broad brushstrokes of the viewpoints offered by interviewees, these could summarized as shown in Table 7.1.

The German firms exhibit German CME traits, albeit from different perspectives given that one is a volume producer (Volkswagen) and the other a premium producer (BMW). They both do not react to consumer demand, so much as attempt to be ahead of it, and then social attitudes are more important than actual demand. They do not meet government regulations, so much as exceed them (BMW) or move in the same direction as government in a spirit of partnership (Volkswagen). Being based in Germany and the EU, the role of government is stronger for them particularly because of the political mainstreaming of environmental regulations, leading to the EU's international regulatory leadership. BMW, as a prestige car firm, is more internally driven than reactive to exogenous factors, whereas in true German CME fashion a balance of stakeholder viewpoints internal and external to the company is what shapes Volkswagen's approach to environmental strategies. Overall, this means that for Volkswagen there is no clear strong driver for environmental initiatives, but a balance between exogenous and endogenous forces, whereas although BMW shares similar viewpoints to its German volume counterpart, its prestige perspective skews its focus more to internal company strategies.

Similar sentiments are evident for Toyota. As a Japanese CME firm, it sees itself as very much part of the fabric of society with resulting social obligations to lead environmental debate and educate society. It leads markets (on the basis of social attitudes, or 'nascent consumer demand'). However, it goes beyond cooperating with government to assume a leadership position, and desires greater government cooperation. As a firm based in a techno-nationalist CME with a philosophical commitment to the environment, it is technologically driven to produce petrol-electric hybrids such as the Prius. Toyota's distinguishing feature is one that characterizes Japanese CME firms more generally: a high importance placed on internal strategic drivers. The result is it is now branding itself as an environmental car firm with environmental leadership a core management objective.

Ford, with its headquarters in the archetypal LME, is more focused on reacting to weak environmental consumer demand than addressing

Table 7.1 Summary of interview findings

	Importance of market forces	Importance of state regulations	Importance of internal company strategies	Timeframes	Materialist versus post-materialist values	The future
Volkswagen	Social attitudes: Medium, respond and lead Consumer demand: Low, respond and lead	Medium: German/EU regulatory leadership and embedding of environmental principles, partnership approach	Medium to high: A balance of exogenous and endogenous factors through a stakeholder approach	Medium term	Post-materialism driven by materialist rationality	Environmental factors are a key challenge to be addressed
BMW	Social attitudes: Medium, lead Consumer demand: Low, lead	Medium: German/EU regulatory leadership and embedding of environmental principles, design for future regulations	High: Product development driven by an internal vision	Medium term	Post-materialism driven by materialist rationality	Environmental factors are a key challenge to be addressed

Table 7.1 (continued)

	Importance of market forces	Importance of state regulations	Importance of internal company strategies	Timeframes	Materialist versus post-materialist values	The future
Ford	Social attitudes: Low to medium, respond Consumer demand: High, respond	High: Constraint on responding to market forces	Low: Except for the role of senior executives: vision of the Chairman/CEO	Short term	Materialist	More of the same: the environment is one of a range of product attributes to be addressed and balanced
Toyota	Social attitudes: Medium, lead and respond Consumer demand: Low, lead	Low: Firm leads government	High: Corporate philosophy drives environmental initiatives	Long term	Transition to post-materialism	Shaping the future of environmental car attributes is a key factor. Competition on the basis of environmental attributes is envisaged

stronger social attitudes. Similarly, it meets government regulations rather than exceeds them. Its main objectives are profitability and economic success, and therefore the firm is more exogenously, materially driven. The 'wild card' in the case of Ford is the role of the company's Chairman and CEO given his environmental awareness, and the family heritage he brings to his firm of a concern for corporate citizenship. This forms the foundation for Ford's internal drive to address environmental concerns, despite market forces exerting contrary material incentives. Given the greater power of top management to make unilateral decisions and set strategy in LME-based firms, this is primarily where the impetus for Ford's environmental initiatives comes from.

These findings extend the analysis of environmental reports in Chapter 6 which showed, in broad terms, that German firms are more driven by social concerns and a more balanced approach than simply responding to market forces, and that Japanese firms are more internally driven for their strategies. US firms are more predisposed to approach environmental initiatives from a market perspective. There are further implications of these observations that relate to the timeframes and attitudes to post-materialism that come from different emphases related to firms' home state VOC: a tendency to longer timeframes and greater weight to post-materialist values for CME firms by comparison to those based in LMEs. Ford has a shorter-term timeframe than the other firms, being more focused on current market conditions, current regulatory requirements, and profitability within the current product cycle. It remains the most materialist in its perspective on environmental product developments. The German firms have a more medium-term perspective based on being ahead of markets and regulatory requirements, and being more stakeholder, rather than market, driven in how these exogenous factors are addressed. Toyota has the longest timeframe, being so strongly internally driven on environmental matters that this significantly overrides exogenous factors. It could be said that for Toyota this is associated with a shift to post-materialist values in how it conducts its business, whereas for the German firms such a shift is occurring for more materialist reasons – that is post-materialism is good for business given the inevitable environmental constraints to be faced.

Ultimately, for Toyota this means that it envisages competing on the basis of its products' environmental attributes, and therefore proactively driving the environmental agenda. For Volkswagen and BMW, environmental considerations are now a key strategic consideration to be addressed. However, for Ford, the environment remains one of a range of strategic considerations, and not necessarily the most pressing one, to be factored into its ongoing material success.

CONCLUSION

All the firms that participated in interviews are committed to demonstrating the environmental performance of their products. Volkswagen and BMW are doing so with advanced diesels in the short term and alternative fuels in the longer term. Ford is the first non-Japanese company to launch a petrol-electric hybrid vehicle, and the first in the world to do so in the form of an SUV. Toyota is a pioneer in petrol-electric hybrids and has committed to applying the technology across its model range. It is likely that these firms self-selected themselves for participation in interviews because of commitments they have made such as these. However, whether this is the case or not, what has clearly emerged is that far from a global perspective on the environment being the case, or even an Australian perspective, interviewees from each firm had very distinct 'lenses' through which they saw the environmental performance of the cars their firms produce. These lenses were 'made' in their firms' home states.

It is also important to concede that there are no absolutes, that these are complex issues, firms are complex organizations, and the intersection of various factors and the forces they exert on firm strategies are not straightforward. For example, it should not be assumed that these firms in no way tailor their operations for the different jurisdictions in which they operate. Similarly, beyond the national distinctions highlighted by the insights of the VOC approach, a firm such as Ford is obviously concerned about social attitudes and Toyota is obviously concerned about making profits. And characterizing German firms' embrace of advanced diesels as an incremental rather than radical step like hybrids was challenged by the Volkswagen interviewee who made the point that the research and development that went into advanced diesels is not dissimilar to that for hybrids. There is a danger of drawing national caricatures, and a complex mixture of national and specific firm traits are bound up in these conclusions.

Even so, there are clear points of difference in emphasis. These points of difference have implications for which firms are setting the environmental agenda and which are following. They also suggest which firms are likely to dominate future environmental initiatives, and redefine the global market for passenger cars in a more environmentally sustainable manner. The answer is obvious: Japanese and German firms. In the course of undertaking research for this book, several people (although none from Toyota) expressed the view that Toyota developed its Prius opportunistically to take advantage of emerging attitudinal trends, the signing of the Kyoto Protocol, and likely emerging market forces. It is simply motivated by a desire to increase its market share. This may be true, but the question has to be asked, if this is the case, why were there not a whole range of

Prius-like models introduced in the late 1990s by car firms of all nationalities, or cars with similar environmental pretensions? Similarly, it might be expedient to explain the move of European producers to advanced diesels in terms of the price differential between diesel and petrol. There are internal corporate technological advantages for European firms in so doing and specific market factors, particularly in terms of social attitudes, that tend to get overlooked in such a simple rationalist explanation of the shift to diesels.

The result of differing national institutional bases for corporate strategies is that Toyota is leading the industry in the commercialization of hybrid technologies, while the German firms are doing likewise with diesels and alternative fuels. Ford is attempting to catch up, yet this may not rule out considerable success if it manages to successfully compete in the markets established by other firms. In this regard, the commitment of its Chairman and CEO to environmental initiatives may serve it in good stead.

NOTES

1. In constructing the interviews this way, the intention was not to get authors to answer in a 'yes' or 'no' manner, but to engage in reflective and critical thinking about their firm's operations, and motivations, in respect of the key areas of interest. Therefore, they were guided in terms of what they should comment on, but only semi-guided in the sense that there was much scope for them to answer the questions in different ways. The literature informing such an approach includes Denscombe (1998: especially Chapter 7); May (2001: especially Chapter 6); Arksey and Knight (1999); Yin (2003a and b); Peavey (1995 and no date); Kvale (1996); and Stanfield (2000).
2. Although, to be precise, in the case of Nissan, an interview was granted, but in the course of the interview the interviewee repeatedly declared that he knew little about environmental matters. This was a curious response given the information he received and phone discussions prior to the interview. His responses have been omitted from the following analysis because analysing non-responses would be counterproductive.
3. The evidence on fuel taxes presented in Chapter 4 would tend to support such a view.
4. Examples given by interviewees included Euro3 noxious emissions regulations being superseded by Euro4 regulations, and more stringent fuel economy standards.
5. For the US, this interviewee referred to the historically long-standing strict Californian noxious emissions regulations and recent Californian CO_2 emission regulations. However, on Californian regulations it was noted in Chapter 3 that while the state of California has historically had much stricter regulations for non-CO_2 emissions than national regulations for the US as a whole, it actually lags national regulations when it comes to CO_2 emissions. This is because although California passed a law requiring 'maximum feasible reductions' in greenhouse gas emissions from cars and light trucks in 2002, no specific standards were mandated under this law, and car manufacturers were not required to take any action to reduce emissions until 2009. Therefore this may effectively be ruled out in terms of any comparison being undertaken here on the basis of CO_2 emissions (Austin et al., 2003: 6; OECD, 2004: 110–112).

6. This is an Australian Commonwealth Government program under which firms make voluntary commitments to reduce CO_2 emissions.
7. The imagery is along the lines that Ford reaches for the ceiling, much the way that the US industry as a whole struggles to comply with CAFE regulations as demonstrated in Chapter 4. Therefore, regulations represent a maximum level of regulatory compliance that must be 'reached' for, rather than a minimum level of compliance easily exceeded.
8. This point was qualified by two other Ford interviewees who even saw the possibility that environmental attributes could have a negative effect on sales. One of them said that 'market forces have worked in the reverse if anything [because] there's a focus on more features, quieter cars which result in more sound deadening material, safer cars which involve stiffer structures, and airbags which of course add weight'. These factors were said to 'act against [Ford] in producing environmental outcomes'.
9. This point was indeed mentioned by Ford interviewees.
10. He did not mention that diesels are also more expensive to manufacture, but this would certainly be a related point as to why their purchase price is higher.
11. This echoes the sentiments of Ford's Chairman and CEO expressed in the firm's environmental reporting, as discussed in Chapter 6.
12. Such a car has now been introduced. It is the Lexus GS450h.

8. Conclusion

This book opened with the observation that changing the behavior of firms is usually seen as unlikely without changes in market forces or effective state regulation. These changes are seen as necessary for internalizing environmental externalities. However, the aim has been to open up the question of addressing environmental externalities by shifting attention away from purely material aspects towards institutional differences in capitalist relations of production in firms' home states. To empirically ground the analysis, the car industry has been the focus. This is because it is the world's largest manufacturing sector, dominated by a handful of large multinational corporations whose products are a major contributor to environmental damage, particularly the pressing global issue of climate change.

By focusing on the industry's contribution to the problem of climate change through the carbon dioxide emissions of passenger cars in use, it has been shown that firms' commitments are not happening equally (that is, in terms of magnitude), nor in the same manner (that is, there are qualitative differences). Firms' strategies are dependent on where they have their home bases. Institutional variations in capitalist relations of production between firms' home states, revealed by the Varieties of Capitalism approach, have been shown to be important for explaining variations in car firms' responses to climate change. In fact, there is a two-way relationship such that the insights of the VOC approach support the results of the empirical analysis, and in turn the results support the insights of the VOC approach.

The key insights of the VOC approach applied to the empirical analysis, and their relation to firms' actions in respect of environmental product developments, are reprised below. The question of casting firms as rational economic actors, as per the liberal economic model, versus seeing them as institutionally embedded in their home states, as per institutional approaches, is summarized. In particular, the idea that the material perspective of firms as rational economic actors in the liberal economic model is only really a useful approximation for liberal market economy-based firms, but not for coordinated market economy-based firms.

The main findings of the book are then summarized. What firms are actually doing, and the national differences in their environmental product developments, is considered first, particularly from the perspective of whether this represents radical or incremental change. The point is made that national differences are a reflection of the LME versus CME divide of the major firms' home states. The role of state regulations is then considered, particularly the conclusion that the extent to which state regulations establish minimum floors (in the case of CMEs) versus maximum ceilings (in the case of LMEs) is a matter of firms' home state variety of capitalism. The role of market forces is then addressed, particular differences in the way market forces are perceived depending on firms' home state variety of capitalism. LME-based firms are most concerned with material factors, and therefore discount social attitudes in favor of focusing on the material impacts of factors such as consumer demand and short-term profit motivations. However, CME-based firms give higher priority to social attitudes. Turning to internal strategic drivers, the findings demonstrate that the importance of these revolves around whether firms may be conceived more as rational business calculators (LME-based firms) or motivated more by beliefs (CME-based firms). In the light of the findings, conclusions are also presented on the extent to which a positive shift in business attitudes is occurring in respect of the environment. It is in the case of CME-based firms, but less so in the case of LME-based firms.

Finally, answers to the questions posed at the outset are presented. These are that the factors that motivate firms to see environmental issues as central to their business interests are contingent on national institutional differences. Therefore, car firms' primary motivators for embracing environmental improvements are specific to their nationalities, and to some extent their individual cultures (although individual cultures are themselves a reflection of nationalities). As such, there is the crucial finding that it is not sufficient to say that material factors such as state regulations or consumer demand are the primary motivators for all firms, or at least they do not necessarily produce the same material outcomes. The reason why the car industry should be concerned about the environment is therefore best answered in terms of institutionalized norms that lead firms of different nationalities to perceive environmental issues in different ways. There is no single answer to such a question, because the VOC of nations have implications not just for the type of products that their corporations produce, and the competitive advantages they develop,[1] but also the way they address related issues arising as a result of their activities, such as environmental degradation.

RATIONAL ECONOMIC ACTORS OR NATIONAL INSTITUTIONAL EMBEDDING?

Two contrasting perspectives on addressing environmental externalities were considered in Chapter 2: the mainstream liberal economic model versus institutional approaches. The liberal economic model is based on a rationalist approach that sees firms as motivated by material concerns. They seek profits in markets, and act instrumentally to do so. They are primarily motivated by a logic of consequentialism (March and Olsen, 1989 and 1998). Based on a priori assumed motivations of them as materially-driven profit seekers, a rationalist analysis is applied the result of which is that, *ceteris paribus*, environmental externalities can only be addressed by state intervention. Alternatively,[2] consumer preferences must change so that market signals provide incentives for them to alter their behavior on the basis of their instrumental profit-seeking goals.

Institutional approaches do not make assumptions about actors' rationality, but instead focus on norms of behavior that become institutionalized over time (see, for example, Finnemore and Sikkink, 1998). They are based not just on a logic of consequentialism defined in terms of *a priori* assumptions regarding actors' rationality, but on a logic of appropriateness based on norms. As such, the relative importance of material, rationalist, instrumental motivations for action need to be weighed against normative rationales that become institutionalized over time. In order to do this, the VOC approach was adopted as the framework for analysis because both material and normative rationales for action are encompassed within it, and because it says that the degree to which firms conform to, or deviate from, the liberal economic model is a question of institutional embedding in their home states.

The VOC approach makes a series of observations on the institutional basis of firms' home state capitalist relations of production that are useful for predicting their motivations. Specifically, firms' motivations are ascribed on the basis of whether their home states lean more towards LMEs, as in the case of the US, versus CMEs, as in the case of Germany (and to some extent Europe more broadly) and Japan. The VOC approach was applied in an innovative way to demonstrate why national variations in capitalist relations of production should be central to any analysis of how firms may ameliorate environmental impacts. The analysis used the dichotomous LME versus CME categorization to do this for the sake of parsimony. This means it runs the risk of employing 'a kind of rough, tough macho-theory that concentrates on the big picture and ignores detail' (Crouch, 2005a: 450). Perhaps the car industry is a rough, tough macho industry, so the approach suits! More seriously, it is to be hoped that the foregoing analysis represents an attempt to empirically study the complexities of national variations in capitalist relations of production not just in a big picture way, but as applied to a particular issue area, a particular industry sector, and a handful of key firms from that industry's hubs of ownership, production and consumption.

WHAT FIRMS ARE DOING: RADICAL OR INCREMENTAL CHANGE?

A range of environmental product development initiatives being under-taken by car firms that address the contribution of their products in use to climate change were outlined in Chapter 3. These include incremental technologies, petrol and diesel-electric hybrid drivetrains, hydrogen fuel cell vehicles (FCVs) and alternative fuels. Developments in these areas all aim to improve fuel economy and reduce passenger cars' contribution to CO_2 emissions. However, an analysis of car firms' environmental reports demonstrated that divergent, rather than convergent, strategies are being employed by firms, and that their strategies diverge on the basis of their nationalities.

Japanese firms are focused on petrol-electric hybrids, and on introduc-ing alternative vehicles more broadly as soon as possible. Not waiting for markets to mature, they are keen to introduce new, radical technologies *now*. By contrast, German firms are focused on incremental technologies in the form of advanced diesels, largely to meet the requirements of their co-regulatory CO_2 emission reduction agreements with the European Commission. German and US firms are focused on alternative fuels, but in different ways. For US firms, this is a strategy for addressing the fuel consumption of their larger light trucks, which have come to dominate sales for the US market and US-based firms. However, for German firms it is an across the board strategy for all vehicles. While FCVs are a relatively distant prospect for all firms, Japanese firms want to introduce them as soon as possible (in the manner of their technologically-driven environ-mental initiatives more generally), whereas German and US firms want to be ready to introduce them when market, regulatory and infrastructure conditions are conducive. A stronger emphasis on reacting to market forces and developing products to suit different markets was noticeable for US firms than German and Japanese firms which have determined clear (and differentiated) technological strategies.

These divergent strategies appear related to firms' home state VOC in three ways. First, the technonationalist version of the Japanese CME is manifested in Japanese car firms' more radical embrace of hybrid tech-nologies, and radical leading-edge technological advances generally. The focus is then on being first on the market with such technologies. Second, LME-style, US firms appear to be more driven by market forces, hence their diversified strategy with different products for different markets, than CME-based Japanese and German firms for whom non-price, internally-driven strategies are more the case. Third, the time frame for the introduc-tion of these technologies is commensurate with the divide between LME

US-based firms on the one hand, and CME German and Japanese-based firms on the other. The timeframes for the latter are less determined by market forces. Japanese firms in particular appear to be driven by a desire to be first on the market with new technologies and new products, regardless of market forces.

Such broad observations were supported and developed through a detailed analysis of the role of state regulations, the nature of market forces, and the internal strategic drivers of firms.

STATE REGULATION: FLOORS OR CEILINGS?

The liberal economic model holds that well-targeted regulations, in the form of penalties or incentives, are required to internalize environmental externalities. These must be enforced by the appropriate authorities to ensure compliance. In Chapter 4, regulations in the form of market mechanisms and command-and-control standards were considered. Market mechanisms were found to be less important in altering industry behavior in all cases than standards. In the case of standards, the material facts of regulations were found to be insufficient to explain the degree of compliance with them, and therefore industry support for them. There were implications for whether the industry leads or follows regulations. These are normative questions, because they do not only ask whether firms comply with regulations, but go beyond this to seek answers to qualitative questions of how well they comply, whether they are likely to continue doing so and whether they are likely to lead change in future or only respond to what is demanded of them. In a nutshell, they go to illuminating the degree to which regulations are 'floors' that establish minimum requirements (for minimal behavioral change) that are easily exceeded by firms, versus 'ceilings' that establish the maximum effort they are inclined to make in addressing environmental externalities.

The VOC of firms' home states explains the extent to which regulations establish floors or ceilings. The nature of state–firm relations, and how this informs the development of regulations, was seen to be the key factor in the industry's performance in respect of them. Closer state–business relations in CMEs were found to mean that firms based there are more likely to be proactive in suggesting and implementing initiatives to reduce CO_2 emissions. Regulation is based more on co- to self-regulatory relations with regulators, and the result is that the industry exceeds regulations which may be thought of as floors that they are well above. By contrast, LME-based US firms, more arm's length from the state in setting standards and therefore having standards imposed on them, act more as lobbyists in respect of the state against regulatory strengthening. They barely meet regulatory requirements. Therefore, regulations are ceilings that the US industry struggles to reach.

These findings were found to have an international dimension because of their ramifications beyond the borders of firms' home states. Firms export the institutional features of their home states' regulations in the products they sell. In all the territories in which they operate, regardless of specific market factors, Japanese and German/European firms sell cars that are more fuel efficient and produce fewer CO_2 emissions than US firms. The institutional importance of national regulatory environments, in terms of state–business relations, how these inform the setting of regulatory standards, and the resulting floor versus ceiling conception of these standards, were shown to override any notions of the universal, stateless corporation driven primarily by global market forces.

MARKET FORCES: CONSUMER DEMAND OR SOCIAL ATTITUDES?

In the absence of state regulatory intervention, the liberal economic model posits that internalization of environmental externalities occurs when market forces in the form of consumer demand mean that such externalities are incorporated in the price mechanism. When they are, an 'invisible hand' efficiently takes environmental concerns into account. Combined with this view is the post-materialist values thesis that such an outcome is increasingly likely because of changing social attitudes. However, the extent to which market forces drive corporate strategic change on the environment was shown to be institutionally dependent on whether markets (in LMEs) or more relational, cooperative relations between economic actors and society (in CMEs) coordinate economic activity. It was found that because material concerns are most important to US LME-based firms, social concern for the environment is discounted in favor of consumer demand and the short-term profit motivations to which it gives rise. By contrast, German and Japanese CME-based firms give higher priority to social attitudes.

Therefore, the key finding of Chapter 5 was the relative importance of short-term material returns in LMEs versus longer-term social attitudes in CMEs. Social concern for the environment in Germany and Japan was found, in a manner similar to the way in which regulations are developed in these CMEs, to produce a willingness to lead markets that is not as evident for US LME-based firms. Predisposed to react to the material returns possible from consumer demand in markets, US firms discount social concerns. This is related to the findings in Chapter 4 in respect of state regulations, in the sense that states that have a co-regulatory approach, or one where regulations have highly voluntaristic components, have firms that are more likely to lead markets. For example, in addressing their CO_2 emission commitments, the German industry is promoting advanced diesel vehicles, which is also commensurate with a CME preference for incremental technological advances. Japanese firms are taking a more radical technology-driven approach befitting their technonationalist version of a CME. In both cases, by proactively acting in concert with, and possibly ahead of, the state, and certainly ahead of markets, they are more internally driven in their environmental initiatives, and more concerned with social attitudes than actual consumer demand.

INTERNAL STRATEGIC DRIVERS: RATIONAL BUSINESS CALCULATIONS OR BELIEFS?

The analysis in Chapters 6 and 7 of individual firms' rationales for their environmental product development strategies expressed in their environmental reports, and in interviews with key personnel, further illuminated the industry-wide conclusions reached in respect of state regulations and market forces. LME-based US firms are focused on material factors – that is, the actual demands of state regulations and consumer demand in markets. In contrast, CME-based firms are more focused on social attitudes (German firms) and internal strategies (Japanese firms). They have a more normative perspective of their business interests. A key exception to the rule, yet suggested by the VOC approach, is that while endogenous sources of change are not as important as exogenous, material (mainly market) imperatives for LME-based firms, in the case of Ford the perspective of the firm's Chairman and Chief Executive Officer results in environmental concerns coming to the fore. This is commensurate with senior management's more unilateral control over firm strategies in LMEs. Environmental sustainability is important for Ford, even if not clearly supportive of immediate material economic interests, because senior management commitment is present.

Unpacking the German and Japanese firms' differences in approach was further illuminated by the analysis in Chapter 6 and 7. The German CME model sees firms as bearing public responsibility for their actions and looking to social attitudes in upholding such responsibilities. Their image and standing matters to them from a material perspective, but also in terms of their role in society. They couple their concern for social attitudes with a desire to be proactive in the policy process to achieve consensus-based agreements that serve environmental, as well as material/business focused goals. Close and cooperative, consensus-based state–business relations are therefore central to their perspective on state regulation, and they are thus likely to develop internal corporate policies to further their environmental goals in the light of social concerns and their close relations with the state.

Japanese firms have similar drivers to German firms, but the enterprise community aspects of Japanese CME capitalist relations are more to the fore. This reflects the more 'organic' way in which Japanese firms conceive their relations with the state and society as opposed to the negotiated consensus, legally mandated *modus operandi* of German firms. Thus, Japanese firms are particularly driven by their internal cultures, as predicted by the importance ascribed to group, consensus-based strategy development and implementation within the Japanese CME model. They are internally driven by a belief in the importance of the environment and a company-specific vision of the strategies required to act on this belief. Less driven by the material imperatives of market forces in the short term, they aim to lead the market in new and uncharted directions with more radical products. They want to lead not just in material competitive terms, but in meeting broader strategic (in this case environmental) goals.

WHICH FIRMS BELIEVE ENVIRONMENTAL CONCERNS ARE IMPORTANT?

Taken together with the observations on state regulation and market forces, the findings on internal strategic drivers lead to key conclusions on the extent to which firms have truly internalized concern for the environment.

The German firms do not meet government regulations, so much as exceed them or move forward with regulators in a spirit of partnership. They do not react to consumer demand, so much as attempt to be ahead of it, and social attitudes are more important to them than actual demand. They are more likely to seek a balance of stakeholder viewpoints external and internal to the company in developing environmental strategies, so that a balance between exogenous and endogenous factors is achieved.

The Japanese firms go beyond cooperating with government to assume a leadership position on the environment. As firms based in a technonationalist CME with philosophical commitment to the environment, they are driven to produce technologically radical environmentally-friendly vehicles such as Toyota's Prius. In so doing, a high importance is placed on internal strategic drivers. The result for firms such as Toyota is that they are increasingly branding themselves as environmental firms as part of being technological leaders. In so doing, environmental leadership is becoming a core management objective.

The US firms remain, LME-style, more focused on reacting to weak (environmental) consumer demand than addressing stronger social attitudes. As well as reacting to market forces in the form of consumer demand, they are predisposed to reacting to and meeting state regulations, rather than exceeding them. With material motivators of profitability and economic success to the fore, they are more exogenously driven. However, in the case of Ford the role of the company's Chairman and CEO is important because of his environmental awareness, and family heritage of corporate citizenship values. This forms the foundation for Ford's internal drive to address environmental concerns, despite market forces exerting contrary material incentives. Given the greater power of top management to make decisions and set strategy in LME-based firms, this is primarily where the impetus for Ford's environmental initiatives comes from.

In the end, as suggested in the conclusion to Chapter 7, there is no doubt that all firms are to some degree driven by both materialist and post-materialist values, but there are clear differences in degree and rationale. A shift to more post-materialist perspectives is a matter of material rationality for German firms – that is, post materialist values are affecting materialist perspectives. Japanese firms are displaying their environmental credentials for both materialist and post-materialist reasons. They are in transition from materialist to post-materialist values as drivers of their business strategies. US firms are predisposed, as a result of the LME variety of capitalism of their home state, to materialist approaches to the environment. The exception is the role of senior management in the case of Ford.

ANSWERS TO QUESTIONS

In finding an answer to what motivates car firms to make environmental commitments, three questions were asked at the outset. The first, and central question, was: what institutional factors are likely to motivate firms in the car industry to see environmental issues as central to their business interests? Japanese car firms are indeed potentially the 'saviours of the environment' (Koshiba et al., 2001; see also Bleviss, 1990; Parker, 1996) because they have *chosen* as a matter of internal company strategy to embrace environmental technologies as a way of enhancing corporate performance. Parker (2001: 109) sums this up neatly as follows:

Rather than being 'lucky' as suggested by some commentators on the fast sale of hybrids when they were launched in North America at a time of rising gasoline prices (2000), the success of the new hybrid technology can be traced to the foresight and planning of firms that recognized mounting environmental pressures and responded. Supportive policies were created by government, industry associations and competing firms, with the end result being a race to deliver new technologies for cars in the 20th century that are less damaging to the environment.

But Japanese firms' actions are, at their root, due more to their home state's CME variety of capitalism than an altruistic concern for environmental sustainability. First, the co- to self-regulatory manner in which regulations are set means firms tend to lead the state and markets with their environmental product development initiatives. They have a longer-term strategic timescale. Second, the technonationalist CME model that typifies Japanese capitalist relations of production leads its car industry to apply radical technological solutions and commercially release the results as soon as possible. Third, the Japanese industry's leadership role on the environment is the least associated with changes in social attitudes and willingness to act on these of the three, but its CME variety of capitalism means the fact of the existence of social concern is more strategically important. Finally, internal strategic drivers are to the fore for Japanese firms. They are increasingly, as a result of the path dependence of previous actions and their core beliefs, internalizing a concern for environmental sustainability in their business strategies.

The case is similar for German car firms. Advanced diesels are their focus, so (arguably) a less technologically-radical approach has been the result. It is certainly true that diesel is cheaper in Europe and that diesel has been embraced by the industry and EU policy-makers, but as the analysis in Chapter 4 and the opinions of the Volkswagen interviewee in Chapter 7 suggest, such market factors are not necessarily the driving force behind these developments. It is more a matter of path-dependent expertise in such technologies, and a technologically incremental approach to addressing climate change that allows them to meet CO_2 emission regulations, voluntarily proposed, in the most cost-effective manner possible and to exceed the targets set. In addition, social concern, willingness to act on this concern and actual consumer behavior also favor such a course of action. Again, the CME basis of capitalist relations is at the core of the strategies being adopted by the German industry, as it is acting more on social concern, in partnership with state regulators, and on a longer-term cooperative strategy to incrementally move towards more environmentally-friendly technologies for its products.

It therefore appears that it is Japanese and German firms that will capitalize on the relative recalcitrance of the US industry. Waiting for, or reacting to, market conditions in the form of material returns as a result of consumer demand, or reacting to (and often opposing) state regulations, they are lagging the Japanese and German industry in environmental product development initiatives. Without competitive pressures from Japanese and German firms, the VOC approach and the analysis in this book supports the finding that for institutional reasons they are unlikely to lead strategic change towards more environmentally responsible technologies, at least in terms of their introduction in cars commercially available for sale. If they do, as in the case of Ford with vehicles such as the petrol-electric hybrid Escape SUV, it is because of a commitment by senior management. Institutional factors that give management the power to act more unilaterally in LMEs are at the root of explaining why this should be the case.

Therefore, answering the question of what motivates car firms to make environmental commitments, or more specifically what institutional factors are likely to motivate firms in the car industry to see environmental issues as central to their business interests, hinges on the impact of differing national institutional factors. It is not so much a question of whether car firms are concerned about the environment and whether or not they have *real* environmental product development strategies (they all do to one degree or another), as what would drive them, or has driven them, to do so. The question of 'greenwashing' versus real commitment to reduce the environmental impact of the industry's products remains relevant, but so do nationally appropriate and conducive paths to environmental commitments. Although ensuring firms make credible environmental commitments is an important consideration, and that these commitments effectively address environmental problems, the question of nationally conducive paths to so doing is no less important.

The second question, contingent on the answer to the first one, was: are the motivators for firms to embrace environmental improvements universal, or are they specific to firms based on their nationality or, possibly, individual cultures? Clearly, it cannot be said that the motivators for firms to embrace environmental improvements are universal. The answer is that the motivators are both nationally specific, and firm-specific. Therefore, the crucial finding is that it is not sufficient to say that material factors, such as state regulations or consumer demand, are the primary motivators for all firms. They cannot be said, by the fact of their existence, to even necessarily produce the same material outcomes.

These findings in respect of the second question are important because of their broader implications. The mainstream liberal economic perspective is a somewhat cynical (although adherents might prefer 'realistic' or 'rational') one that any concern for the environment must be the result of materially-driven instrumental behavior based on a logic of consequential-ism. The aim is purely self-interested profit seeking on the part of firms. However, what has been shown is that far from a global perspective on the environment being the case, firms have very distinct lenses through which they view the environmental performance of their products. Employing the insights of the VOC approach, empirical evidence has been presented for why the liberal economic model only approximates the behavior and motivations of US-based car firms. This is because they are based in the archetypal LME. However, for CME-based German and Japanese firms, a different institutional basis for capitalist relations leads them to focus on more normative factors. In turn, such normative factors influence the way they view their material interests, and the consequences of their actions. They are inclined to take a more holistic view in which their role in society occupies a more central strategic position, internal corporate strategies proactively drive environmental product initiatives, and leadership over, or partnership with, regulators is a feature of their strategic planning.

The third question, contingent on answers to the first two and re-phrasing the central question more accurately, was: why should the car industry be concerned about the environment, particularly given its global economic significance and resulting political power? Institutionalized norms have implications for the way in which firms of different nationalities approach important issues such as the environment and, specifically in this thesis, the issue of climate change. The VOC approach has been employed to demon-strate that it is the institutional basis of different capitalisms that is particu-larly relevant when one considers MNCs such as those in the car industry whose operations may be truly global, but whose 'spirit' remains rooted in the nation that gave them birth. It has been shown that the VOC of nations has implications not just for the type of products these transnational eco-nomic actors produce, and the competitive advantages they develop, but also the way they address related issues arising as a result of their activities, such as environmental degradation. Thus, while their attitude and actions relating to environmental concerns have been the focus, non-environmental institutional factors relating to states' VOC have been shown to be salient for explaining their actions. Therefore, the VOC approach has implications for the way in which non-economic issues, such as environmental externali-ties, are addressed by these transnational actors.

THE ROAD AHEAD

Any piece of research raises as many questions as it answers, and this book is no exception. A reality check is therefore in order. Despite finding that the CME variety of capitalism is producing superior results in respect of the environment, it is premature to celebrate the salvation of the planet through cooperative market relations. For example, whatever the reductions in EU emissions per car, the European Commission finds that 'even though there have been significant improvements in vehicle technology – in particular in fuel efficiency which also means lower CO_2 emissions – this has not been enough to neutralize the effect of increased traffic and car size. While the EU as a whole has reduced its emissions by just under 5 per cent over the 1990–2004 period, CO_2 emissions from road transport have increased by 26 per cent' (Commission of the European Communities, 2007b:2). In addition, whatever the emission reductions made previously, resistance from the European car industry today means that the EU is now actively considering further legislation (Commission of the European Communities, 2007b; *The Economist*, 2008).

Clearly there is a need for more effective transport alternatives to cars, and perhaps private mobility in general. This has not been considered here, but I would venture that the reality is that none of us seem inclined to get out of our cars and on to our bikes, buses, trains or other alternative transportation solutions any time soon unless, perhaps, the price of petrol and diesel starts to approach US$10 a litre. LME, CME or otherwise, no democratically elected government will ever embrace a regulatory regime with the electoral impacts that would flow from a set of policies that achieved this.

Even so, as we go into the 21st century, with climate change perhaps the most pressing global issue faced by all nations, imagine a world in which the effects become so acute that there is the political possibility of not just a moderate approach to taxing CO_2 emissions, but a broad-based comprehensive tax system to address the crisis of climate change. Or, imagine a world in which market realities mean that the price of oil is suddenly so high that it rules out the sale of big gas guzzlers, coupled with the social stigma that goes with being seen driving them. Which countries' industries would be most in trouble versus those that could more easily rise to the challenges? As a result, which countries' economic power and influence on the world stage in addressing the ongoing/ upcoming crisis is likely to be enhanced, versus eroded? The answer to all these questions is all too clear. Even if the European industry is resistant to further initiatives to reduce CO_2 emissions, any more stringent regulations introduced now will build on the industry's own initial efforts, rather than being the primary response to the problem. The Japanese industry is already on a path to coping well with the potential shocks by effectively leading regulators. A much less favorable scenario is the case for the US.

Yet, Germany, the US and Japan are increasingly not the only states that matter. As emerging economies such as China and India continue to develop their own car industries, and indeed as they develop in general, how are the capitalist relations of production of the established LMEs and CMEs relevant to them? This is not clear. The VOC approach's use of the CME/LME divide is a useful heuristic device, but there is a danger of drawing caricatures of states based on a simple categorization of them as LMEs or CMEs. As a leading exponent of the VOC approach, Hall himself concedes that 'there is still an implicit emphasis in [the VOC] literature on a few ideal-typical countries', even if 'it has generated an important set of propositions of wide potential applicability' (Hall, 1999: 145; see also Coates, 2005b). If a country possesses attributes of both CMEs and LMEs, in other words we are not at the extremes of the continuum, the VOC approach is not so useful and there is the danger of concept stretching (i.e. over-extension) in order to encompass states that do not fit the categories (Collier and Mahon, 1993). In future research, it will therefore be important to extend the insights of the VOC approach beyond the extreme cases of LMEs versus CMEs, and beyond the usual suspects of the largest industrialized states.

Given the demonstrated importance of institutional perspectives, and the need to extend the analysis both theoretically and empirically, future research suggested from this book revolves around two related key themes. First, the global versus national/international debate. While the focus has been on the environmental initiatives of the car industry, the issues considered speak to larger debates about the extent to which a shift in power has occurred from states to markets and the forces of transnational capital, versus the enduring relevance of states in international capitalist relations. The former may be thought of as a global perspective, the latter a more statist perspective that holds that economic relations are more international (that is, between states) than global (that is, a borderless world). To a large extent this is a book about the VOC implications for MNCs and their corporate/ environmental responsibility as much, if not more, than a book about the car industry. At its core, this book takes issue with arguments that the world is becoming homogenized because of the greater permeability of states' borders as a result of the globalization of markets. Instead, the story told is one of enduring and vital differences, and preliminary research aimed at extending the analysis in Mikler (2008) demonstrates its broader applicability.

It would perhaps be best to expand the field of inquiry to other non-economic (or perhaps more accurately, non-material) issues, such as human rights, corporate social responsibility and ethical business practice, and to examine these across industrial sectors. This would allow the insights gained here via studying one industrial sector in detail, to be applied more broadly to the role of MNCs in addressing such non-economic issues. This is because there are implications for whether the institutional basis of different states' capitalisms facilitates (or does not facilitate) addressing such aspects of economic activity, as well as how they are addressed. It means that studies at the level of the firm and individual industrial sectors may, to some extent, be set aside for an analysis that focuses on the institutional structures of states and the environment they provide for their flagship corporations to address such concerns. Far from being irrelevant, differences in states' capitalist relations are institutionally embedded in their MNCs (as MNCs are in turn institutionally embedded in their home states) that disseminate the norms of their home state's capitalist relations internationally with global effects.

The second theme is the role of private versus public authority. At the outset of the book it was noted that a significant implication of taking a normative institutional approach is that at some stage self-regulation may be effective for normative reasons, as opposed to the traditional liberal economic view that it cannot for rationalist reasons. While the OECD (2001a) observes that firms themselves are the primary source of new codes of conduct, suggesting that responsibility for regulation is moving from the private to the public sphere, the important question to ask is whether or not this really represents a shift of power to markets. The findings of this book suggest that the institutional embedding of firms in their home states, and the manner in which this impacts on their strategic thinking, means that what we have is a case of 'freer markets, more rules' (Vogel, 1996), or perhaps that national institutional differences impact on the manner in which private authority is exercised for addressing the non-economic impacts of economic activity (as suggested in OECD, 2001b).

Either way, it appears that as Harrod (2006) notes, firms are political actors as much as economic ones, and that national institutional differences do matter. This means that it is important to investigate how these differences impact on firms when they develop their codes of conduct, what these contain, the relevance of national institutional differences which they may embody, and whether or not these differences mean that global codes of conduct can ever be effective. Indeed, it raises questions of whether the various global codes of conduct proposed by international organizations represent attempts to homogenize rules in a manner that reflects more one institutional perspective than another. If this is the case, they are likely to be at least partially ineffective.

NOTES

1. While Hall and Soskice (2001a) focus on 'the institutional foundations of comparative advantage', I am more comfortable speaking in terns of competitive advantage. This is because the concept of comparative advantage is most accurately associated with the endowments and efficiencies of states, rather than the way in which firms from them compete.
2. That is to say, relaxing the *ceteris paribus* assumption.

Appendix A: questions asked in the world values survey

As a global survey, the World Values Survey (WVS) is useful for comparatively analysing attitudes to a range of social concerns across countries. Questions relating to respondents' attitude to the environment were singled out for examination as they are of direct relevance to the questions asked in Chapter 5. The WVS is also useful because it covers all the countries examined, as well as the time frame for analysis. However, like any global survey conducted over time there are data gaps, and variations in questions asked and responses to them which cause problems. There is no such thing as the perfect survey or dataset, so one must acknowledge and work within the limitations of what is available.

Reponses to the second (1990–1993), third (1995–1997) and fourth (1999–2000) WVS waves were analysed. All questions on the environment asked in the WVS that relate to the three concerns here (that is, concern for the environment; willingness to take direct action in markets; and willingness to take non-market action) are analysed in Chapter 5. However, not all the questions were asked in all the waves of the WVS. German respondents were not asked certain questions in Wave 4 that were asked of US and Japanese respondents. In Wave 4, one of the questions was asked in a different format to Waves 3 and 4. The waves in which they were asked, and where applicable the countries that were covered, are shown in Table A.1.

In addition, two categories of responses were eliminated to enhance the clarity of the analysis:

1. For many questions, some waves included a category 'don't know' as a possible response to the question posed, while in others such a category of response was not available. Furthermore, waves that did include such a category did not include it uniformly for all countries covered (for example, in Wave 3 'don't know' was a possible response for Germany, but not for the US or Japan). For the sake of comparison, all 'don't know' responses have been eliminated in percentage calculations.

Table A.1   Environmental questions asked in the World Values Survey

Question	Asked in Wave 2?	Asked in Wave 3?	Asked in Wave 4?
Now I am going to read off a list of voluntary organizations; for each one, could you tell me whether you are an active member, an inactive member or not a member of that type of organization?			
Environmental organization	YES	YES	YES, although the question was asked in two parts: respondents were asked whether they were a member, and then asked in another question if they had done unpaid work. For the sake of analysis, doing unpaid work was taken as being equivalent to being an active member of an organization.
I am now going to read out some statements about the environment. For each one I read out, can you tell me whether you agree strongly, agree, disagree or disagree strongly?			
I would agree to an increase in taxes if the extra money were used to prevent environmental damage.	YES	YES	YES
I would buy things at 20% higher than usual prices if it would help protect the environment.	NO	YES	NO
I would give part of my income if I were certain that the money would be used to prevent environmental pollution.	NO	NO	YES

Government should reduce environmental pollution but it should not cost me any money

NO   NO   YES

Here are two statements people sometimes make when discussing the environment and economic growth. Which of them comes closer to your own point of view?

NO   YES   YES

1. Protecting the environment should be given priority, even if it causes slower economic growth and some loss of jobs.
2. Economic growth and creating jobs should be the top priority, even if the environment suffers to some extent
3. Other answer

Which, if any, of these things have you done in the last 12 months, out of concern for the environment?

Have you chosen household products that you think are better for the environment?

NO   YES   NO

Have you decided for environmental reasons to reuse or recycle something rather than throw it away?

NO   YES   NO

Have you tried to reduce water consumption for environmental reasons?

NO   YES   NO

Have you attended a meeting or signed a letter or petition aimed at protecting the environment?

NO   YES   NO

Have you contributed to an environmental organization?

NO   YES   NO

239

Table A.1 (continued)

Question	Asked in Wave 2?	Asked in Wave 3?	Asked in Wave 4?
For each of the following pairs of statements, please tell me which one comes closest to your own views:	NO	YES	YES, but not for Germany
1. Human beings should master nature; or			
2. Humans should coexist with nature.			
Now I'd like you to look at this card. I'm going to read out some different forms of political action that people can take, and I'd like you to tell me, for each one, whether you have actually done any of these things, whether you might do it or would never, under any circumstances, do it.			
Signing a petition	YES	YES	YES
Joining in boycotts	YES	YES	YES
Attending lawful demonstrations	YES	YES	YES
Joining unofficial strikes	YES	YES	YES
Occupying buildings or factories	YES	YES	YES

2. 'Other' was a possible answer for the question on preferencing protecting the environment versus economic growth. 'Other' responses were eliminated, as it is not clear what answer was given when such a response is indicated. It therefore cannot be said with any certainty what such a response indicates. In addition, 'other' responses accounted for under 10 per cent of all valid responses for the countries analysed.

The total number of 'don't know' and 'other' responses has been subtracted from total responses and the calculation of response percentages made on the basis of this reduced total number of responses.

Appendix B: car class definitions

As noted in Chapter 5, there are variations in the definition of car classes across the three territories. The exact definitions are given here.

EUROPEAN UNION

The data presented for the European Union is from the Association des Constructeurs Européens d'Automobiles (ACEA), which receives it in aggregated form from a private data collection agency. Phone discussions with ACEA personnel indicated that data disaggregated by country are not available, nor a uniform definition for car classes across countries and manufacturers. Furthermore, they were unsure how the private agency that aggregated the data into classes across EU member states did so. However, the ACEA personnel were able to provide examples of cars in each class which indicates the following:

1. 'Small' cars are cheap, economical four-cylinder cars that correspond with the definition of mini and small Japanese cars (see below) – for example the Peugeot 106 and 206; Ford Ka and Fiesta; Honda Logo and Civic; and Volkswagen Polo and Lupo.
2. 'Lower-medium' cars are more expensive, slightly larger cars – for example, the Renault Megane; Opel Astra and Tigra; Toyota Corolla; and Volkswagen Golf and Beetle.
3. 'Upper-medium' cars are larger cars – for example, the Citroen Xantia; Opel Vectra; and Subaru Legacy.
4. 'Executive' cars are generally larger, more luxurious models, although in some cases they are sports and performance vehicles – for example, the BMW 3 and 5 series; Alfa Romeo 166 and Spider; Opel Omega; Audi A8; and Toyota Lexus.
5. 'Others' are mostly four-wheel drives, people-movers and cross-over vehicles – for example, the Jeep Grand Cherokee; Ford Courier; Honda CRV and HRV; Mitsubishi Pajero; and Toyota RAV4 and Land Cruiser.

GERMANY

The data for Germany were provided on request from the Verband der Automobilindustrie (VDA) which sources it from the Kraftfahrt-Bundesamt (KBA). The classes are for passenger vehicles (*personenkraft-wagen*) and are similar to those available for the EU, except that:

1. The 'small' class is disaggregated into 'mini' and 'small' classes.
2. The 'others' class is disaggregated into four-wheel drives (*gelandewa-gen*), vans, utilities and cabriolets.
3. The disaggregation employed may, somewhat perversely, have under-mined the explanatory power of the data. For example, it is unclear whether a cabriolet is a large powerful car (for example, a top-of-the-line Mercedes convertible) or a smaller compact car (for example, a Peugeot 206). It is similarly unclear whether a van is a 'people-mover' or a more utility-based vehicle, and its size is indeterminate.

In phone discussions, both VDA and KBA personnel confirmed that aggregate car class data are only available from 1999 onwards. The KBA was able to provide disaggregated data on a per-model sales basis before 1999. However, it was unclear exactly which classes individual models sold should fall into. I was therefore unwilling to risk arbitrary assignment of models to classes without detailed information on each model offered for sale.

UNITED STATES

For the United States, the classes identified are those used by the US Environment Protection Agency (EPA) and US Department of Energy. They classify cars on the basis of interior passenger and cargo volume as follows (Hellman and Heavenrich, 2003b; US Department of Energy and US Environment Protection Agency, 2004):

1. 'Small' cars and wagons include the three EPA categories for cars of minicompact (under 85 cubic feet), subcompact (85–99 cubic feet) and compact (100–109 cubic feet) and for station wagons under 130 cubic feet.
2. 'Mid-size' cars and wagons includes cars of 110–119 cubic feet and station wagons of 130–159 cubic feet.
3. 'Large' cars and wagons includes cars of 120 or more cubic feet and station wagons of 160 or more cubic feet.

US light trucks are classified on the basis of wheelbase length as follows (Hellman and Heavenrich, 2004c):

1. SUVs: 'small' is less than 100 inches, 'mid-size' is 100–110 inches and 'large' is over 110 inches.
2. Vans: 'small' is less than 109 inches, 'mid-size' is 109–124 inches and 'large' is over 124 inches.
3. Pickup trucks: 'small' is less than 105 inches, 'mid-size' is 105–115 inches and 'large' is over 115 inches.

JAPAN

For Japan, cars are classified according to the Road Vehicles Act. These classifications are used for registration statistics and vehicle inspections. For passenger cars, there are three categories (JAMA, 2004a: 64):

1. 'Mini' vehicles are under 660cc in engine displacement, under 2 metres in height, under 1.48 metres in width and under 3.4 metres in length.
2. 'Small' vehicles are between 661–2000cc in engine displacement, except for diesel engines, under 2 metres in height, 1.45–1.7 metres in width and 3.4–4.7 metres in length.
3. 'Ordinary/standard' motor vehicles are over 2000cc in engine displacement, over 2 metres in height, over 1.7 metres in width and over 4.7 metres in length.

The Japan Automobile Manufacturers Association (JAMA, 2004b: 168) notes that cars are categorized primarily on the basis of engine displacement, so a car with less than 2000cc engine displacement that has a width greater than 1.7 metres is still classified as a small vehicle.

For four-wheel drives, no definition is provided by JAMA for its categorization of them in either the 'mini' or 'other' class of four-wheel drives, but one may presume that this categorization is along similar lines to that for passenger cars. Another potential problem is that JAMA's data for four-wheel drives exclude sales of imported four-wheel drives, but given the predominance of Japanese manufacturers in the Japanese market (that is, nearly 94 per cent of total sales) this is not a critical problem.

Appendix C: coding of environmental reports

The text of firms' environmental reports was analysed using QSR NVivo 2.0 qualitative analysis software. This software allows codes to be applied to the text for recurring concepts expressed. Coding was applied to those sections of environmental reports where rationales for action are outlined, rather than the action itself. Thus, codes were applied to executive statements at the front of reports, sections on the company's 'vision' vis-à-vis the environment, and the firm's actual environmental policy guidelines. The rules employed for coding are based on authoritative literature outlining appropriate methodologies (for example, see Bazeley and Richards, 2000; Gibbs, 2002; Bryman, 2004; Denscombe, 1998; Yin, 2003a and b). The definitions of the factors to which codes were applied, and their subcategories, are defined below.

Material factors are split between the subcategories of market forces and state regulation. These are largely the material factors already examined in Chapters 4 and 5. For the sake of coding, market forces are defined in material terms as statements that identify forces that affect the firm's financial bottom line and its economic performance as a result of the products it sells. Therefore, codes applied within this subcategory related to the following concepts:

1. Competition, in terms of:
   a. *Consumer demand*: The need to take account of consumer preferences or demand – for example, tying efforts on the environment to demand for these, or saying that market forces temper what can be done.
   b. *Competitive pressure from other firms*: Competitive pressures from other firms in markets or within the industry as a whole.
2. Safeguarding financial returns, in terms of:
   a. *Profits and sales*: References to profits and sales, whether associated with environmental concerns or otherwise.
   b. *Shareholder value*: Providing value to shareholders, or stock performance generally.
   c. *Risk management*: Identification of environmental factors as a significant business risk factor that needs to be addressed.

3. Proactive action, in terms of:
   a. *Market share/leadership*: Being first to market new products, or leading in them, as a business strategy that drives environmental product development initiatives.
   b. *Business opportunity*: The idea that being environmentally responsible and producing products that reflect this represents a business opportunity.

State regulation is defined as references to regulations, including complying with them, exceeding them, acting on the future likelihood of them, etc. Codes applied within this sub-category related to the following concepts:

1. International regulation: Internationally agreed conventions, protocols, etc. on environmental issues, including:
   a. *International meetings*: Meetings convened by international organizations such as the United Nations Conference on Environment and Development (UNCED), the United Nations Environment Programme (UNEP), etc., or participation in international forums where environmental performance is addressed including meetings held by industry groups such as the World Business Council for Sustainable Development (WBCSD).
   b. *International protocols*: Ratified international agreements that states have decided to adopt (for example, the Montreal Protocol and Kyoto Protocol).
   c. *International voluntary agreements*: Adherence to, or participation in, international non-binding international agreements, such as the Global Reporting Initiative (GRI), Coalition of Environmentally Responsible Economies (CERES) Principles, etc.
2. National regulation: National regulations, policies, agreements, etc. on environmental issues, in terms of:
   a. *National legislation*: Meeting or exceeding the requirements of national legislation.
   b. *National voluntary agreements*: National voluntary agreements agreed and supported jointly between the industry and regulatory authorities.
   c. *Input to policy/regulations*: Input to/the provision of advice on national regulations and regulatory settings.

Normative factors are split between the subcategories of social attitudes and internal company strategies. Social attitudes were considered in Chapter 5. However, internal company strategies, which are endogenous to individual firms, have not been considered so far because the analysis in Chapters 4 and 5 has been at a national, rather than individual firm, level. Social attitudes are defined as non-market forces to do with social perceptions of environmental concerns, and the way this indirectly affects perceptions of the firm's business or the firm's reaction to them for other reasons. Codes applied within this subcategory related to the following concepts:

1. General social concern/raised awareness of environmental issues: A recognition of increased social concern for the environment and a response to this.
2. Firm image, in terms of:
   a. *Brand value*: The value of the name of the company and what it represents, especially in terms of loyalty and price premiums that it can extract for its products.
   b. *Building trust*: References to trust, respect and generally high standing in a more general sense than brand value.
3. Responsibility to society on various levels, including:
   a. *Responsibility to society*:
      - *Unspecified*: The firm has a responsibility to society generally.
      - *Global*: The firm has a responsibility to society globally.
      - *Nation*: The firm has a responsibility to society nationally.
   b. *Responsibility to stakeholders*: The firm has a responsibility to those directly affected by the company's operations, specifically customers, suppliers, employees and government.

Internal company strategies are defined simply as endogenous factors that lead firms to take the environment seriously. Codes applied within this subcategory related to the following concepts:

1. Corporate policy: A statement that indicates not just that environmental impact is something for which the firm must take responsibility, and take action in respect of it, but that it is a:
   a. *Corporate belief*: Environmentally responsible behavior is a clear strategic commitment, or corporate goal. In a sense, everything done by a company is because it believes it is a 'good thing' to do/ is in its interest, but this code relates to statements that represent a clear belief company-wide that the environmental impact of its products is important. It is a statement along the lines that 'we do this because we believe it is a good/right thing to do'.
   b. *Guiding principle*: Not just a statement of belief, but reference to actual internal guiding principles, or guidelines for operation, or policies that codify or implement the environmental performance

of the company. To some extent this represents a rationale based on circular reasoning (for example, along the lines that 'we do it because we have guideline that says we do it') but it still indicates a rationale for action based on internal company strategies that in this case are clearly codified.

2. *History/path dependence*: The firm characterizes itself as one that takes the environmental impacts of its actions seriously, and thus continues to be one where concern for the environment is part of how it does business. This is not a change in direction but a continuation of a commitment and strategy.[1]

3. *Leader's vision*: The leader her/himself identifies, or is identified as having, a commitment to the environment and action that is aimed at reducing the environmental impacts of the company's products.

No preconceived notions of what codes might be applied within the subcategories were established *a priori*. The idea was that the reports 'speak for themselves'. Therefore, codes under the subcategories emerged in the course of reading and re-reading the reports over a period of six months in 2005. In so doing, it was also realized that another category of coding was required due to the fact that the theme of 'sustainability' recurred in the texts. This occurred in two ways. First, the overarching concern of the concept of sustainability was mentioned. Second, the link between environmental and economic sustainability was made by several firms and given as the reason behind their environmental product development initiatives. Coding was applied in respect of both these concepts, which are defined as follows:

1. *Environmental sustainability*: Specific reference to the concept in terms of environmental sustainability itself, or sustainable development, environmentally sustainable economic development, sustainable mobility or similar. Any use of the word 'sustainable' in an environmental context.

2. *Environmental and economic sustainability linked*: An expressed belief that environmental sustainability is connected with economic sustainability. This may be the idea that there is a double dividend in looking after the environment: not only does the environment benefit, but the business benefits through being more economically sustainable as a result. Or it may be that the two are linked and need to be balanced.

Coding of Nissan's *Environmental Report* (2004a) and *Sustainability Report* (2004b) was combined, and likewise for Honda's *Environmental*

Annual Report (2004) and *Ecology* (2002). The rationale for so doing is that these companies intend the reports to be complementary and inform one another. They should be read together and, as such, coded together.

NOTE

1. This has undertones of path dependence as described in Pierson (2000) and Pierson and Skocpol (2000).

Appendix D: interview questions

Interviews were conducted in 2005. The interviews were recorded and transcribed in order to facilitate analysis. However, the full transcribed text of the interviews is not available, this being a condition of the University of Sydney Ethics Committee. Therefore, in the analysis presented in Chapter 7, interviewees' quotations and views are not referenced to these transcripts, which have been kept confidential as required. Instead, it is made clear to which firm's interviewee(s) the views expressed pertain. The questions asked were as follows:

1. What would you say are the major initiatives your firm is taking in producing vehicles that are more environmentally friendly? Why has your firm taken these initiatives?
2. In a business sense, how do you believe improvements in the environmental performance of the vehicles produced by your firm may be encouraged: government regulations, consumer preferences (market forces), internal company strategies? Please feel free to expand on your answer.
3. Do you believe the approach of government on environmental issues has changed in the last ten years? How?
4. What do you think the role of government should be in encouraging the production of more environmentally-friendly vehicles? [*prompt*: standards, taxes, subsidies, penalties, rewards]
5. Does government policy shape the strategic direction taken by your firm with respect to the environment? If so how? Has this changed the strategic direction taken by your firm over the last ten years?
6. What major market conditions, if any, have prompted your firm to improve the environmental performance of the vehicles it produces?
7. What changes have you noticed in consumer attitudes or demand in the last ten years with respect to the environment? Has this changed your firm's business significantly? How?
8. Which is most important in shaping your firms' long-term planning: consumer attitudes or actual consumer demand?
9. What do you believe are the major challenges facing your firm in the next ten to twenty years with respect to the environmental perform-

ance of the vehicles it produces? How do you think your firm will respond to these challenges?

Questions 1 and 2 are in the form of open questions that seek the interviewee's opinion on what their company is doing and why. It allows them the opportunity to state the activities their firm is taking with respect to the environment, and the rationales for environmental strategies that have been adopted.

Questions 3 to 8 are designed to allow the interviewee to reflect on the statements made in questions 1 and 2. They broadly cover two themes. Questions 3 to 5 probe, from a variety of angles, the interviewee's conception of the role of government vis-à-vis the company's environmental product development strategies, and how the company operates in the light of government action. Questions 6 to 8 are designed to elucidate opinions in a similar manner with respect to market forces. Hence, these two sets of questions examine how personnel in different firms that hail from different countries perceive their firms' strategies as related to exogenous material factors, or the 'lens' through which such factors are interpreted.

Question 9, like questions 1 and 2, is an open question that seeks the interviewee's opinions on what their company is likely to do in future and why. Coming at the end of the interview, it is designed to produce a response on what is likely to be the strategy of the company in future and the challenges it will face, 'colored' by the issues and the perspectives on them already covered in the preceding questions. Posing a 'crystal ball gazing' question at the end of the interview also gave the interviewee an opportunity to reflect on what they have said in the course of the interview, and add anything they believe is important that may not have already been highlighted.

Apart from questions 1, 2 and 9, there are no questions where interviewees were asked specifically about firm strategies that are not associated with external forces. In fact, only in question 2 is the possibility raised that firm strategies may have been generated internally with no relation to government regulations or market conditions, although the possibility for answering in this way is implicit in questions 1 and 9. The reason for this is twofold. First, the hypothesis that firms can generate such strategies independently should be spontaneously given rather than suggested in order to avoid confirmation bias. Second, this book is not so much concerned with the possibility that material factors are irrelevant (it would be incredibly naive to believe this) but that their importance and how they are perceived differs between different companies on the basis of their nationality.

In almost all cases, questions permitting simple 'yes' or 'no' answers were avoided, and where they were asked (questions 3 and 5) this was done

to get a clear response to the influence of government on business strategies, given that a key aspect of this book is whether regulation is a key
factor in the internalization of environmental externalities and because
the Varieties of Capitalism approach, which strongly focuses on the role
of government and government–business relations, underpins the institutional analysis conducted.

Bibliography

AAM (Alliance of Automobile Manufacturers) (no date a), *What is Corporate Average Fuel Economy (CAFE)?*, http://autoalliance.org/archives/fact2.pdf, accessed 24 March 2004.

AAM (no date b), 'Our Position on CAFE', *Fuel Economy*, http://autoalliance.org/fuel/cafe101_position.php, accessed 24 March 2004.

AAM (no date c), *Consumers and Fuel Economy*, http://autoalliance.org/archives/CAFE9.pdf, accessed 23 July 2004.

ACEA (Association des Constructeurs Europeens d'Automobiles) (2002), *ACEA's CO_2 Commitment*, www.acea.be/ACEA/brochure_co2.pdf, accessed 11 June 2003.

ACEA (2003), *Monitoring of ACEA's Commitment to CO_2 Emission Reductions from Passenger Cars 2002*, final report, www.acea.be/ACEA/20040317PublicationEmissions.pdf, accessed 14 May 2004.

ACEA (2004a), *Why Diesel?*, www.acea.be/ACEA/20040212Publications WhyDiesel.pdf, accessed 5 July 2004.

ACEA (2004b), *EU15 Economic Report*, www.acea.be/ACEA/ER-0204-Internet.pdf, accessed 9 June 2004.

ACEA (no date a), *Passenger Cars in EU15: Breakdown by Segments and Bodies*, www.acea.be/ACEA/Segment-Bodies.pdf, accessed 9 June 2004.

ACEA (no date b), *New Passenger Car Registrations in W. Europe, Breakdown by Specifications: Average Cubic Capacity*, www.acea.be/images/uploads/st/20080131_CC%2090-07.pdf, accessed 21 April 2008.

ACEA (no date c), *New Passenger Car Registrations in W. Europe, Breakdown by Specifications: Share of Diesel*, www.acea.be/images/uploads/st/20080131_Diesel%2090-07.pdf, accessed 21 April 2008.

ACEA (no date d), *New Passenger Car Registrations in W. Europe, Breakdown by Specifications: Share of 4x4*, www.acea.be/images/uploads/st/20080131_4x4%2090-07.pdf, accessed 21 April 2008.

ADB (Asian Development Bank) (no date), *Vehicle Emissions Reduction: European Union*, www.adb.org/vehicle-emissions/General/Standards-eu.asp, accessed 7 January 2004.

Adcock, R. and D. Collier (2001), 'Measurement validity: a shared standard for qualitative and quantitative research', *American Political Science Review*, **95** (3), 529–46.

Adler, E. (1997), 'Seizing the middle ground: constructivism in world politics', *European Journal of International Relations*, **3** (3), 319–63.

Arima, J. (2000), 'Top runner program', presentation at the Workshop on Best Practices in Policy and Measures, Copenhagen, 11–13 April, http://unfccc.int/sessions/workshop/000411/jpnja.pdf, accessed 28 April 2004.

Arksey, H. and P. Knight (1999) *Interviewing for Social Scientists*, London: Sage Publications.

Austin, D., N. Rosinki, A. Sauer and C. le Duc (2003), *Changing Drivers: the Impact of Climate Change on Competitiveness and Value Creation in the Automotive Industry*, report for the Sustainable Asset Management and World Resources Institute, http://pdf.wri.org/changing_drivers_full_report.pdf, accessed 10 January 2004.

Barrett, S. (2003), *Environment and Statecraft: the Strategy of Environmental Treaty-Making*, New York: Oxford University Press.

Bazeley, P. and L. Richards (2000), *The NVivo Qualitative Project Book*, London: Sage Publications.

Beder, S. (2002), *Global Spin: The Corporate Assault on Environmentalism*, Foxhole: Green Books.

Berger, S. (1996), 'Introduction', in S. Berger and R. Dore (eds), *National Diversity and Global Capitalism*, Ithaca, NY: Cornell University Press, pp. 1–25.

Berger, S. and R. Dore (eds) (1996), *National Diversity and Global Capitalism*, Ithaca, NY: Cornell University Press.

Bleviss, D. (1990), 'Policy options to encourage low emission/low fuel consumption vehicles', in *Low Consumption/Low Emission Automobile, Proceedings of an Expert Panel*, conducted in Rome, 14–15 February, International Energy Agency, OECD: Paris.

Blyth, M. (1997), 'Any more bright ideas? The ideational turn of comparative political economy', *Comparative Politics*, **29** (1), 229–50.

Blyth, M. (2003), 'Structures do not come with instruction sheets: interests, ideas and progress in political science', *Perspectives on Politics*, **1** (4), 695–706.

BMW Group (2003a), *Sustainable Value Report 2003/2004: Innovation. Efficiency. Responsibility*, Munich, Germany: Bayerischen Motoren Werke.

BMW Group (2003b), *Environmental Protection: BMW Group Environmental Guidelines*, www.bmwgroup.com/e/0_0_www_bmwgroup_com/5_verantwortung/5_4_publikationen/5_4_4_downloads/pdf/BMWGroup_Umweltleitlinen_E.pdf, accessed 13 January 2005.

Boadway, R. and D. Wildasin (1984), *Public Sector Economics*, Boston, MA: Little, Brown.

Boniface, D. and J. Sharman (2001), 'An analytical revolution in comparative politics?', *Comparative Politics*, **34** (4), 475–93.

Boyer, R. (1996), 'The convergence hypothesis revisited: globalization but still the century of nations?', in S. Berger and R. Dore (eds), *National Diversity and Global Capitalism*, Ithaca, NY: Cornell University Press, pp. 29–59.

Bradsher, K. (2002), *High and Mighty – SUVs: The World's Most Dangerous Vehicles and How they Got That Way*, New York: Public Affairs.

Braithwaite, J. and P. Drahos (2000), *Global Business Regulation*, Cambridge: Cambridge University Press.

Broadbent, J. (2002), 'Japan's environmental regime: the political dynamics of change', in U. Desai (ed.), *Environmental Politics and Policy in Industrialized Countries*, Cambridge, MA: MIT Press, pp. 295–355.

Bryman, A. (2004), *Social Research Methods*, 2nd edn, Oxford: Oxford University Press.

Burchill, S. (1996), 'Liberal internationalism', in S. Burchill and A. Linklater (eds), *Theories of International Relations*, New York: St Martin's Press, pp. 67–92.

Bürgenmeier, B. (1997), 'Economic instruments and social acceptability: a debate about values', in C. Jeanrenaud (ed.), *Environmental Policy Between Regulation and Market*, Basel, Switzerland: Birkhauser Verlag, pp. 288–301.

Burns, L., J. McCormick and C. Borroni-Bird (2002), 'Vehicle of change', *Scientific American*, **287** (4), 64–73.

Carson, R. ([1962] 1999), *Silent Spring*, London: Penguin.

CCFA (Comite' des Constructeurs Français d'Automobiles) (2003), *Analysis and Statistics*, Paris: CCFA, www.ccfa.fr/pdf/2003eng.pdf, accessed 10 January 2004.

Clegg, S. and S. Redding (1990), *Capitalism in Contrasting Cultures*, Berlin: Walter de Gruyter.

The Club of Rome (1972), *The Limits to Growth*, London: Earth Island.

Coase, R. (1960), 'The problem of social cost', *Journal of Law and Economics*, **3** (October), 1–44.

Coates, D. (2005), 'Paradigms of explanation', in D. Coates (ed.), *Varieties of Capitalism, Varieties of Approaches*, Basingstoke: Palgrave Macmillan, pp. 1–25.

Coates, D. (ed.) (2005), *Varieties of Capitalism, Varieties of Approaches*, Basingstoke: Palgrave Macmillan.

Collier, D. and R. Adcock (1999), 'Democracy and dichotomies: a pragmatic approach to choices about concepts', *Annual Review of Political Science*, **2**, 537–65.

Collier, D. and J. Mahon (1993), 'Conceptual stretching revisited: adapting categories in comparative analysis', *American Political Science Review*, **87** (4), 845–55.

Commission of the European Communities (2002), *Monitoring of ACEA's Commitment on CO₂ Emission Reductions from Passenger Cars (2001)*, joint report of the European Automobile Manufacturers Association and the Commission Services, SEC(2002) 1338.

Commission of the European Communities (2005), *Monitoring of ACEA's Commitment on CO₂ Emission Reductions from Passenger Cars 2003*, SEC(2005) 826.

Commission of the European Communities (2006a), *Implementing the Community Strategy to Reduce CO₂ Emissions from Cars: Sixth Annual Communication on the Effectiveness of the Strategy*, COM(2006) 463.

Commission of the European Communities (2006b), *Implementing the Community Strategy to Reduce CO₂ Emissions from Cars: Monitoring of ACEA's Commitment on CO₂ Emission Reductions from Passenger Cars 2004*, SEC(2006) 1078.

Commission of the European Communities (2007a), *Accompanying Document to the Communication from the Commission to the European Parliament and Council on the Review of the Community Strategy to Reduce and Improve Fuel Efficiency from Passenger Cars and Light Commercial Vehicles*, SEC(2007) 61.

Commission of the European Communities (2007b), *Results of the Review of the Community Strategy to Reduce CO₂ Emissions from Passenger Cars and Light-Commercial Vehicles*, COM(2007) 19 final.

Crandall, R. (2003), 'The changing rationale for motor vehicle fuel-economy regulation', in *Regulation: the Cato Review of Business and Government*, www.cato.org/pubs/regulation/reg13n3-crandall.html, accessed 13 January 2004.

Crane, G. and A. Amawi (1997), 'Classic liberalism' in G. Crane and A. Amawi (eds), *The Theoretical Evolution of International Political Economy: A Reader*, 2nd edn, Oxford: Oxford University Press, pp. 55–82.

Crouch, C. (2005a), 'Models of capitalism', *New Political Economy*, **10** (4), pp. 339–456.

Crouch, C. (2005b), *Capitalist Diversity and Change: Recombinant Governance and Institutional Entrepreneurs*, Oxford: Oxford University Press.

Crouch, C. and W. Streeck (1997a), 'Introduction: the future of capitalist diversity', in C. Crouch and W. Streeck (eds), *Political Economy of Modern Capitalism: Mapping Convergence and Diversity*, London: Sage Publications, pp. 1–18.

Crouch, C. and W. Streeck (eds) (1997b), *Political Economy of Modern Capitalism: Mapping Convergence and Diversity*, London: Sage Publications.

Cutler, A.C. (2006), 'Transnational business civilization, corporations and the privatization of global governance', *Global Corporate Power*, vol 15, *International Political Economy Yearbook*, Boulder, CO: Lynne Rienner Publishers, pp. 199–225.

Cutler, A.C., V. Haufler and T. Porter (1999a), 'The contours and significance of private authority in international affairs', in A.C. Cutler, V. Haufler and T. Porter (eds), *Private Authority and International Affairs*, Albany, NY: State University of New York Press, pp. 333–76.

Cutler, A.C., V. Haufler and T. Porter (1999b), 'Private authority and international affairs', in A.C. Cutler, V. Haufler and T. Porter (eds), *Private Authority and International Affairs*, Albany, NY: State University of New York Press, pp. 3–28.

DaimlerChrysler (2004), *360 Degrees: Environmental Report 2004: Alliances for the Environment*, Stuttgart, Germany: DaimlerChrysler Communications, including accompanying CD ROM.

de Vaus, D. (1991), *Surveys in Social Research*, 3rd edn, St Leonards: Allen and Unwin.

Denscombe, M. (1998) *The Good Research Guide for Small Scaled Social Research Projects*, Buckingham: Open University Press.

Denzau, A. and D. North (1994), 'Shared mental models: ideologies and institutions', *Kyklos*, **47** (1), 3–31.

Desai, U. (2002a), 'Institutions and environmental policy in developed countries', in U. Desai (ed.), *Environmental Politics and Policy in Industrialized Countries*, Cambridge, MA: MIT Press, pp. 1–27.

Desai, U. (2002b), 'Institutional profiles and policy performance: summary and conclusion', in U. Desai (ed.), *Environmental Politics and Policy in Industrialized Countries*, Cambridge, MA: MIT Press, pp. 357–81.

DeSombre, E. (2000), *Domestic Sources of International Environmental Policy: Industry, Environmentalists and US Power*, Cambridge, MA: MIT Press.

Deutsche Bank (2002), *The Drivers: How to Navigate the Auto Industry*, Frankfurt am Main: Deutsche Bank.

Deutsche Bank (2004), *The Drivers: How to Navigate the Auto Industry*, Frankfurt am Main: Deutsche Bank.

Dicken, P. (1998), *Global Shift: Transforming the World Economy*, 3rd edn, London: Paul Chapman Publishing.

Dicken, P. (2003), *Global Shift: Reshaping the Global Economic Map in the 21st Century*, 4th edn, London: Sage Publications.

Dore, R. (1997), 'The distinctiveness of Japan', in C. Crouch and

W. Streeck (eds), *Political Economy of Modern Capitalism: Mapping Convergence and Diversity*, London: Sage Publications, pp. 19–32.

Dore, R. (2000a), *Stock Market Capitalism: Welfare Capitalism: Japan and Germany versus the Anglo Saxons*, Oxford and New York: Oxford University Press.

Dore, R. (2000b), 'Will global capitalism be Anglo-Saxon capitalism?', *New Left Review*, **6**, 101–19.

Dore, R., W. Lazonick and M. O'Sullivan (1999), 'Varieties of capitalism in the twentieth century', *Oxford Review of Economic Policy*, **15** (4), 102–20.

Doremus, P., W. Keller, L. Pauly and S. Reich (1999), *The Myth of the Global Corporation*, Princeton, NJ: Princeton University Press.

DOT (Department of Transportation) (2003), *Summary of Fuel Economy Performance*, www.nhtsa.dot.gov/cars/rules/CAFE/docs/242873_web. pdf, accessed 15 January 2004.

Dowling, J. (2006), 'Ours are bigger than yours, says US . . . but it's all torque', *Sydney Morning Herald*, 11 January 2006, www.drive.com.au, accessed 11 January 2006.

Dowling, J. (2008), 'GMC Yukon hybrid', *Sydney Morning Herald*, 21 January 2008, www.drive.com.au, accessed 24 January 2008

Dunne, T. (2005), 'Liberalism', in J. Bayliss and S. Smith (eds), *The Globalization of World Politics: An Introduction to International Relations*, 3rd edn, Oxford: Oxford University Press, pp. 185–203.

Dunning, J. (1993), *Multinational Enterprises and the Global Economy*, Wokingham: Addison-Wesley, pp. 79–137.

Eckstein, H. (1975), 'Case study and theory in political science', in F. Greenstein and N. Polsby (eds), *Strategies of Enquiry*, Reading: Addison-Wesley.

ECMT (European Conference of Ministers of Transport) (1997), CO_2 *Emissions from Transport*, Paris: OECD.

ECMT (2001), *Vehicle Emission Reductions*, Paris: OECD.

ECMT (2003), *Monitoring of CO_2 Emissions from New Cars*, CEMT/CM(2003)10.

The Economist (2002a), *Pocket World in Figures 2003 Edition*, London: Profile Books.

The Economist (2002b), 'Storm clouds over Detroit', *The Economist*, 16 November, pp. 55–6.

The Economist (2003), 'Ford's troubles – one hell of a birthday bill', *The Economist*, 14 June, pp. 57–60.

The Economist (2004), 'Driven by the oil price', *The Economist*, 26 August.

The Economist (2005), 'The $10 billion man', *The Economist*, 26 February, p. 62.

The Economist (2006), 'The business of giving: a survey of wealth and philanthropy', *The Economist*, 25 February.

The Economist (2008), 'Face value: climate of fear', *The Economist*, 25 October, p.78.

EIA (Energy Information Administration) (2005), *Historical Data: Alternative Transportation Fuels (ATF) and Alternative Fueled Vehicles (AFV)*, www.eia.doe.gov/cneaf/alternate/page/atftables/afv_hist_data. html, accessed 22 April 2008.

EIA (2008), 'All countries spot price FOB weighted by estimated export volume (dollars per barrel)', *Petroleum Navigator*, http://tonto.eia.doe. gov/dnav/pet/hist/wtotworldw.htm, accessed 9 April 2008, Washington, DC: EIA.

EIA (no date a), 'Crude oil prices: world prices', *Historical Petroleum Price Data*, www.eia.doe.gov/neic/historic/hpetroleum2.htm , accessed 9 January 2006.

Ekins, P., C. Folke and R. Costanza (1994), 'Trade, environment and development: the issues in perspective', *Ecological Economics*, **9** (1), 1–12.

Elster, J. (1989), *Nuts and Bolts for the Social Sciences*, Cambridge: Cambridge University Press.

Energy Conservation Centre (no date), *Effects of the Top Runner Program*, www.eccj.or.jp/top_runner/chapter4-2.html, accessed 28 April 2004.

Esping-Andersen, G. (1990), *The Three Worlds of Welfare Capitalism*, Cambridge: Polity Press.

Europa (no date), *Objectives of the Agreement Concluded with the Automobile Industry*, http://europa.eu.int/comm/environment/co2/co2_ agreements.htm, accessed 6 January 2004.

Finnemore, M. and K. Sikkink (1998), 'International norm dynamics and political change', *International Organization*, **52** (4), 887–917.

Finnemore, M. and K. Sikkink (2001), 'Taking stock: the constructivist research program in international relations and comparative politics', *Annual Review of Political Science 2001*, **4**, 391–416.

Fioretos, O. (2001), 'The domestic sources of multilateral preferences: varieties of capitalism in the European Community', in P. Hall and D. Soskice (eds), *Varieties of Capitalism: The Institutional Foundations of Comparative Advantage*, Oxford: Oxford University Press, pp. 213–44.

Florini, A. (2003a), 'Business and global governance: the growing role of corporate codes of conduct', *Brookings Review*, (Spring), 4–8.

Florini, A. (2003b), *The Coming Democracy: New Rules for Running a New World*, Washington, DC: Island Press.

Ford Motor Company (2000), Speech by William Clay Ford, Jr. at the 5th Annual Greenpeace Business Conference, London, 5 October, http://

media.ford.com/article_display.cfm?article_id=6217, accessed 12 April 2006.

Ford Motor Company (2004), *2003/4 Corporate Citizenship Report: Our Principles, Progress and Performance: Connecting with Society*, Dearborn, MI: Ford Motor Company.

Freund, P. and G. Martin (1993), *The Ecology of the Automobile*, Montreal, QC: Black Rose.

Frieden, J. and L. Martin (2002), 'International political economy: global and domestic interactions', in I. Katznelson and H. Milner (eds), *Political Science: The State of the Discipline*, New York: W.W. Norton, pp. 118–46.

Friedman, M. (1970), 'The social responsibility of business is to increase profits', *New York Times Magazine*, 13 September.

Friedman, T. (1999), *The Lexus and the Olive Tree*, London: HarperCollins.

General Motors Corporation (2004), *2004 Corporate Responsibility Report*, Detroit, MI: General Motors Corporation.

Gibbs, G. (2002), *Qualitative Data Analysis: Explorations with NVivo*, Buckingham: Open University Press.

Goldstein, J. and R. Keohane (1993), 'Ideas and foreign policy: an analytical framework', in J. Goldstein and R. Keohane (eds), *Ideas and Foreign Policy: Beliefs, Institutions and Political Change*, Ithaca, NY: Cornell University Press, pp. 3–30.

Graham, D., and S. Glaister (2002), 'The demand for automobile fuel: a survey of elasticities', *Journal of Transport Economics and Policy*, **36** (1), 1–26.

Graham, D. and S. Glaister (2004), 'Road traffic demand elasticity estimates: a review', *Transport Reviews*, **24** (3), 261–74.

Green Car Congress (2006), 'Prius passes 500,000 sales mark worldwide', www.greencarcongress.com/2006/06/prius_passes_50.html, accessed 15 February 2008.

Green, D. and I. Shapiro (1994), *Pathologies of Rational Choice Theory: A Critique of Applications in Political Science*, New Haven, CT, and London: Yale University Press.

Greene, O. (2005), 'Environmental issues', in J. Bayliss and S. Smith (eds), *The Globalization of World Politics: An Introduction to International Relations*, 3rd edn, Oxford: Oxford University Press, pp. 451–78.

GRI (2002), *Sustainability Reporting Guidelines: 2002*, www.globalreporting.org/guidelines/2002/GRI_guidelines_print.pdf, accessed 10 December 2004.

Haigh, N. (1996), 'Climate change policies and politics in the European Community', in T. O'Riordan and J. Jager (eds), *Politics of Climate*

Change: A European Perspective, London and New York: Routledge, pp. 155–85.

Hall, J. (1993), 'Ideas and the social sciences', in J. Goldstein and R. Keohane (eds), *Ideas and Foreign Policy: Beliefs, Institutions and Political Change*, Ithaca, NY: Cornell University Press, pp. 31–54.

Hall, P. (1997), 'The role of interests, ideas and institutions in the comparative political economy of industrialised nations', in M. Lichbach and A. Zuckerman (eds), *Comparative Politics: Rationality, Culture and Structure*, Cambridge: Cambridge University Press, pp. 174–207.

Hall, P. (1999), 'The political economy of Europe in an era of interdependence', in H. Kitschelt, P. Lange, G. Marks and J. Stephens (eds), *Continuity and Change in Contemporary Capitalism*, Cambridge: Cambridge University Press, pp. 135–63.

Hall, R. and T. Biersteker (eds) (2002), *The Emergence of Private Authority in Global Governance*, Cambridge: Cambridge University Press

Hall, P., and D. Soskice (2001), 'An introduction to varieties of capitalism', in P. Hall and D. Soskice (eds), *Varieties of Capitalism: The Institutional Foundations of Comparative Advantage*, Oxford: Oxford University Press, pp. 1–68.

Hall, P. and D. Soskice (eds) (2001), *Varieties of Capitalism: The Institutional Foundations of Comparative Advantage*, Oxford: Oxford University Press.

Hampden-Turner, C., and A. Trompenaars (1993), *The Seven Cultures of Capitalism: Value Systems for Creating Wealth in the United States, Japan, Germany, France, Britain, Sweden and the Netherlands*, New York: Currency Doubleday.

Hardin, G. (1968), 'The tragedy of the commons', *Science*, **162**, 1243–8.

Harrington, W. and V. McConnell (2003), *Motor Vehicles and the Environment*, Washington, DC: Resources for the Future, www.rff.org/Documents/RFF-RPT-carsenviron.pdf, accessed 2 January 2004.

Harrison, N. (2000), *Constructing Sustainable Development*, Albany, NY: State University of New York Press.

Harrod, J. (2006), 'The century of the corporation', in C. May (ed.), *Global Corporate Power*, vol 15, *International Political Economy Yearbook*, Boulder, CO: Lynne Rienner Publishers, pp. 23–46.

Haufler, V. (1999), 'Self-regulation and business norms: political risk, political activism', in A.C. Cutler, V. Haufler and T. Porter (eds), *Private Authority and International Affairs*, Albany, NY: State University of New York Press, pp. 199–222.

Haufler, V. (2006), 'Global governance and the private sector', in C. May (ed.), *Global Corporate Power*, vol 15, *International Political Economy Yearbook*, Boulder, CO: Lynne Rienner Publishers, pp. 85–103.

Hawken, P., A. Lovins and H. Lovins (1999), *Natural Capitalism: Creating the Next Industrial Revolution*, New York: Little Brown.

Hay, C. (2002), *Political Analysis*, Basingstoke: Palgrave.

Hay, C. (2004), 'Ideas, interests and institutions in the political economy of great transformations', *Review of International Political Economy*, **11** (1), 204–26.

Hay, C. (2005), 'Two can play at that game . . . or can they? Varieties of capitalism, varieties of institutionalism', in D. Coates (ed.), *Varieties of Capitalism, Varieties of Approaches*, Basingstoke: Palgrave Macmillan, pp. 106–21.

Hay, C. (2006a), 'Constructivist institutionalism . . . or, why ideas into interests don't go', paper presented at the American Political Science Association Conference, Philadelphia, PA, 31 August to 3 September 2006.

Hay, C. (2006b), 'Constructivist institutionalism', in R. Rhodes, S. Binder and B. Rockman (eds), *The Oxford Handbook of Political Institutions*, Oxford: Oxford University Press, pp. 56–74.

Hay, C. (2006c), 'Globalization and public policy', in M. Moran, M. Rein and R.E. Goodin (eds), *The Oxford Handbook of Public Policy*, Oxford: Oxford University Press, pp. 587–604.

Hay, C. and D. Marsh (eds) (2000), *Demystifying Globalisation*, Basingstoke: Palgrave.

Healey, J. (1993), *Statistics: A Tool for Social Research*, 3rd edn, Belmont, CA: Wadsworth Publishing.

Held, D. (2006), 'Reframing global governance: apocalypse soon or reform!', *New Political Economy*, **11** (2), 157–76.

Held, D., A. McGrew, D. Goldblatt and J. Perraton (1999), *Global Transformations: Politics, Economics, Culture*, Cambridge: Polity Press.

Helleiner, E. (2003), 'Economic liberalism and its critics: the past as prologue', *Review of International Political Economy*, **10** (4), 685–96.

Hellman, K. and R. Heavenrich (2003a), *Light Duty Automotive Technology and Fuel Economy Trends: 1975 Through 2003*, United States Environment Protection Agency, www.epa.gov/otaq/cert/mpg/fetrends/r03006.pdf, accessed 17 February 2004.

Hellman, K. and R. Heavenrich (2003b), *Light Duty Automotive Technology and Fuel Economy Trends: 1975 Through 2003, Appendix A*, United States Environment Protection Agency, www.epa.gov/otaq/cert/mpg/fetrends/r03006.pdf, accessed 17 February 2004.

Hellman, K. and R. Heavenrich (2004a), *Light Duty Automotive Technology and Fuel Economy Trends: 1975 Through 2004*, United States Environment Protection Agency, www.epa.gov/otaq/cert/mpg/fetrends/420r04001.pdf, accessed 13 May 2004.

Hellman, K. and R. Heavenrich (2004b), *Light Duty Automotive Technology and Fuel Economy Trends: 1975 Through 2004, Appendix F*, United States Environment Protection Agency, www.epa.gov/otaq/cert/mpg/fetrends/420r04001-f.pdf, accessed 13 May 2004.

Hellman, K. and R. Heavenrich (2004c), *Light Duty Automotive Technology and Fuel Economy Trends: 1975 Through 2004, Appendix A*, United States Environment Protection Agency, www.epa.gov/otaq/cert/mpg/fetrends/420r04001.pdf, accessed 13 May 2004.

Hirst, P. and G. Thompson (1996), *Globalisation in Question*, Cambridge: Polity Press.

Hirst, P. and G. Thompson (1997), 'Globalisation in question: international economic relations and forms of public governance', in J. Hollingsworth and R. Boyer (eds), *Contemporary Capitalism: The Embeddedness of Institutions*, Cambridge: Cambridge University Press, pp. 337–60.

Hoffman, A. (1999), 'Institutional evolution and change', *Academy of Management Journal*, **42** (4), 351–71.

Holliday Jr, C., S. Schmidheiny and P. Watts (2002), *Walking the Talk*, Sheffield: Greenleaf.

Hollingsworth, J. (1997a), 'Continuities and changes in social systems of production: the cases of Japan, Germany, and the United States', in J. Hollingsworth and R. Boyer (eds), *Contemporary Capitalism: The Embeddedness of Institutions*, Cambridge: Cambridge University Press, pp. 265–310.

Hollingsworth, J. (1997b), 'The institutional embeddedness of American capitalism', in C. Crouch and W. Streeck (eds), *Political Economy of Modern Capitalism: Mapping Convergence and Diversity*, London: Sage Publications, pp. 133–47.

Honda Motor Company (2002), *Honda Ecology*, Tokyo: Honda Motor Company.

Honda Motor Company (2004), *Honda Environmental Annual Report 2004*, Tokyo: Honda Motor Company.

IEA (International Energy Agency) (1991), *Fuel Efficiency of Passenger Cars*, Paris: OECD.

IEA (1993), *Cars and Climate Change*, Paris: OECD.

IEA (1997), *Transport, Energy and Climate Change* Paris: OECD.

Inglehart, R. (1997), *Modernization and Postmodernization: Cultural, Economic and Political Change in 43 Societies*, Princeton, NJ: Princeton University Press.

Interviews conducted in 2005 with three personnel from Toyota Australia, five from Ford Australia, and one each from Volkswagen Group and BMW Australia.

Jacoby, S. (2005), *The Embedded Corporation: Corporate Governance and Employment Relations in Japan and the United States*, Princeton, NJ and Oxford: Princeton University Press.

JAMA (2003), *2003: The Motor Industry of Japan*, www.jama.or.jp/eng/pdf/MIJ2003.pdf, accessed 18 January 2004.

JAMA (2004a), *2004: The Motor Industry of Japan*, Tokyo: JAMA.

JAMA (2004b), *World Motor Vehicle Statistics Vol.3 2004*, Tokyo: JAMA.

JAMA (2007a), *Motor Vehicle Statistics of Japan 2007*, www.jama-english.jp/publications/motor_vehicle_statistic2007.pdf, accessed 21 April 2008.

JAMA (2007b), *2007: The Motor Industry of Japan*, Tokyo: JAMA, www.jama-english.jp/publications/MIJ2007.pdf, accessed 15 April 2008.

JAMA (no date a), *A Better Environment for Future Generations*, www.jama.or.jp/eco/eco_car/en/en/, accessed 13 January 2004.

JAMA (no date b), 'Controlling exhaust emissions', *A Better Environment for Future Generations*, www.jama.or.jp/eco/eco_car/en/en_1_08a.html, accessed 13 January 2004.

JAMA (no date c), 'Curbing global warming', *A Better Environment for Future Generations*, www.jama.or.jp/eco/eco_car/en/en_1_06a.html, accessed 13 January 2004.

Jain, J. and J. Guiver (2001), 'Turning the car inside out: transport, equity and environment', *Social Policy and Administration*, **35** (5), 569–86.

Karliner, J. (1997), *The Corporate Planet*, San Francisco, CA: Sierra Club Books.

Katzenstein, P. (1996), *Cultural Norms and National Security: Police and Military in Postwar Japan*, Ithaca, NY: Cornell University Press.

King, G., R. Keohane and S. Verba (1994), *Designing Social Inquiry: Scientific Inference in Social Research*, Princeton, NJ: Princeton University Press.

Kitschelt, H., P. Lange, G. Marks and J. Stephens (1999a), 'Convergence and divergence in advanced capitalist democracies', in H. Kitschelt, P. Lange, G. Marks and J. Stephens (eds), *Continuity and Change in Contemporary Capitalism*, Cambridge: Cambridge University Press, pp. 427–60.

Kitschelt, H., P. Lange, G. Marks and J. Stephens (eds) (1996), *Continuity and Change in Contemporary Capitalism*, Cambridge: Cambridge University Press.

Korten, D. (1999), *The Post-Corporate World: Life After Capitalism*, San Francisco, CA: Berrett-Koehler.

Koshiba, T., P. Parker, T. Rutherford, D. Sanford and R. Olson (2001), 'Japanese automakers and the NAFTA environment: global context', *Environments*, **29** (3), 1–14.

Kraft, M. (2002), 'Environmental policy and politics in the United States: toward environmental sustainability?', in U. Desai (ed.), *Environmental Politics and Policy in Industrialized Countries*, Cambridge, MA: MIT Press, pp. 29–69.

Kvale, S. (1996), *Interviews: An Introduction to Qualitative Research Interviewing*, Thousand Oaks, CA: Sage Publications.

Lamy, S. (2005), 'Contemporary mainstream approaches: neo-realism and neo-liberalism', in J. Bayliss and S. Smith (eds), *The Globalization of World Politics: An Introduction to International Relations*, 3rd edn, Oxford: Oxford University Press, pp. 205–24.

Lawrence, A., J. Weber and J. Post (2005), *Business and Society: Corporate Strategy, Public Policy, Ethics*, 11th edn, Boston, MA: McGraw Hill.

Legro, J. (1997), 'Which norms matter? Revisiting the "failure" of internationalism', *International Organization*, **51** (1), 31–63.

Leveque, F. (1996), *Environmental Policy in Europe*, Cheltenham, UK and Brookfield, VT, USA: Edward Elgar.

Levy, D. and S. Rothenberg (2002), 'Heterogeneity and change in environmental strategy: technological and political responses to climate change in the global automobile industry', in A. Hoffman and M. Ventresc (eds), *Organizations, Policy, and the Natural Environment: Institutional and Strategic Perspectives*, Stanford, CA: Stanford University Press, pp. 173–93.

Liefferink, D., M. Andersen and M. Enevoldsen (2000), 'Interpreting joint environmental policy-making: between deregulation and political modernisation', in A. Mol, V. Lauber and D. Liefferink (eds), *The Voluntary Approach to Environmental Policy: Joint Environmental Policy-making in Europe*, Oxford: Oxford University Press, pp. 10–31.

Lowndes, V. (2002), 'Institutionalism', in D. Marsh and G. Stoker (eds), *Theory and Methods in Political Science*, 2nd edn, Basingstoke: Palgrave Macmillan, pp. 90–108.

Luterbacher, U. and D. Sprinz (2001), 'Problems of global environmental cooperation', in U. Luterbacher and D. Sprinz (eds), *International Relations and Global Climate Change*, Cambridge, MA: MIT Press.

Macroy, R. and M. Hession (1996), 'The European Community and climate change: the role of law and legal competence', in T. O'Riordan and J. Jager (eds), *Politics of Climate Change: A European Perspective*, London and New York: Routledge, pp. 106–54.

March, J. and J. Olsen (1989), *Rediscovering Institutions, The Organizational Basis of Politics*, New York: Free Press.

March, J. and J. Olsen (1998), 'The institutional dynamics of international political orders', *International Organization*, **52** (4), 943–69.

Margarita, E., T. Iversen and D. Soskice (2001), 'Social protection and the formation of skills: a reinterpretation of the welfare state', in P. Hall and D. Soskice (eds), *Varieties of Capitalism: The Institutional Foundations of Comparative Advantage*, Oxford: Oxford University Press, pp. 145–83.

Martell, L. (2007), 'The third wave in globalisation theory', *International Studies Review*, **9** (2), 173–96.

Maxton, G. and J. Wormald (2004), *Time for a Model Change: Re-engineering the Global Automotive Industry*, Cambridge: Cambridge University Press.

May, T. (2001) *Social Research*, 3rd edn, Buckingham: Open University Press.

McDonald, N. (2004), 'Green hybrids clean up in local market', *The Australian*, 29 January, p. 7.

Mearsheimer, J. (1990), 'Back to the future: instability on Europe after the Cold War', *International Security*, **15** (1), 5–56.

Mikler, J. (2008), 'Framing responsibility: national variations in corporations' motivations', *Policy and Society*, **26** (4), 67–104.

Mol, A., D. Liefferink and V. Lauber (2000a), 'Introduction', in A. Mol, V. Lauber and D. Liefferink (eds), *The Voluntary Approach to Environmental Policy: Joint Environmental Policy-making in Europe*, Oxford: Oxford University Press.

Mol, A., D. Liefferink and V. Lauber (2000b), 'Epilogue: conclusions and policy implications', in A. Mol, V. Lauber and D. Liefferink (eds), *The Voluntary Approach to Environmental Policy: Joint Environmental Policy-making in Europe*, Oxford: Oxford University Press.

National Research Council (2002), *Effectiveness and Impact of Corporate Average Fuel Economy (CAFE) Standards*, http://books.nap.edu/openbook.php?isbn=0309076013&page=111, accessed 10 October 2008.

Newell, P. and D. Levy (2006), 'The political economy of the firm in global environmental governance', in C. May (ed.), *Global Corporate Power*, vol 15, *International Political Economy Yearbook*, Boulder, CO: Lynne Rienner Publishers.

Newell, P. and M. Paterson (1998), 'A climate for business: global warming: the state and capital', *Review of International Political Economy*, **5** (4), 679–703.

Newton-Small, J. (2003), 'Detroit's fuel economy woes', *Global Exchange*, www.globalexchange.org/campaigns/oil/1217.html, accessed 13 January 2004.

National Highway Traffic Safety Administration (NHTSA) (2003), 'Automotive fuel economy program annual update calendar year 2002', accessed 15 January, 2004 at www.nhtsa.dot.gov/cars/rules/CAFE/Fuel EconUpdates/2002/2002AnnualUpdate.pdf.

NHTSA (2005), *Automotive Fuel Economy Program Annual Update Calender Year 2004*, www.nhtsa.dot.gov/staticfiles/DOT/NHTSA/ Vehicle%20Safety/CAFE/2004_Fuel_Economy_Program.pdf, accessed 15 April 2008.

NHTSA (no date), *CAFE Overview: Frequently Asked Questions*, www. nhtsa.dot.gov/cars/rules/CAFE/overview.htm, accessed 15 January 2004.

Nissan Motor Company (2004a), *Environmental Report 2004*, Tokyo: Nissan Motor Company.

Nissan Motor Company (2004b), *Sustainability Report 2004*, Tokyo: Nissan Motor Company.

Nordstrom, H., and S. Vaughan (1999), *Trade and Environment*, WTO special studies 4, Geneva: WTO Publications.

North, D. (1990), *Institutions, Institutional Change and Economic Performance*, Cambridge: Cambridge University Press.

Norusis, M. (1990), *The SPSS Guide to Data Analysis for Release 4*, Chicago, IL: SPSS.

O'Brien, R., A. Goetz, J. Scholte and M. Williams (2000), *Contesting Global Governance: Multilateral Economic Institutions and Global Social Movements*, Cambridge: Cambridge University Press.

OECD (Organisation for Economic Co-operation and Development) (1996), *Environmental Performance Reviews: United States*, Paris: OECD.

OECD (2000), *Frameworks to Measure Sustainable Development*, Paris: OECD.

OECD (2001a), *Corporate Responsibility: Private Initiatives and Public Goals*, Paris: OECD.

OECD (2001b), *OECD Guidelines for Multinational Enterprises, Global Instruments for Corporate Responsibility*, annual report 2001, Paris: OECD.

OECD (2002a), *Environmental Performance Reviews: Japan*, Paris: OECD.

OECD (2002b), *Strategies to Reduce Greenhouse Gas Emissions from Transport*, Paris: OECD.

OECD (2002c), 'Transport', *OECD Environmental Data Compendium 2002*, Paris: OECD, www.oecd.org/dataoecd/52/59/2958321.pdf, accessed 12 January 2004.

OECD (2002d), 'Air', *OECD Environmental Data Compendium 2002*, Paris: OECD, www.oecd.org/dataoecd/8/62/2958142.pdf, accessed 12 January 2004.

OECD (2003), *CO_2 Emissions from Fuel Combustion 1971–2002*, Paris: OECD.

OECD (2004), *Can Cars Come Clean? Strategies for Low-Emission Vehicles*, Paris: OECD.

Official Journal of the European Communities (1999), *Commission Recommendation of 5 February 1999 on the Reduction of CO_2 Emissions from Passenger Cars*, 1999/125/EC, http://europa.eu.int/comm/environment/co2/99125/en.pdf, accessed 19 July 2004.

Ohmae, K. (1990), *The Borderless World: Power and Strategy in the Interlinked Economy*, London: Collins.

OICA (International Organization of Motor Vehicle Manufacturers) (2004), *World Motor Vehicle Production by Manufacturer: World Ranking 2003*, www.oica.net/htdocs/Main.htm, accessed 29 November 2004.

OICA (2006), *The World's Automotive Industry: Some Key Figures*, http://oica.net/wp-content/uploads/2007/06/oica-depliant-final.pdf, accessed 7 February 2007.

OICA (2007), *Motor Vehicle Production by Manufacturer: World Ranking of Manufacturers*, http://oica.net/wp-content/uploads/2007/07/ranking06.pdf, accessed 11 February 2008.

OICA (no date), *Production Statistics*, http://www.oica.net/htdocs/Main, accessed 25 July 2005.

O'Riordan, T. and A. Jordan (1996), 'Social institutions and climate change', in T. O'Riordan and J. Jager (eds), *Politics of Climate Change: A European Perspective*, London and New York: Routledge, pp. 65–105.

Orssatto, R. and S. Clegg (1999), 'The political ecology of organizations', *Organization and Environment*, **12** (3), 263–79.

Ostrom, E. (1990), *Governing the Commons: The Evolution of Institutions for Collective Action*, Cambridge: Cambridge University Press.

Ostrom, E. (1999), 'Coping with tragedies of the Commons', *Annual Review of Political Science 1999*, **2**, 493–535.

Palmer, K., W. Oates and P. Portney (1995), 'Tightening environmental standards: the benefit-cost or the no cost paradigm?', *Journal of Economic Perspectives*, **9** (4), 119–32.

Parker, P. (1996), 'Japan and the global environment: leadership in environmental technology', in D. Rumley, T. Chiba, A. Takagi and Y. Fukushima (eds), *Global Geopolitical Change and the Asia-Pacific*, Aldershot: Avebury, pp. 93–112.

Parker, P. (2001), 'Environmental initiatives among Japanese automakers: new technology, EMS, recycling and lifecycle approaches', *Environments*, **29** (3), 91–113.

Paterson, M. (1996), 'IR theory: neorealism, neoinstitutionalism and the Climate Change Convention', in M. Imber and J. Vogler (eds),

The Environment and International Relations: Theories and Processes, London and New York: Routledge, pp. 59–76.

Paterson, M. (2000), 'Car culture and global environmental politics', *Review of International Studies*, **26** (2), 253–70.

Paterson, M. (2007), *Automobile Politics*, Cambridge: Cambridge University Press.

Pauly, L. and S. Reich (1997), 'National structures and multinational corporate behaviour: enduring differences in the age of globalisation', *International Organization*, **51**(1), 1–30.

Peavey, F. (1995), 'Strategic questioning, an approach to creating personal and social change', *In Context*, **40** (Spring), 36–8.

Peavey, F. (no date), *Strategic Questioning, an Approach to Creating Personal and Social Change*, www/jobsletter.org.nz/pdf/stratq97.pdf, accessed 12 May 2004.

Pierson, P. (2000), 'Increasing returns, path dependence and the study of politics', *American Political Science Review*, **94** (2), 251–67.

Pierson, P. and S. Skocpol (2000), 'Historical institutionalism in contemporary political science', in I. Katznelson and H. Milner (eds), *Political Science: The State of the Discipline*, New York: W.W. Norton, pp. 643–721.

Pontusson, J. (2005), *Inequality and Prosperity: Social Europe versus Liberal America*, Ithaca, NY: Cornell University Press.

Porter, G. and J. Brown (1996), *Global Environmental Politics*, Boulder, CO: Westview Press.

Porter, M. (1990), *The Competitive Advantage of Nations*, New York: Free Press.

Porter, M. and C. van der Linde (1995a), 'Towards a new conception of the environment-competitiveness relationship', *Journal of Economic Perspectives*, **9** (4), 97–118.

Porter, M. and C. van der Linde (1995b), 'Green and competitive: ending the stalemate', *Harvard Business Review*, **73** (5), 120–34.

Prakash, A. (2000), *Greening the Firm: The Politics of Corporate Environmentalism*, Cambridge: Cambridge University Press.

Price, R. and C. Reus-Smit (1998), 'Dangerous liaisons? Critical international relations theory and constructivism', *European Journal of International Relations*, **4** (3), 259–94.

Productivity Commission (2002), *Review of Automotive Assistance*, inquiry report no.25, Melbourne, VIC: Productivity Commission.

Pye, L. and M. Pye (1985), *Asian Power and Politics: The Cultural Dimension of Authority*, Cambridge, MA: Harvard University Press.

Redding, S. and R. Whitley (1990), 'Beyond bureaucracy: towards a comparative analysis of forms of economic resource coordination and control', in S. Clegg and S. Redding (eds), *Capitalism in Contrasting Cultures*, Berlin: Walter de Gruyter, pp. 79–104.

Renault (2001), *2000 Annual Report Summary*, Boulogne Billancourt, France: Renault, www.renault.com/docs/finance_gb/synthese_2000_gb.pdf, accessed 17 January 2006, pp. 12–15.

Risse, T. (2000), '"Let's argue!": communicative action in world politics', *International Organisation*, **54** (1), 1–39.

Risse, T. (2002), 'Constructivism and international institutions: toward conversations across paradigms', in I. Katznelson and H. Milner (eds), *Political Science: The State of the Discipline*, New York: W.W. Norton, pp. 597–623.

Ropke, I. (1994), 'Trade, development and sustainability: a critical assessment of the free trade dogma', *Ecological Economics*, **9** (1), 13–22.

Ruggie, J. (1998a), *Constructing the World Polity*, New York: Routledge.

Ruggie, J. (1998b), 'What makes the world hang together? Neo-utilitarianism and the social constructivist challenge', *International Organization*, **52** (4), 855–87.

Rugman, A. (2005), *The Regional Multinationals: MNEs and 'Global' Strategic Management*, Cambridge: Cambridge University Press.

Sartori, G. (1970), 'Concept misinformation in comparative politics', *American Political Science Review*, **6** (4), 1033–53.

Schmidt, V. (2002), *The Futures of European Capitalism*, Oxford: Oxford University Press.

Schnitter, P. (1997), 'The emerging Europolity and its impact upon national systems of production', in J. Hollingsworth and R. Boyer (eds), *Contemporary Capitalism: The Embeddedness of Institutions*, Cambridge: Cambridge University Press, pp. 395–430.

Schreurs, M. (2002), *Environmental Politics in Japan, Germany and the United States*, Cambridge: Cambridge University Press.

Scientific American (2002a), 'Greenwashing the car', *Scientific American*, **287** (4), 8.

Scruggs, L. (2003), *Sustaining Abundance: Environmental Performance in Industrial Democracies*, Cambridge: Cambridge University Press.

Soskice, D. (1999), 'Divergent production regimes: coordinated and uncoordinated market economies in the 1980s and 1990s', in H. Kitschelt, P. Lange, G. Marks and J. Stephens (eds), *Continuity and Change in Contemporary Capitalism*, Cambridge: Cambridge University Press, pp. 101–34.

Source Watch (no date), *Global Climate Coalition*, www.sourcewatch.org/index.php?title=Global_Climate_Coalition, accessed 12 April 2006.

Stanfield, B. (2000), *The Art of Focused Conversation: 100 Ways to Access Group Wisdom in the Workplace*, Gabriola Island, BC: New Society Publishers and Toronto, ON: Canadian Institute of Cultural Affairs.

Stempeck, B. (2003), 'DOT proposes revamp of fuel economy regulations', *Greenwire*, 23 December, http://knowledge.fhwa.dot.gov/cops/italladdsup.nsf/docs/51AE2D33EC82E2AD85256E0500839744?open document&CurrentCategory=Other%20Transportation%20and%20 Air%20Quality%20Technical%20Assistance, accessed 28 January 2004.

Strange, S. (1996), *The Retreat of the State: The Diffusion of Power in the World Economy*, Cambridge: Cambridge University Press.

Strange, S. (1997), 'The future of global capitalism; or will divergence persist forever?', in C. Crouch and W. Streeck (eds), *Political Economy of Modern Capitalism: Mapping Convergence and Diversity*, London: Sage Publications, pp. 182–91.

Streeck, W. (1997), 'German capitalism: does it exist? Can it survive?', in C. Crouch and W. Streeck (eds), *Political Economy of Modern Capitalism: Mapping Convergence and Diversity*, London: Sage Publications, pp. 31–54.

Suzuki, D. (1993), *Time to Change*, St Leonards, NSW: Allen and Unwin.

Suzuki, D., and H. Dressel (2002), *Good News for a Change: Hope for a Troubled Planet*, Toronto, ON: Allen and Unwin.

Thatcher, M. (2007), *Internationalisation and Economic Institutions*, Oxford: Oxford University Press.

Tiberghien, Y. (2007), *Entrepreneurial States: Reforming Corporate Governance in France, Japan and Korea*, Ithaca, NY: Cornell University Press.

Toner, M., C. White and L. Rotherham (1999), *The Bluffer's Guide to the EU,* London: Oval Books.

Toyota Motor Corporation (2004), *Environmental and Social Report 2004*, Tokyo: Toyota Motor Corporation.

UN (United Nations) (no date a), *Earth Summit: UN Conference on Environment and Development*, www.un.org/geninfo/bp/enviro.html, accessed 8 February 2006.

UN (no date b), *The Global Compact*, http://www.unglobalcompact.org/Portal/, accessed 25 August 2003.

UNCTAD (United Nations Conference on Trade and Development) (2006), *World Investment Report 2006*, New York and Geneva: United Nations.

UNEP (United Nations Environment Programme) (2002), *Industry as a Partner for Sustainable Development – 10 Years After Rio: the UNEP Assessment*, www.uneptie.org/Outreach/wssd/contributions/publications/pub_global.htm, accessed 13 June 2003.

UNEP (2003), *Transport*, http://www.uneptie.org/energy/act/tp/index.htm, accessed 26 May 2003.

UNEP (no date), *Environmental Action Already Undertaken by Auto Manufacturers*, http://www.uneptie.org/energy/act/tp/amf/action.htm, accessed 7 January 2005.

UNEP and ACEA (2002), *Industry as a Partner for Sustainable Development: Automotive*, http://www.unepti.e.org/outreach/wssd/docs/sectors/final/automotive.pdf, accessed 14 May 2003.

UNEP and International Institute for Sustainable Development (2000), *Environment and Trade: A Handbook*, Winnipeg, MB: International Institute for Sustainable Development.

UNFCCC (United Nations Framework Convention on Climate Change) (no date a), *Kyoto Protocol*, http://unfccc.int/essential_background/kyoto_protocol/items/2613.php, accessed 12 February 2005.

UNFCCC (no date b), *Status of Ratification*, http://unfccc.int/essential_background/kyoto_protocol/status_of_ratification/items/2613.php, accessed 12 February 2006.

UNFCCC (no date c), *Kyoto Protocol: Status of Ratification*, http://unfccc.int/files/essential_background/kyoto_protocol/application/pdf/kpstats.pdf, accessed 12 February 2006.

US Department of Energy (no date a), www.eia.doe.gov/cneaf/alternate/page/datatables/afvtable1_03.xls, accessed 6 October 2004.

US Department of Energy (no date b), *Renewable and Alternative Fuels*, www.eia.doe.gov/fuelalternate.html, accessed 11 October 2004.

US Department of Energy and US Environment Protection Agency (2004), 'Introduction', *Fuel Economy Guide*, www.fueleconomy.gov/feg/FEG2004intro.pdf, accessed 12 July 2004.

VDA (Verband der Automobilindustrie) (2003), *Annual Report 2003*, Frankfurt: VDA, www.vda.de/en/service/jahresbericht/files/VDA_2003EN.pdf, accessed 17 March 2004.

VDA (2004), *Annual Report 2004*, Frankfurt: VDA, www.vda.de/en/service/jahresbericht/files/VDA_2004_en.pdf, accessed 20 March 2005.

VDA (2005), *Annual Report 2005*, Frankfurt: VDA, www.vda.de/en/service/jahresbericht/files/VDA_2005_en.pdf, accessed 21 April 2008.

VDA (no date), *Fuel Consumption*, www.vda.de/en/aktuell/kraftstoffverbrauch/marktgewichtet.html, accessed 29 July 2005.

Vitols, S. (2001), 'Varieties of corporate governance: comparing Germany and the UK', in P. Hall and D. Soskice (eds), *Varieties of Capitalism: The Institutional Foundations of Comparative Advantage*, Oxford: Oxford University Press.

Vlasic, B. and B. Stertz (2001), *Taken for a Ride: How Daimler-Benz Drove Off with Chrysler*, New York: Harper Business.

Vogel, S. (1996), *Freer Markets, More Rules: Regulatory Reform in Advanced Industrial Countries*, Ithaca, NY: Cornell University Press.

Vogel, S. (2001), 'The crisis of German and Japanese capitalism: stalled on the road to the liberal market model?', *Comparative Political Studies*, **34** (10), 1103–33.

Volkswagen AG (2001) *Environmental Report 2001/2002: Mobility and Sustainability*, Wolfsburg, Germany: Volkswagen AG.

Volkswagen AG (2003), *Environmental Report 2003/2004: Partners in Sustainability*, Wolfsburg, Germany: Volkswagen AG.

Volpi, G. and S. Singer (2000), *Will Voluntary Agreements at EU Level Deliver on Environmental Objectives? Lessons from the Agreement with the Automotive Industry*, World Wide Fund for Nature discussion paper, Brussels: WWF www.panda.org/downloads/europe/agreementonfueleconomy.pdf, accessed 12 December 2003.

von Moltke, K. and A. Rahman (1996), 'External perspectives on climate change: a view from the United States and the Third World', in T. O'Riordan and J. Jager (eds), *Politics of Climate Change: A European Perspective*, London and New York: Routledge, pp. 330–45.

Wade, R. (1996), 'Globalization and its limits: reports of the death of the national economy are greatly exaggerated', in S. Berger, and R. Dore (eds), *National Diversity and Global Capitalism*, Ithaca, NY: Cornell University Press, pp. 60–88.

Wallerstein, I. (1995), *After Liberalism*, New York: New Press.

Wapner, P. (1996), *Environmental Activism and World Civic Politics*, Albany, NY: State University of New York Press.

WBCSD (World Business Council for Sustainable Development) (2000), *Annual Review 2000: Ten Years of Achievement*, Geneva: WBCSD, www.wbcsd.org/DocRoot/fQ4x089Xp5OEnrs0Gp2i/ar2000.pdf, accessed 17 August 2003.

WBCSD (2004), *Mobility 2030: Meeting the Challenges of Sustainability*, Geneva: WBCSD.

Weiss, L. (1998), *The Myth of the Powerless State: Governing the Economy in a Global Era*, Cambridge: Polity Press and Ithaca, NY: Cornell University Press.

Weiss, L. (2003), 'Introduction: bringing domestic institutions back in', in L. Weiss (ed.), *States in the Global Economy: Bringing Domestic Institutions Back in*, Cambridge: Cambridge University Press, pp. 1–33.

Weiss, L. and J. Hobson (1995), *States and Economic Development: A Comparative Economic Analysis*, Cambridge: Polity Press.

Wendt, A. (1995), 'Constructing international politics', *International Security*, **20** (1), 71–81.

Wendt, A. (1998), 'On constitution and causation in international relations', *Review of International Studies*, **24** (4), 101–17.

Wendt, A. (1999), *Social Theory of International Politics*, Cambridge: Cambridge University Press.

Whitley, R. (1999), *Divergent Capitalisms: the Social Structuring and Change of Business Systems*, Oxford: Oxford University Press.

Wilks, S. (1990), 'The embodiment of industrial culture in bureaucracy and management', in S. Clegg and S. Redding (eds), *Capitalism in Contrasting Cultures*, Berlin: Walter de Gruyter, pp. 131–52.

Williams, M. (1996), 'International political economy and global environmental change', in M. Imber and J. Vogler (eds), *Environment and International Relations: Theories and Processes*, London and New York: Routledge, pp. 41–58.

Womack, J., D. Jones and D. Roos (1990), *The Machine that Changed the World*, New York: Rawson Associates.

World Values Survey (no date), www.worldvaluessurvey.org, accessed 15 January 2004.

Wright, P. (1979), *On a Clear Day You Can See General Motors: John Z. de Lorean's Look Inside the Automotive Giant*, Grosse Point, MI: Wright Enterprises.

Yin, R. (2003a), *Applications of Case Study Research*, 2nd edn, Thousand Oaks, CA: Sage Publications.

Yin, R. (2003b), *Case Study Research: Design and Methods*, 3rd edn, Thousand Oaks, CA: Sage Publications.

Index